The Complete Book of Bible Prophecy

THE COMPLETE BOOK OF

BIBLE PROPHECY

MARK HITCHCOCK

TYNDALE HOUSE PUBLISHERS, INC. WHEATON, ILLINOIS

Library of Congress Cataloging-in-Publication Data

Hitchcock, Mark.
  The complete book of Bible prophecy / Mark Hitchcock.
    p.   cm.
  Includes bibliographical references and index.
  ISBN 0-8423-1831-3 (sc : alk. paper)
  1. Bible—Prophecies.   I. Title.
BS647.2.H58   1999
220.1'5—dc21   99-22148

Printed in the United States of America

06   05   04
8   7   6

To Cheryl

who each day exceeds my expectations
of what a wife and mother should be.
Thank you for the best thirteen years of my life!
"There are many virtuous and capable women in the world,
but you surpass them all!" (Proverbs 31:29)

Table of Contents

Introduction

A few months ago, as I was driving on SE Fifteenth Street near my house in Edmond, Oklahoma, a momentous event occurred. The odometer in my car rolled over 100,000 miles. Of course, this was no big deal to anyone else (even my wife and kids failed to share my excitement). But I had been watching the odometer off and on since it turned over 99,000 miles, and I wanted to witness the big rollover at 100,000 because I knew that I probably would not own the car when the next big rollover would occur at 200,000.

Today something far more momentous is occurring in our world. The odometer of the universe is turning over a new millennium. While one in three people is privileged to experience the beginning of a new century, only one in thirty is alive to witness the rolling over of a new millennium (McGinn, Bernard. *Antichrist: Two Thousand Years of Human Fascination with Evil*. San Francisco: Harper Collins, 1994, p. xi.). With the dawn of the next millennium approaching, there is a flood of renewed interest in Bible prophecy, the end times, and the coming apocalypse. Books on Bible prophecy—including everything from hidden Bible codes to personal identification numbers to the mark of the Beast, 666—have been spinning off the presses in record numbers. You can find a prophecy book on practically everything from Arafat to Zionism, from Armageddon to Zhirinovsky.

What may be even more remarkable than this deluge of renewed interest is the fact that most people have heard that Jesus is coming back someday and believe that this is true. Consider these facts from a *U.S. News & World Report* poll in 1997:

- Sixty-six percent of Americans, including a third of those who admit they never attend church, say they believe Jesus Christ will return to earth someday. This is an increase from 61 percent in 1994.
- Nearly six in ten Americans believe that the world will end or be destroyed, and a third of those think it will happen within the next few years or decades.
- Forty-four percent believe the world will face the apocalypse with true believers being whisked away to heaven.
- Forty-nine percent believe there will be an Antichrist.

In a more recent survey, 20 percent of Americans said they believe the Second Coming will occur sometime around the year 2000 (*Dallas Morning News*, 10/24/98, p. 24A).

However, while the majority of people believe in the second coming of Christ, the apocalypse, the Antichrist, and the end of the world, Bible prophecy remains a confusing, frustrating, even bewildering morass of differing views, strange symbols, confusing charts, and bizarre visions. For far too many people, Bible prophecy remains shrouded in mystery and irrelevance.

Have you ever wished you could understand what the Bible says about the last days of the planet earth? Have you ever wished you could find one book that helped put all the pieces of the puzzle in place in a simple, straightforward fashion? If you have, there is no need to despair any longer. I wrote this book with you in mind. You might say that this book is Bible Prophecy 101, written solely to help the average person gain a foundational understanding of the basics of Bible prophecy. The express purpose of *The Complete Book of Bible Prophecy* is to present what the Bible says about the last days in a straightforward, easy-to-follow format.

As you read this book, my prayer is that God will use it to give you wisdom and understanding about the last days and, more important, about the glorious return of our Lord and Savior, Jesus Christ.

Prophecy and Prophets

Twenty-seven percent of the Bible's content can be characterized as prophecy, and 20 percent of its books are prophetic.[1] These facts alone make knowledge of Bible prophecy indispensable to anyone wanting to understand what the Bible is all about. However, this information also presents quite an overwhelming challenge. Trying to understand and digest this much material is like traveling through a maze. Where do we start? What is Bible prophecy? Who or what is a prophet?

For many people, Bible prophecy is all the negative, catastrophic, cataclysmic warnings about how God is going to destroy everything someday. And prophets? They are those strange people wearing strange clothes, eating strange foods, preaching strange sermons, and doing strange things that no one understands. The popular image of a prophet is of some crusty old sage gazing into a crystal ball.

Since this book is about Bible prophecy, let's start by getting acquainted with the men and women the Bible calls prophets and prophetesses. Let's find out who they are, what they said, and how one could verify their authority.

TITLES OF A PROPHET

The title for any job usually reveals a lot about the person who fills that position and what he or she does. For instance, people call me a pastor, teacher, minister, elder, or reverend—and sometimes a few names I can't repeat here. Each of these titles gives people insight into the job I fulfill. Likewise, the Bible contains several titles for the office of prophet that help us to understand who these people were and what they did.

Old Testament Titles The English translations of the Old Testament use five main titles for those who spoke on God's behalf. Each of these titles emphasizes a different aspect of the prophet's job description.

PROPHET This title, the most commonly used, emphasizes that the person was an authoritative spokesman for God.

SEER This word focuses on the way in which the prophet received God's message.

MAN OF GOD This title identifies the prophet as one who knew God and one whom God had commissioned for a specific task.

SERVANT OF THE LORD   This term stresses the close relationship between God and his faithful messenger.

MESSENGER OF THE LORD   This term focuses on the mission and the message rather than on the person. It emphasizes the fact that God sent a prophet to deliver a message—the word of God.

Old Testament Terms   Three Hebrew words in the Old Testament are translated "prophet" or "seer." The first two terms occur less frequently than the third. The first term, *ro'eh*, appears only twelve times, and the second term, *hozeh*, appears eighteen times. These words are both "revelational" terms. They come from words that basically mean to see, look at, or behold. The prophet or seer, therefore, is one who can see things that others cannot. The prophet is one to whom God directly and uniquely reveals his word and his will—usually through dreams or visions.

The third term, *nabbi'*, appears 309 times in its noun form and almost 600 times in its verb forms. When we trace this term through the Old Testament, it becomes clear that *nabbi'* refers primarily to one who speaks for someone else, someone who acts as a "mouth" for another (Exod. 7:1). Whenever God assigned a specific task to a prophet, the assignment always focused on speaking God's message. Therefore, the basic meaning of the term *nabbi'* is "to speak God's message," to be a "speaker for God," "one who is a spokesman for God" (Deut. 18:18; Jer. 1:7; Isa. 1:20). The *nabbi'* was a divinely inspired preacher who faithfully spoke the message God had revealed. When the prophet spoke, God spoke.

THE RELATIONSHIP BETWEEN "PROPHET" AND "SEER"[2]

NAME	BASIC CONCEPT	FOCUS	EMPHASIS
Prophet	Spokesman	Proclamation of divine revelation	Output (what he does)
Seer	One who Sees	Reception of divine revelation	Input (how he knows)

New Testament Terms   The primary New Testament term for a prophet or prophetess is the Greek noun *prophetes*, and the Greek verb *propheteuo* means "to prophesy." These words, like their Old Testament counterparts, refer to one who speaks for God, one who speaks the word and will of God. The New Testament prophet brought God's word to his fellowman.

TRAITS OF A PROPHET

It was a great and distinct honor to be a prophet of the living God. That's why there were so many false prophets in Israel. Prophets anointed kings, performed miracles, and predicted the future. But at the same time, a prophet's assignment could also bring great danger, difficulty, and even death. The prophet was called to speak God's undiluted, uncompromising, unvarnished message to an often rebellious people. This frequently brought reproach, fierce opposition, harsh criticism, and even execution to the man of God. For this reason not just anyone could be a prophet. There were at least two major qualifications that a person had to possess in order to be a true prophet of God.

The Prophet Must Be Called. Unlike the offices of king and priest, the office of a prophet was not inherited by being born into a prophetic family or tribe. The son of a prophet did not automatically receive a commission as a prophet. Rather, God individually selected and called each prophet to a specific work that God wanted accomplished. The divine call is what made a man a true prophet, and the lack of this call is what made so many false prophets. Here are just a few examples of the divine call of a prophet.

- Moses received the call at the burning bush (Exod. 3:4).
- Isaiah responded to the divine call through a vision he had of the Lord high and lifted up in the temple (Isa. 6:1-8).
- Jeremiah was called by God as a prophet while still in his mother's womb (Jer. 1:5).
- Ezekiel was called by God near the Kebar River in Babylon (Ezek. 1:1; 2:2-3).
- Amos remembers his call in Amos 7:14-15.

The Prophet Must Be Courageous. In light of the rigors and responsibility of this office, the prophet had to be a special kind of person. The prophet had to be a bold, fearless individual. He had to be able to handle both persecution and praise, both accolades and antagonism. Leon Wood summarizes the courage needed by a prophet:

A person had to be an outstanding individual to qualify as a prophet. Prophets had to be people of outstanding character, great minds, and courageous souls. They had to be this by nature and then, being dedicated to God, they became still greater because of the tasks and special provisions assigned them. Thus they became the towering giants of Israel, the formers of public opinion, the leaders through days of darkness, people distinguished from all those about them either in Israel or the other nations of the day.[3]

Let's look at some of the tasks God assigned to his prophets.

- Samuel's first task as a prophet was to inform the high priest Eli that God had rejected his house (1 Sam. 3:4-18).
- Nathan had to confront King David about his sin with Bathsheba (2 Sam. 12:1-12).
- God gave David a choice of three punishments for his sinful census (2 Sam. 24:10-17).
- Elijah warned King Ahab of a terrible drought and famine (1 Kings 17:1).
- Jonah called the wicked city of Nineveh to repentance (Jon. 1:2; 3:1-2).

TASKS OF A PROPHET

When most people think of the job description for a prophet, they immediately think of dramatic dreams and visions of the future apocalypse. The common image of a prophet is of a predictor and prognosticator. Biblical prophets foretold the future with 100 percent accuracy and announced the coming Messiah, the coming of Antichrist, and the end of the world. This aspect of the prophet's ministry is often called "foretelling." The prophet was God's mouthpiece and spokesman for predicting and previewing the future of Israel and other nations.

This future-predicting aspect of the prophet's mission—the unfulfilled Bible prophecies of the last days or end times—is the primary focus of this book. However, it is important to remember that the prophets also had a powerful, pertinent message for the people of their own day. This aspect of the prophet's ministry is sometimes called "forthtelling." The prophet echoed forth God's message to his or her own generation.

In both of these aspects of the prophetic office, the overall purpose was the same. Whether the prophet was forthtelling to the people of his or her own day or foretelling about future events, the goal was to call people to trust the Lord, obey God's Word, and submit to his will for their lives. In essence, the ministry of the prophet was to call people to live their lives in conformity with God's law.

It is also important to understand that even in the forthtelling function of the prophet, the foretelling element is always present to some degree. When the prophets spoke to their contemporaries about current situations, they generally included warnings and encouragements about the future in their message. Almost every prophet appears first as a foreteller. The notion of prediction seems to be the very essence of the prophetic office and function (Deut. 18:20-22). Nevertheless, while always recognizing the future aspect of all prophecy, it is important for us to also remember the important function of the prophets to their contemporary society.

In the Scriptures there are at least five specific tasks, functions, or missions that the prophets fulfilled as they announced God's message to the people of their day. Let's briefly consider the five functions of forthtelling:

Reformers The prophets served as reformers. They consistently called the people to obey the law of God. The prophets were ethical and moral preachers who denounced all the moral, religious, and social evils of the day. The prophet of God was called on to fearlessly rebuke idolatry, marital infidelity, oppression of the poor and needy, injustice, and social, moral, and political corruption. The prophets called people to turn back from their sinful ways and to live in conformity to God's Word.

Statesmen The prophets confronted kings and played the role of statesman in national affairs. Interestingly, the first two kings of Israel, Saul and David, were also prophets. But the two roles even in that day were clearly separate. The prophet Samuel confronted Saul about his disobedience (1 Sam. 15:13-23), and the prophet Nathan confronted David when he committed murder and adultery (2 Sam. 12:1-12).

Watchmen The prophets served as watchmen among the people. God raised up the prophets to point out the people's religious apostasy and to trumpet forth warnings of judgment for the people's failure to turn from idolatry.

Intercessors The prophets served as intercessors for God's people. While the priests were the primary intercessors, offering sacrifices for the people, the prophets also assumed this role, apart from sacrificial and ceremonial activity. There are numerous instances of prophets praying for the needs of people.

REFERENCE	INTERCESSION
1 Kings 13:6	An anonymous man of God prayed for King Jeroboam.
1 Kings 17:17-24	Elijah prayed for the widow's son.
2 Kings 4:18-37	Elisha prayed for the son of the woman from Shunem.
Jeremiah 7:16; 14:7	Jeremiah continuously prayed for God's mercy on the rebellious nation.
Amos 7:2	Amos asked God to forgive Israel.

Comforters and Encouragers The prophets comforted and encouraged God's people. Prophets are often caricatured as negative doomsayers who spent all their time going around lambasting people for their sins. As we have seen, this was certainly a principal part of their calling. But we often forget that a key aspect of the prophet's ministry was to console and comfort. First Corinthians 14:3 says, "One who prophesies is helping others grow in the Lord, encouraging and comforting them." The prophets were called by God again and again to remind the people of his faithfulness, love, mercy, and compassion. By urging the people to conform their lives to God's law, the prophets edified and encouraged the Lord's people. In Isaiah 40:1-2, the Lord tells the prophet, "'Comfort, comfort my people,' says your God. 'Speak tenderly to Jerusalem. Tell her that her sad days are gone and that her sins are pardoned.' "

The prophet Nahum, whose name means "comfort" or "consolation," brought comfort to the nation of Israel by predicting and previewing the savage destruction of the wicked city of Nineveh. (Nahum is often called the book Jonah would like to have written.) In this short book of three chapters, Nahum clearly presents judgment and comfort side by side. This is not unique to Nahum. While almost all the prophets spoke about God's judgment and wrath on the unrepentant, many also closed their message with the promise of a glorious future in the messianic kingdom. So even in the midst of judgment, there is a beautiful message of hope, comfort, and encouragement. Hobart Freeman summarizes the task of the prophet in this way:

The prophets boldly rebuked vice, denounced political corruption, oppression, idolatry and moral degeneracy. They were preachers of righteousness, reformers, and revivalists of spiritual religion, as well as prophets of future judgment or blessing. They were raised up in times of crisis to instruct, rebuke, warn and comfort Israel, but interwoven with their ethical and moral teaching are to be found numerous predictions of future events concerning Israel, the nations and the Messianic kingdom.[4]

THEMES OF A PROPHET

As you can imagine, the messages the prophets spoke were as varied as the situations they encountered. Yet there are several key themes in the prophetic messages, repeated with amazing regularity throughout Israel's history. These messages or themes can be distilled under four main headings:

Impending Judgment A consistent diatribe of the prophets is that God will rain his judgment and wrath on those who fail to repent of their evil ways. God's judgment reaches its climax during the coming Tribulation or Day of the Lord, of which the prophets spoke so frequently.

Social Reform The prophets repeatedly called the people to have love and compassion for their fellowman.

Condemnation of Idolatry The people of Israel worshiped idols again and again. One of the main prophetic themes was to call the people to put away their false gods and to turn in faith and dependence to the only true God.

The Coming of Messiah and His Kingdom The prophets consistently spoke of the coming of Messiah and the future kingdom he would bring. This message of hope and comfort radiates through all the prophets. The first prophecy announcing a coming deliverer is found in Genesis 3:15. Hundreds of later prophecies fill in the details of his person and his work. There are more than three hundred prophecies that Christ fulfilled at his first coming, while hundreds more await fulfillment at his second coming. Following is a list of forty-five of the most significant messianic prophecies fulfilled during the first advent of Christ.

1. He was born of a woman (Gen. 3:15; Gal. 4:4).
2. He was a descendant of Abraham (Gen. 12:3, 7; Matt. 1:1; Gal. 3:16).
3. He was of the tribe of Judah (Gen. 49:10; Heb. 7:14; Rev. 5:5).
4. He was of the house or family of David (2 Sam. 7:12-13; Luke 1:31-33; Rom. 1:3).
5. He was born of a virgin (Isa. 7:14; Matt. 1:22-23).
6. He was called Emmanuel (Isa. 7:14; Matt. 1:23).
7. He had a forerunner (Isa. 40:3-5; Mal. 3:1; Matt. 3:1-3; Luke 1:76-78).
8. He was born in Bethlehem (Mic. 5:2; Matt. 2:5-6; Luke 2:4-6).
9. He was worshiped by wise men and given gifts (Ps. 72:10-11; Isa. 60:3, 6, 9; Matt. 2:11).
10. He was in Egypt for a season (Hos. 11:1; Matt. 2:15).
11. His birthplace was a place where infants were slaughtered (Jer. 31:15; Matt. 2:16).
12. He was zealous for the Father (Ps. 69:9; John 6:37-40).
13. He was filled with God's Spirit (Isa. 11:2; Luke 4:18-19).
14. He was a mighty healer (Isa. 35:5-6; Matt. 8:16-17).
15. He ministered to the Gentiles (Isa. 9:1-2; 42:1-3; Matt. 4:13-16; 12:17-21).
16. He spoke in parables (Isa. 6:9-10; Matt. 13:10-15).
17. He was rejected by the Jewish people (Ps. 69:8; Isa. 53:3; John 1:11; 7:5).
18. He made a triumphal entry into Jerusalem, riding on a donkey (Zech. 9:9; Matt. 21:4-5).
19. He was praised by little children (Ps. 8:2; Matt. 21:16).
20. He was the rejected cornerstone (Ps. 118:22-23; Matt. 21:42).
21. His miracles were not believed (Isa. 53:1; John 12:37-38).
22. He was betrayed by his friend for thirty pieces of silver (Ps. 41:9; Zech. 11:12-13; Matt. 26:14-16, 21-25).
23. He was a man of sorrows (Isa. 53:3; Matt. 26:37-38).
24. He was forsaken by his disciples (Zech. 13:7; Matt. 26:31, 56).
25. He was beaten and spit upon (Isa. 50:6; Matt. 26:67; 27:26).
26. His betrayal money was used to purchase a potter's field (Zech. 11:12-13; Matt. 27:9-10).
27. He was executed by means of piercing his hands and feet (Ps. 22:16; Zech. 12:10; John 19:34, 37).
28. He was crucified between two thieves (Isa. 53:12; Matt. 27:38).
29. He was given vinegar to drink (Ps. 69:21; Matt. 27:34).
30. His garments were divided, and soldiers gambled for them (Ps. 22:18; Luke 23:34).
31. He was surrounded and ridiculed by enemies (Ps. 22:7-8; Matt. 27:39-44).
32. He was thirsty on the cross (Ps. 22:15; John 19:28).
33. He commended his spirit to the Father (Ps. 31:5; Luke 23:46).
34. He uttered a forsaken cry on the cross (Ps. 22:1; Matt. 27:46).
35. He committed himself to God (Ps. 31:5; Luke 23:46).

36. He was hated without a cause (Ps. 69:4; John 15:25).
37. People shook their heads as they saw him on the cross (Ps. 109:25; Matt. 27:39).
38. He was silent before his accusers (Isa. 53:7; Matt. 27:12).
39. His bones were not broken (Exod. 12:46; Ps. 34:20; John 19:33-36).
40. He was stared at in death (Zech. 12:10; Matt. 27:36; John 19:37).
41. He was buried with the rich (Isa. 53:9; Matt. 27:57-60).
42. He rose from the dead (Ps. 16:10; Matt. 28:2-7).
43. He was and is a high priest greater than Aaron (Ps. 11:4; Heb. 5:4-6).
44. He ascended to glory (Ps. 68:18; Eph. 4:8).
45. He was and is seated at the right hand of the Father (Ps. 110:1; Heb. 10:12-13).

In addition to these messianic prophecies, there are hundreds of presently unfulfilled messianic prophecies associated with the last days and the second coming of Christ. These future prophecies of Messiah, his second coming, and his kingdom will be outlined in subsequent chapters.

THE TEST OF A PROPHET

Imitators and counterfeiters have always plagued the true Word and way of God. For this reason the Lord established a clear set of tests a person had to pass in order to be received as a true spokesman for God. There are four main passages in the Old Testament that deal with the subject of false prophets: (1) Deuteronomy 13:1-18; (2) Deuteronomy 18:9-22; (3) Jeremiah 23:9-40; and (4) Ezekiel 12:21–14:11.

In examining these four passages and many others, Scripture presents at least seven marks of a true prophet. While all of these marks may not have been present in every prophet, certainly some prophets had each one. However, for any follower of God who really wanted to know who was true and who was false, there would have been no question about a prophet's authenticity.

The Seven Distinguishing Marks of a True Prophet[5]

1. The true prophet never used divination, sorcery, or astrology (Deut. 18:9-14; Mic. 3:7; Ezek. 12:24). The source of the prophet's message was God himself (2 Pet. 1:20-21).
2. The true prophet never tailored his or her message to cater to the cravings or desires of the people (Jer. 8:11; 28:8; Ezek. 13:10). The false prophets, or "pillow prophets," as some describe them, spoke a message that would bring them popularity and money. They were the Fortune 500 prophets, the religious opportunists (Mic. 3:5-6, 11). The

true prophet spoke God's unadulterated message regardless of personal loss, shame, and even physical harm.
3. The true prophet maintained personal integrity and character (Isa. 28:7; Jer. 23:11; Hos. 9:7-9; Mic. 3:5, 11; Zeph. 3:4). Jesus said that true and false prophets would be known by their fruit—that is, by what they did and said (Matt. 7:15-20).
4. The true prophet was willing to suffer for the sake of his message (1 Kings 22:27-28; Jer. 38:4-13; Ezek. 3:4-8).
5. The true prophet announced a message that was consistent with the law and with the messages of other true prophets (Jer. 26:17-19). The message never contradicted nor disagreed with any previous revelation of truth but confirmed and built upon that body of truth (Deut. 13:1-3).
6. The true prophet, when predicting future events, had a 100 percent success rate (Deut. 18:21-22). Unlike modern psychics, any success rate short of perfect was not good enough! If the alleged prophet was not 100 percent accurate, the people were to take him outside the city and stone him to death (Deut. 18:20).
7. The true prophet sometimes had his or her message authenticated by the performance of a miracle or miracles (see Exod. 5–12). This test was not conclusive evidence, however, because false prophets also produced miracles on occasion (Exod. 7:10-12; 8:5-7; Mark 13:22; 2 Thess. 2:9). Therefore, Moses gave a further aspect to this test in Deuteronomy 13:1-3:

> *Suppose there are prophets among you, or those who have dreams about the future, and they promise you signs or miracles, and the predicted signs or miracles take place. If the prophets then say, "Come, let us worship the gods of foreign nations," do not listen to them. The Lord your God is testing you to see if you love him with all your heart and soul.*

The true test was the content of the message, not the miracles. The true prophet spoke only in the name of the Lord and called people to God, not away from God.

THE TABULATION OF THE PROPHETS

The Bible records a number of true prophets and prophetesses as well as several false prophets and prophetesses. Certainly not all of those who spoke for God or pretended to speak for God are specifically mentioned in the Bible. However, the following is a tabulation or list of those who are set forth in the pages of Scripture as false and true speakers for God.

Old Testament Pre-Monarchy Prophets
1. Abel (Luke 11:49-51)
2. Enoch (Jude 1:14)

3. Noah (Gen. 9:24-27)
4. Abraham (Gen. 20:7)
5. Jacob (Gen. 48–49)
6. Aaron (Exod. 7:1)
7. Moses (Deut. 18:15; 34:10)
8. An anonymous prophet (Judg. 6:7-10)
9. An anonymous prophet who predicted the death of Eli's sons (1 Sam. 2:27-36)

10. Samuel (1 Sam. 3:20)
11. A band of prophets (1 Sam. 10:5-10; 19:18-20)

Old Testament Monarchy Prophets (Nonwriting Prophets)
1. Nathan (2 Sam. 7:2; 12:25)
2. Gad (2 Sam. 24:11)
3. Zadok the priest (2 Sam. 15:27)
4. Heman and fourteen of his sons (1 Chron. 25:1-5)
5. Asaph and four of his sons (1 Chron. 25:1-5)
6. Jeduthun and six of his sons (1 Chron. 25:1-5)
7. Ahijah (1 Kings 11:29; 14:2-8)
8. A man of God who spoke against Jeroboam's altar (1 Kings 13:1-10)
9. An old prophet in Bethel (1 Kings 13:11-32)
10. Shemaiah (2 Chron. 11:2-4; 12:5-15)
11. Iddo (2 Chron. 9:29; 12:15; 13:22)
12. Azariah (2 Chron. 15:1-8)
13. Hanani (2 Chron. 16:7; 19:2)
14. Jehu, son of Hanani (1 Kings 16:1-12)
15. Jahaziel (2 Chron. 20:14)
16. Eliezer (2 Chron. 20:37)
17. Elijah (1 Kings 17–19)
18. Elisha (1 Kings 19:19-21)
19. An unnamed prophet (1 Kings 20:13-28)
20. Micaiah (1 Kings 22:8-28)
21. Zechariah (2 Chron. 24:20-22; Luke 11:49-51)
22. An unnamed prophet (2 Chron. 25:15)
23. Uriah (Jer. 26:20)
24. Oded (2 Chron. 28:9-11)
25. King Saul, who prophesied on two occasions (1 Sam. 10:1-13; 19:18-24)
26. King David (Pss. 2; 16; 22; 110; Acts 2:30-35)

Old Testament Monarchy Prophets (Writing Prophets)
Preexilic Prophets (Ninth Century B.C.)
1. Obadiah
2. Joel

(Eighth Century B.C.)
1. Amos
2. Hosea
3. Isaiah

4. Micah
5. Jonah

(Seventh Century B.C.)
1. Nahum
2. Jeremiah
3. Zephaniah
4. Habakkuk

Exilic Prophets
1. Daniel
2. Ezekiel

Postexilic Prophets
1. Haggai
2. Zechariah
3. Malachi

Old Testament Prophetesses
1. Deborah (Judg. 4:4)
2. Miriam (Exod. 15:20)
3. Huldah (2 Kings (22:14-17)
4. Isaiah's wife (Isa. 8:2-3, KJV)

Old Testament False Prophets and Prophetesses
1. Balaam (Num. 22–24)
2. Zedekiah (1 Kings 22:11-24)
3. Hananiah (Jer. 28:1-17)
4. Shemaiah (Jer. 29:24-32)
5. Ahab (Jer. 29:21)
6. Zedekiah (Jer. 29:21)
7. Noadiah (Neh. 6:14)
8. A group of false prophets (Ezek. 13:1-16)
9. A group of false prophetesses (Ezek. 13:17-23)

New Testament Prophets and Prophetesses
1. John the Baptist (Matt. 11:9)
2. Anna (Luke 2:36)
3. Agabus (Acts 11:28; 21:10)
4. Judas Barsabbas (Acts 15:32)
5. Silas (Acts 15:32)
6. The four daughters of Philip (Acts 21:8-9)
7. The two witnesses of the last days (Rev. 11:4, 10)
8. John the apostle (Rev. 22:6-18)
9. Jesus Christ (Matt. 24–25; John 4:19, 44; 7:40; 9:17)

New Testament False Prophets and Prophetesses
1. Elymas (Acts 13:6-8)
2. Jezebel (Rev. 2:20)
3. A parade of false prophets in the last days (Matt. 24:24)
4. The false prophets (Rev. 13:11-18)

FOCUS ON THE FUTURE

As we have seen, the prophet often spoke a divine message for his or her own day. The message was always closely tied to a prediction of future judgment or future blessing, depending on how the audience responded to the message. Many of these prophecies have already been fulfilled. In addition, the hundreds of messianic prophecies associated with the first coming of Christ have also been fulfilled. This book will not focus on prophecies that have already been fulfilled but on the currently unfulfilled prophecies commonly referred to as the last days or end times.

14

[1]According to the calculations of J. Barton Payne (*Encyclopedia of Bible Prophecy.* New York: Harper and Row, 1973, pp. 631–82), there are 8,352 verses (out of a total of 31,124 for the whole Bible) that contain predictive material. This means that 27 percent of the Bible is prophecy. In the Old Testament, 6,641 out of 23,210 verses contain predictive material (28.5 percent), while 1,711 of the New Testament's 7,914 verses include predictive material (21.5 percent). These verses discuss 737 separate prophetic topics.

[2]This chart was taken from Dr. Charles Dyer, "Preexilic and Exilic Prophets," unpublished class notes, Dallas Theological Seminary.

[3]Leon J. Wood, *The Prophets of Israel* (Grand Rapids: Baker Book House, 1979), 16.

[4]Hobart E. Freeman, *An Introduction to the Old Testament Prophets* (Chicago: Moody Press, 1968), 14.

[5]These marks were adapted from Wood, 109–13 and Freeman, 102–17.

Ten Key Reasons Why Bible Prophecy Is Important

There's no doubt that people are fascinated with the future. Psychic hot lines, tabloid newspapers, and astrologers make livings preying on people's innate interest in the future. Like Dwight Eisenhower once said, "I'm interested in the future because that's where I'm going to spend the remainder of my life." But is this interest the only incentive for studying Bible prophecy? Was prophecy given just to satisfy our curiosity about the signs of the times and the end of the world?

In this chapter we are going to briefly consider ten key reasons why it is important to understand Bible prophecy.

PROPHECY IS A MAJOR PART OF DIVINE REVELATION

As we have already seen, 27 percent of the Bible is prophecy, and 20 percent of the books of the Bible are prophetic. For example, lengthy books such as Isaiah, Ezekiel, Daniel, Zechariah, and Revelation are almost entirely prophetic in content. These facts alone warrant serious study of this aspect of God's revelation.

Let's consider the importance of this fact from other perspectives: Who would study American history and ignore 27 percent of the material? Who would dare to call himself or herself a doctor if he or she failed to understand 27 percent of body functions? Likewise, if we call ourselves followers of Jesus Christ, it is critical that we understand at least the basics of Bible prophecy.

GOD PROMISES A SPECIAL BLESSING TO THOSE WHO STUDY AND PAY ATTENTION TO PROPHECY

Revelation is the final book of the Bible and records the consummation of God's program for humanity and the world. When people think of Bible prophecy, the first book they think of—and maybe the only one—is Revelation. In Revelation 1:3, the Lord promises a special blessing on those who study Bible prophecy: "God blesses the one who reads this prophecy to the church, and he blesses all who listen to it and obey what it says."

Revelation is the only book in the Bible that contains this specific, unique promise. The inclusion of this blessing seems to anticipate that many would ignore and neglect the study of Bible prophecy, especially the book of Revelation.

Seven such blessings or beatitudes appear throughout Revelation's pages (1:3; 14:13; 16:15; 19:9; 20:6; 22:7; 22:14). This blessing in 1:3 is the first and most comprehensive one. It is a blessing that anyone reading these words can enjoy. Notice that this blessing is threefold:

The One Who Reads In the early church, not everyone had a copy of the Scriptures, so someone would read them aloud to the people.

Today this blessing extends to all who read this grand climax to God's prophetic program.

The One Who Listens Just to hear the book of Revelation (as well as other Bible prophecies) read is a great blessing in troubled times like those of our modern world.

The One Who Obeys It is not only important to read and hear Bible prophecy but also to observe, pay attention to, and obey what is written. After reading and listening to what Revelation teaches us, we should diligently pay attention to and watch for the events of the last days to come to pass.

Any believer in Christ can receive the unmitigated blessing of God by simply reading, hearing, and paying attention to the things written in the book of Revelation and other Scriptures that reveal the consummation of human history.

JESUS CHRIST IS THE SUBJECT OF PROPHECY

Theologians have frequently noted that Jesus is the center of theology because all of the great purposes of God depend on Christ's person and work. What is true of theology in general is especially true of eschatology, or Bible prophecy.

Revelation 19:10 says, "The essence of prophecy is to give a clear witness for Jesus." The truth of this verse is certainly born out in Scripture. Prophecy is all about Christ.

Bible prophecy finds its beginning and ending in the person and work of the Savior. The very first prophecy in the Bible (Genesis 3:15) is about the coming of the Deliverer, who will crush the head of the serpent. Enoch's ancient prophecy recorded in Jude 1:14-15 predicts the Flood judgment but also previews the second coming of Christ. From Genesis to Revelation, the Bible overflows with prophecies that ultimately point in one way or another to the Savior. We saw forty-five of these fulfilled messianic prophecies in the last chapter. Here are twenty-five more prophetic references to the person and work of Jesus Christ:

1. The coming seed of the woman, who will crush the serpent's head (Gen. 3:15)
2. Shiloh ("the one to whom it belongs") (Gen. 49:10)
3. The Passover Lamb (Exod. 12:1-51; John 1:29; 1 Cor. 5:7)

COMPLETE BOOK OF BIBLE PROPHECY

4. The star from Jacob (Num. 24:17)
5. The great High Priest (Ps. 110)
6. The prophet (Deut. 18:18)
7. The King (2 Sam. 7:11-16; Luke 1:32-33)
8. "Wonderful Counselor, Mighty God, Everlasting Father, Prince of Peace" (Isa. 9:6)
9. A righteous king (Isa. 32:1)
10. "My servant" (Isa. 53:2)
11. A man of sorrows (Isa. 53:3)
12. The smiting stone, the smashing rock (Dan. 2:31-35)
13. The Son of man (Dan. 7:13, KJV)
14. The Anointed One (Dan. 9:25-26)
15. The Son who will rule the world (Ps. 2)
16. "My Shepherd," "my partner" (Zech. 13:7)
17. The Lord of the temple (Mal. 3:1)
18. The resurrection and the life (John 11:1-44)
19. The glorified, risen Savior (Rev. 1:9-19)
20. The Lord of the church (Rev. 2–3)
21. The Lamb of God (Rev. 4–5)
22. The judge of the nations (Rev. 6:1-17)
23. The miracle-born man child (Rev. 12–13)
24. The coming King (Rev. 14–19)
25. The Lord of heaven and earth (Rev. 20–22)

Studying Bible prophecy is vital because its very essence gives witness to Jesus.

PROPHECY GIVES US A PROPER PERSPECTIVE IN LIFE

The story is told of an airplane lost over the ocean in the middle of a hurricane. The captain decided it was time to inform the passengers of their dilemma, so he turned on the intercom. "I have some good news and some bad news," he began. "The bad news is that we've lost our guidance system and have no way of knowing where we are or which way we are going. The good news is, we're making great time!"

Most people today are like the people in that plane. They are making great time, moving quickly through life, but they have no clue where they are, which way they're going, or where they are going to land. As a result they lack a proper perspective about life, and their focus is only on the here and now.

Bible prophecy is important because it tells us the end of the story. It tells us where we're going. It reveals that just as our world had a definite beginning in Genesis 1:1, it will also have an ending. This world will not continue on forever through infinite cycles of history. History is not an endless recurrence of reincarnations, karma, birth, life, and death. Bible prophecy not only reveals to us that there is an end but that there is a purpose and goal for this world, creation, humanity, and the events of everyday life. Knowing this truth gives us meaning, perspective, and purpose and helps us not to become cynical about life.

If a person really believed that this world would continue on forever with no ultimate goal or purpose, his or her belief would lead to total hopelessness and despair. It would mean there would be no existence beyond the grave, no ultimate justice, no final accounting, no tying together of all the loose ends of human history.

Bible prophecy tells us that there is an end of all things when every wrong will be righted and every right will be rewarded. There is a consummation of human history and this present world. Bible prophecy is the vehicle God has given us to reveal the grand finale of history and to provide a terminus or goal for our thinking about life and its ultimate meaning and purpose.

PROPHECY HELPS US UNDERSTAND THE WHOLE BIBLE

There's a story about a preacher from back east whose parishioners said he was the best they had ever seen at taking the Bible apart; the problem was he couldn't get it back together. Sadly, this story describes far too many Christians, who read their Bible faithfully but have no idea what they're reading. That is because they lack an overall framework for evaluating the pieces of Scripture and putting them in their proper place.

Understanding God's prophetic program for this world gives a person the best overall framework possible for understanding the Bible from Genesis to Revelation. As Randall Price observes, "To be a student of the prophetic Scriptures is to be a student of the Scriptures in their entirety."[1]

Prophecy reveals God's program for the Jewish people, for the Gentile nations, and for the church. A person who doesn't have at least a basic understanding of prophecy will get totally lost in large sections of the Old Testament and in several books of the New Testament. In addition, this person has no hope of accurately handling the Word of Truth as a whole (2 Tim. 2:15).

PROPHECY CAN AND SHOULD BE USED
AS A TOOL FOR EVANGELISM

As I have listened to the testimonies of hundreds of people through the years, I am amazed how many people first began to think about their relationship with God as a result of Bible prophecy. I was talking to a new member of our church one day at lunch. The first Christian book he read back in the 1970s was a book on Bible prophecy. God used the events of the last days and the second coming of Christ to awaken this man to his need for salvation.

This man's story shouldn't surprise us, for Bible prophecy fascinates even unbelievers. That is because everyone has the same basic questions about the future. What's going to happen to the world? Are these the last days of the world as we know it? Is Jesus really coming back? Will the human race survive in the future? Is there life after death? Are heaven and hell real? The Bible answers all of these ultimate questions about the future, and we can and should use this knowledge to share Christ with others as God opens the door of opportunity.

PROPHECY CAN HELP INSULATE PEOPLE FROM HERESY

From the earliest days of Christianity, false teachers have attacked and corrupted the true teachings of the church. Almost every book in the New Testament has a section that deals with false teaching. Some of the more notable sections are 2 Corinthians 10–11; Philippians 3:17-21; 2 Timothy 3:1-17; and Titus 1:5-16. In some cases an entire book is devoted almost entirely to combating false teaching and the corrupt lifestyle it produces (such as Galatians, Colossians, 1 Timothy, 2 Peter, and Jude).

In a few instances, the false teaching that erupted concerned the last days and the second coming of Christ. In 2 Thessalonians 2, Paul corrected a false teaching that the Day of the Lord, or the Tribulation period, had already come. As a result of this false teaching, Paul also had to correct an errant action. In chapter 3, he commanded some of the people to go back to work and quit sponging off the other believers. Apparently, they had applied the false teaching about the Tribulation period to their lives and had quit working since Christ was coming very soon.

In 2 Peter 3, a group of scoffers had arisen who mocked the idea that Jesus was coming back. To them, the idea of God's intervening dramatically in human history to judge mankind was absurd. However, Peter reminds them in verse 6 of the worldwide Flood. God created the world, and he will judge the world. God's delay in sending Christ back to this world is not a delay of powerlessness or indifference but a delay of patience (2 Pet. 3:9). The apparent delay in Christ's return is due to God's mercy in giving sinners more time to repent.

The same kinds of errors have continued from the first century to the present day. Think of all the false teachers who have gained a following by appealing to Bible prophecy. For example, William Miller—a date setter—gained a large following by predicting that Jesus was coming back in 1843. When Christ didn't come, Miller revised the date to 1844. Since Miller's day there have been hundreds of date setters who have led throngs of people to sell their belongings and wait for Jesus on some mountaintop in their pajamas.

Jehovah's Witnesses often appeal to Bible prophecies of the future to gain a listening ear. When they came to our house not long ago, my wife told me that their opening appeal was about the future conditions of life on earth as predicted in the Bible.

Mormons have a confused and corrupt yet very appealing view of the last days and the afterlife that draws in many converts every year.

Theonomists, Reconstructionists, and adherents of dominion theology use their postmillennial view of the last days to promote a proactive, even overtly militant agenda toward secular society.

David Koresh sucked people into his outlandish brand of the Adventist movement primarily by his teachings on the last days. His tirades on the end of the world, Armageddon, and the judgment of God held his followers spellbound. At the time of his death, he was composing his own twisted view of the seven seals in Revelation 6–8.

The Heaven's Gate cult attracted a following through its bizarre views on the last days, alien life, and heaven.

A proper view of Bible prophecy and the last days insulates God's people from these kinds of harmful, heretical teachings.

PROPHECY HELPS US UNDERSTAND OUR WORLD TODAY

There are two main extremes in the study and application of Bible prophecy. One extreme is to try to relate every event—no matter how minor—to the prophecies of the Bible. Every earthquake, disease, disaster, or feud between nations is seen a sign of the times. This extreme position of "newspaper exegesis" is unproductive at best and unbiblical at worst.

The other extreme ignores Bible prophecy and considers signs of the times irrelevant. The following passages from the Word of God, however, clearly call us to observe the signs of the times and to be alert and watchful:

- *One day the Pharisees and Sadducees came to test Jesus' claims by asking him to show them a miraculous sign from heaven. He replied, "You know the saying, 'Red sky at night means fair weather tomorrow, red sky in the morning means foul weather all day.' You are good at reading the weather signs in the sky, but you can't read the obvious signs of the times!" (Matt. 16:1-3)*

- *Now learn a lesson from the fig tree. When its buds become tender and its leaves begin to sprout, you know without being told that summer is near. Just so, when you see the events I've described beginning to happen, you can know his return is very near, right at the door. (Matt. 24:32-33)*

- *There will be strange events in the skies—signs in the sun, moon, and stars. And down here on earth the nations will be in turmoil, perplexed by the roaring seas and strange tides. The courage of many people will falter because of the fearful fate they see coming upon the earth, because the stability of the very heavens will be broken up. Then everyone will see the Son of Man arrive on the clouds with power and great glory. So when all these things begin to happen, stand straight and look up, for your salvation is near! (Luke 21:25-28)*

Let's face it—the vast majority of people have no clue what's going on in our world today. Even most world leaders don't really understand what's happening. They grope around in the darkness, trying to figure out this world. But as God's children, we have a light that helps us see in the darkness of our world. That light is Bible prophecy. "We have . . . confidence in the message proclaimed by the prophets. Pay close attention to what they wrote, for their words are like a light shining in a dark place—until the day Christ appears and his brilliant light shines in your hearts" (2 Pet. 1:19).

Bible prophecy is a light that helps us understand our world and live as lights in the darkness (Phil. 2:15-16). Prophecy doesn't show us every insignificant ripple in our world today, but it does reveal the main currents and trends. Why is religious apostasy on the rise? Why are there so many false teachers in the church today? Why are Israel and the Middle East the focus of the world? Why are the main nations of the Roman Empire coming back together? Why does the world seem to be moving toward a one-world economy that could easily be controlled by one person with enough power? If we understand Bible prophecy, the answers to these questions become clearer and clearer.

First Chronicles 12:32 says that back in the days of King David, there were two hundred men renowned for their unique knowledge of the days in which they lived. "From the tribe of Issachar, there were 200 leaders of the tribe with their relatives. All these men understood the temper of the times and knew the best course for Israel to take." Understanding what the Bible reveals about the last days helps us become modern-day "men of Issachar," who understand the times in which we live and know the best course for our life, our family, and our church to follow.

PROPHECY REVEALS THE SOVEREIGNTY OF GOD OVER TIME AND HISTORY

In order to accurately predict the future, one must be omniscient (know everything), omnipresent (be present everywhere), and omnipotent (possess all power). The true prognosticator must know all things, must be present at all times and places, and must have all power to make sure the prediction is fulfilled.

The God of the Bible issues a challenge to any would-be rivals to his place of supremacy in the universe. The basis of the challenge is that only the true God can accurately predict the future. Read what God says about his ability to disclose the future:

> • *"Can your idols make such claims as these? Let them come and show what they can do!" says the Lord, the King of Israel. "Let*

them try to tell us what happened long ago or what the future holds. Yes, that's it! If you are gods, tell what will occur in the days ahead. Or perform a mighty miracle that will fill us with amazement and fear. Do something, whether good or bad! But no! You are less than nothing and can do nothing at all. Anyone who chooses you becomes filthy, just like you!" (Isaiah 41:21-24)

• *Everything I prophesied has come true, and now I will prophesy again. I will tell you the future before it happens. (Isaiah 42:9)*

• *This is what the Lord, Israel's King and Redeemer, the Lord Almighty, says: "I am the First and the Last; there is no other God. Who else can tell you what is going to happen in the days ahead? Let them tell you if they can and thus prove their power. Let them do as I have done since ancient times. Do not tremble; do not be afraid. Have I not proclaimed from ages past what my purposes are for you? You are my witnesses—is there any other God? No! There is no other Rock—not one!" (Isaiah 44:6-8)*

• *Do not forget this, you guilty ones. And do not forget the things I have done throughout history. For I am God—I alone! I am God, and there is no one else like me. Only I can tell you what is going to happen even before it happens. Everything I plan will come to pass, for I do whatever I wish. (Isaiah 46:8-10)*

• *Praise the name of God forever and ever, for he alone has all wisdom and power. He determines the course of world events; he removes kings and sets others on the throne. He gives wisdom to the wise and knowledge to the scholars. He reveals deep and mysterious things and knows what lies hidden in the darkness, though he himself is surrounded by light. (Daniel 2:20-22)*

Bible prophecy proves beyond any shadow of a doubt that God is the true God, who alone rules over time and history! He not only rules the ages, but he is also in total control over the events of the life of every person. What a comfort and encouragement it is to know that God is in control!

PROPHECY PROVES THE TRUTH OF GOD'S WORD

Just as Bible prophecy establishes that God is the true God, it also proves that God's Word is the true Word. An old Chinese proverb says that it's very difficult to prophesy, especially about the future. That's why Bible prophecy is absolute proof of the truth and veracity of God's Word. The hundreds of prophecies that have come to pass exactly as the Bible has said prove that the Bible is the inspired Word of the sovereign Lord.

Here are just a few examples of some amazing prophecies that prove the divine inspiration of the Bible and separate it from every other book ever written:

- King Cyrus of Persia—Isaiah 44:28–45:7 calls King Cyrus of Persia by name and describes his mighty conquests in detail more than one hundred years before he was even born.
- The Four Great World Empires—Around 530 B.C., the prophet Daniel predicted that there would be four great Gentile powers that would rule the world in succession: Babylon, Persia, Greece, and Rome (Daniel 2:31-45; 7:1-28). He further prophesied that in the last days, the final Gentile world power (Rome) will be reconstituted in a ten-nation confederation that will be ruled over by one man (Antichrist). Amazingly, there have been four—and only four—world empires. As much as others have tried since the fall of the Roman Empire, they have always failed in their lust to rule the world. God's Word stands as the anvil of truth.
- The Fall of Nineveh—Sometime around 650–640 B.C. God revealed an amazing prophecy to a prophet named Nahum. God showed this prophet that the great city of Nineveh, the capital of the Assyrian Empire, would be destroyed. Moreover, God gave a detailed description of exactly how the devastation would occur.

In a state of drunkenness, Nineveh would be destroyed by an invading army racing madly through the streets (Nah. 1:10; 2:3-4). Nineveh would also be flooded with water (Nah. 1:8), burned with fire (Nah. 2:13; 3:13, 15), plundered for her treasures (Nah. 2:9), and totally destroyed (Nah. 3:19).

History records that all of these predictions were fulfilled exactly in 612 B.C., when the Babylonians and Medes invaded, sacked, and utterly destroyed this powerful city.

- The Seventy-Year Babylonian Captivity of Judah—The prophet Jeremiah, who spoke for God from 627 to 582 B.C., prophesied that the wicked people of Judah would be taken into captivity by the

Babylonians and that the captivity would last for seventy years, during which time the land of Judah would rest:

I will take away your happy singing and laughter. The joyful voices of bridegrooms and brides will no longer be heard. Your businesses will fail, and all your homes will stand silent and dark. This entire land will become a desolate wasteland. Israel and her neighboring lands will serve the king of Babylon for seventy years. (Jer. 25:10-11)

The truth is that you will be in Babylon for seventy years. But then I will come and do for you all the good things I have promised, and I will bring you home again. (Jer. 29:10)

• This prophecy, given decades before the event occurred, was fulfilled accurately. Nebuchadnezzar of Babylon first took the people of Israel into captivity in 605 B.C. King Cyrus of Persia allowed the captives to return from Babylon in 538 B.C. Allowing for the time it would take them to return, to plant crops, and to receive a harvest, the land rested for seventy years:

The few who survived were taken away to Babylon, and they became servants to the king and his sons until the kingdom of Persia came to power. So the message of the Lord spoken through Jeremiah was fulfilled. The land finally enjoyed its Sabbath rest, lying desolate for seventy years, just as the prophet had said. (2 Chron. 36:20-21)

These are just a few of the hundreds of prophecies that prove without a doubt that the Bible is the inerrant, inspired Word of the living God. History and the fulfillment of prophecy have proven the Bible to be like the wall that a man built, which was four feet wide and three feet high. When asked why he had been so foolish as to build a wall wider than it was high, the man replied, "I built it this way so that if a storm should come and blow it over, it will be higher afterward than it was before." No book has weathered more storms than the Bible. And after each storm the Bible is left standing higher than it was before.

After seeing how the Bible predicts the future with 100 percent accuracy, the Bible reaches up to the heavens as the tower of God's truth!

[1]Randall Price, *Jerusalem in Prophecy: God's Stage for the Final Drama* (Eugene, Oreg.: Harvest House, 1998), 55.

Three Main Views
of Bible Prophecy

One of the primary reasons average Christians avoid studying Bible prophecy is all the different views. A person picks up a few books to brush up on his or her knowledge of the end times, and before long he or she is hopelessly lost in lengthy explanations of long, unfamiliar words. The average Christian's dilemma reminds me of the little boy

whose father was a preacher. After hearing his dad preach on justifica-
tion, sanctification, and all the other "ations," he was ready to answer
when his Sunday school teacher asked if anyone knew what *procrasti-
nation* meant. The boy immediately replied, "I'm not sure what it
means, but I know our church believes in it!" That's the way many people are when it comes to Bible prophecy. They're not sure what these
big words mean, but they know that they must believe in it.

Bible prophecy novices hear words such as *premillennial, postmillennial, Pretribulational, Posttribulational, dispensational,* and *cove-
nantal* and see enough charts and time lines to last them a lifetime.
Overwhelmed, they finally adopt the position of the "panmillennial."
Essentially, they believe that it will all "pan out" in the end and don't
worry about it anymore.

All the different views, systems, and theories of the last days even
intimidate many pastors and teachers. To most professing Christians, Bible prophecy remains an unsolvable mystery. How can we
hope to make our way through and make sense out of all the conflict-
ing views? Is it possible to boil it all down to the basics so we can
understand at least the main views or systems people hold on the last
days? The answer is a resounding yes! In the next few pages, the three
main views of the last days will be presented in a clear, easy-to-
follow format.

Broadly speaking, there are three main evangelical views, systems, or
frameworks of Bible prophecy and the end times: amillennial, premillennial, and postmillennial. As you can see, the main word in each of
these terms is *millennial* or *millennium,* which means a thousand
years. This term comes from the Latin words *mille* (a thousand) and
annus (year). In the Bible the millennial kingdom is that phase of God's
kingdom when Jesus Christ rules and reigns. Although the word itself
never appears in the Bible, Revelation 20:1-7 specifically states six
times that the duration of this kingdom is one thousand years.

TWO MAIN POINTS OF AGREEMENT

As with most divergent views, there are points on which all of these
positions agree. Two main points of agreement between these views
are essential:

1. All three of these views believe that Jesus Christ is King of kings and Lord of lords and that he rules or will rule over a glorious kingdom.
2. All three of these views hold that Jesus Christ will one day return to this world literally, physically, visibly, and gloriously as the Judge of all the earth.

It is important not to overlook these two key points of agreement. After all, these are part of the essentials that bind us together as believers in Jesus Christ, our soon-coming Lord. However, we must also recognize that there are significant differences between these views that affect how believers understand almost every key event of the last days. Each of these systems presents a very different picture of what will happen both before and after Jesus returns to earth. This is not just some study in irrelevant theory. Which of these views you hold will determine how you understand the characters, chronology, and consummation of the end times. Will there be a literal kingdom on earth? Will there be a literal seven-year Tribulation period before Christ returns? Will there be an individual called the Antichrist? Will the church succeed in Christianizing the world before Christ returns?

THREE MAIN POINTS OF DISAGREEMENT

While there are many differences between these three views of the last days, the main points of disagreement revolve around three key issues: (1) *when* Jesus will reign (the timing of his reign); (2) *how* Jesus will reign (the nature of his reign); and (3) *where* Jesus will reign (the place of his reign). While there are some variations even within these three systems, only the general framework of these views will be presented.

The Amillennial View The amillennial position is the dominant view of the modern church. It is the view held by the Roman Catholic Church, the Greek church, and a large portion of Protestantism. The genesis of this view is usually traced back to St. Augustine (A.D. 354–430). This was also the view of reformers such as John Calvin and Martin Luther.

The prefix *a=* before the word *millennium* denotes a negation of the word and literally means "no millennium." However, this is not exactly true, because the amillennialists do believe in a millennial kingdom of Christ, just not a literal kingdom.

WHEN WILL JESUS REIGN? Amillennialists believe that Christ's kingdom transpires in the present age between his first and second comings. Therefore, the Millennium is not a literal period of one thousand years but is symbolic of a "long period of time." Amillennialists teach that the binding of Satan (Rev. 20:1-3) occurred at the first coming of Christ as a result of Christ's death and resurrection.

HOW AND WHERE WILL JESUS REIGN? Amillennialists deny that the reign of Jesus will be a literal, physical kingdom on earth. For the amillennialist, the reign of Christ is a present spiritual kingdom, where Christ reigns over the church in the hearts of believers and/or in heaven over the souls of the redeemed. The amillennial position is very simple and streamlined. Amillenialists believe that Christ will return someday to judge all people and bring in the eternal state. They deny both a literal seven-year period of Tribulation before the second coming of Christ and a literal one-thousand-year period of reign after his second coming.

CHRONOLOGY OF FUTURE EVENTS ACCORDING
TO THE AMILLENNIAL SYSTEM

- A parallel development of both good (God's kingdom) and evil (Satan's kingdom) during this present age
- The second coming of Christ
- The general resurrection of all people
- A general judgment of all people
- Eternity

THE TIME LINE OF AMILLENNIALISM

CHRIST'S FIRST COMING — Christ reigning in heaven over souls of redeemed / Christ ruling on earth in hearts of believers — CHRIST'S SECOND COMING

? YEARS

Satan Bound — Present Age = Millennial Kingdom — The Eternal State

The Premillennial View Premillennialism was the view of the early church. It was the view held by such early church fathers as Papias, Tertullian, Clement of Rome, Barnabas, Ignatius, Polycarp, and Justin the Martyr. After the third century, it began to wane, and amillennialism replaced it as the prevailing view. Premillennialism began to make a comeback in the mid-nineteenth century and is currently a very popular way of understanding the last days. Some modern premillennialists are Charles Ryrie, John Walvoord, J. Dwight Pentecost, James Montgomery Boice, Hal Lindsey, John MacArthur Jr., and Charles Swindoll.

WHEN WILL JESUS REIGN? Premillennialism teaches that the second coming of Jesus Christ will occur before *(pre)* the millennial kingdom. Christ's return to earth at the end of a literal seven-year period of terrible judgment called the Tribulation inaugurates the millennial kingdom.

HOW AND WHERE WILL JESUS REIGN? Premillennialists hold that the millennial kingdom will be a literal, physical, earthly kingdom of one thousand literal years, during which Jesus Christ will rule and reign over the earth from his throne in Jerusalem. According to this view, the kingdom will not be established by the conversion of souls over an extended period of time but suddenly and powerfully by the glorious coming of Christ from heaven to earth. Satan will be bound for one thousand years during the duration of Christ's reign (Rev. 20:1-3), the curse of the Fall will be reversed, the Jewish people will be restored to their ancient land, and Christ will reign over the earth in righteousness, peace, and joy.

It is important to note that most premillennialists would agree that Jesus rules over the church during this present age as its head and that he certainly rules over the hearts of his people. He was, is, and always will be the Sovereign of the universe. However, premillennialists would contend that this is not to be confused with the millennial kingdom that Christ will rule over as King for one thousand years as described in Revelation 20:1-6. The rule of Christ will be literally fulfilled in the future.

CHRONOLOGY OF FUTURE EVENTS ACCORDING
TO THE PREMILLENNIAL SYSTEM

- Increase of apostasy as the church age draws to a close
- The rapture of the Church (resurrection of dead saints/translation of living saints)—premillennialists disagree among themselves about the timing of the Rapture. This will be discussed in the next chapter.
- Seven-year Tribulation period on earth
- The second coming of Christ to earth

- The campaign of Armageddon
- The millennial reign of Christ on earth
- The Great White Throne Judgment
- The creation of a new heaven and a new earth
- Eternity

THE TIME LINE OF PREMILLENNIALISM

The Postmillennial View Postmillennialism arrived on the scene much later than either of its rivals but enjoyed great popularity, becoming the major millennial view of the eighteenth and nineteenth centuries. With all the advances in technology, science, and the industrial revolution, the idea that man could bring in the kingdom of God made perfect sense. However, the outbreak of World War I, followed closely by World War II, dealt postmillennialism a blow from which it has never fully recovered. Modern reconstructionists, theonomists, and adherents of dominion theology are postmillennialists.

WHEN WILL JESUS REIGN? Postmillennialists maintain that Jesus Christ will return to earth after *(post)* the Millennium. Consequently, the Millennium is the entire period of time between the first and second comings of Christ. Christ returns after the Millennium is completely over.

HOW AND WHERE WILL JESUS REIGN? The nature of Jesus' reign for postmillennialists is spiritual and political. This view teaches that the millennial kingdom is not a literal thousand years but a golden age ushered in by the church's preaching of the gospel during this present age. This golden age will arrive by degrees as the gospel spreads throughout the earth until the whole world is eventually Christianized. The Millennium will grow on earth as believers in Christ exercise more and more influence over the affairs of this earth. Ultimately, the gospel will prevail, and the earth will become a better world, after which time Christ will return to usher in eternity.

The best-known advocate of this view in recent years is Loraine Boettner. He summarizes the postmillennial view very well:

Postmillennialism is that view of the last things which holds that the kingdom of God is now being extended in the world through the preaching of the gospel and the saving work of the Holy Spirit in the hearts of individuals, that the world eventually is to be Christianized and that the return of Christ is to occur at the close of a long period of righteousness and peace commonly called the millennium. It should be added that on the postmillennial principles the Second Coming of Christ will be followed immediately by the general resurrection, the general judgment, and the introduction of heaven and hell in their fullness.

The millennium to which the postmillennialist looks forward is thus a golden age of spiritual prosperity during this present dispensation, that is, the Church Age. This is to be brought about through forces now active in the world. It is to last an indefinitely long period of time, perhaps much longer than a literal one thousand years. The changed character of individuals will be reflected in an uplifted social, economic, political and cultural life of mankind. The world at large will then enjoy a state of righteousness which up until now has been seen only in relatively small and isolated groups: for example, some family circles, and some local church groups and kindred organizations.

This does not mean that there will be a time on this earth when every person will be a Christian or that all sin will be abolished. But it does mean that evil in all its many forms eventually will be reduced to negligible proportions, that Christian principles will be the rule, not the exception, and that Christ will return to a truly Christianized world.[1]

CHRONOLOGY OF FUTURE EVENTS ACCORDING TO THE POSTMILLENNIAL SYSTEM

- Progressive improvement of conditions on earth as the end draws near, culminating in a golden age as the world is Christianized
- The second coming of Christ

- The general resurrection of all people
- A general judgment of all people
- Eternity

THE TIME LINE OF POSTMILLENNIALISM

CHRIST'S FIRST COMING

CHRIST'S SECOND COMING

? YEARS

Satan Bound

The Present Age = The Golden Age
Millennium = ? Years

The Eternal State

SUMMARY OF THE THREE MILLENNIAL VIEWS

VIEWS	WHEN WILL CHRIST REIGN?	HOW AND WHERE WILL CHRIST REIGN?
Amillennial	Between the First and Second Comings (Present reign)	Christ rules over a spiritual kingdom in the hearts of believers on earth and over the souls of the redeemed in heaven. (Spiritual reign)
Premillennial	Immediately after the Second Coming (Future reign)	Christ will rule personally for one thousand years over a literal, physical, earthly kingdom with Satan bound and the curse of the Fall removed. (Earthly reign)
Postmillennial	Between the First and Second Comings but arriving by degrees (Present reign)	Christ rules in the hearts of believers as the church brings in the kingdom by the triumph of the gospel in this world. (Spiritual reign)

WHICH VIEW IS MOST CONVINCING?

As you can see, these three systems are very different in their picture of the end times. Which system of beliefs one holds determines how he or she interprets hundreds of passages in the Bible. Therefore, this is not a trivial matter.

The big question is, Which view is most convincing? Which of these three views most accurately reflects the teachings found in the Bible? The view that I hold and that will be the foundation for the rest of this book is the premillennial view. I believe this view is far superior to either of the other views for four main reasons:

Early Church Tradition As we have already noted, this was the view of the early church for the first two centuries of church history. While this point is not conclusive, it does carry undeniable weight, for those closest in time to the New Testament era should have the clearest understanding of what the apostles taught. Papias (c. A.D. 130), one of the apostolic fathers, was a student of the apostle John. Papias believed in a literal one-thousand-year reign of Christ after his return to earth. It is very possible that Papias received this truth directly from John himself, the author of Revelation.

Correct Method of Interpretation The premillennial position is the only position that consistently interprets Bible prophecy literally. The other two positions consistently spiritualize Old Testament prophecies and apply them to the church, which they interpret as the spiritual Israel.

35

The method for interpreting Bible prophecy is clearly established in Scripture. All the prophecies of Christ's first coming were fulfilled literally in the person and work of our Savior. It makes sense to believe that the prophecies of Christ's second coming will also be fulfilled literally. To spiritualize the prophecies of the last days and deny a literal Tribulation period, a literal Antichrist, a literal battle of Armageddon, a literal restoration of the Jewish people to the land of Israel, and a literal, earthly millennial kingdom violates the method of interpreting Bible prophecy already established in the prophecies of the first coming of Christ.

Fulfillment of Covenants Premillennialism is the only one of these systems that allows for the literal fulfillment of God's covenants with Abraham and David.

God unconditionally and unilaterally promised Abraham three things in Genesis 12:1-3 and 15:18-19:

1. God would bless Abraham personally, and the whole world would be blessed through him.
2. God would give Abraham many descendants.
3. God would give Abraham and his descendants a specific piece of land forever (the boundaries of this land are described in Genesis 15:18-19).

Clearly, the first two prongs of God's promise have been literally fulfilled. God gave Abraham many descendants, and God has blessed the world through Abraham via the Jewish Scripture and the Jewish Savior. If these first two conditions of this covenant have been fulfilled literally, then it seems logical to conclude that the last (the promise of land) will also be literally fulfilled. And since this promise has never been completely fulfilled in history (the Israelites have never possessed the land with the boundaries given in Genesis 15:18-19), the promise must still be future. The promise of land to Abraham fits perfectly with the idea of Christ's reigning on earth for a thousand years, during which time Israel will occupy all the land promised in Genesis 15:18 and Christ will rule from the city of Jerusalem.

In 2 Samuel 7:12-16, God promised King David that one of his descendants would sit on his throne and reign over his kingdom forever. While God did not promise that this rule would continue uninterrupted, he did promise that David's dynasty would maintain the right to rule and that one of David's descendants would rule forever. This promise was applied specifically to Jesus when he was born (Luke 1:32-33).

Amillennialists and postmillennialists argue that this covenant is completely fulfilled in the present age as Christ sits on his throne in heaven, ruling over the church. Premillennialists, on the other hand, contend that Christ must literally sit on David's throne on earth and rule over David's kingdom, which is the nation of Israel.

The New Testament bears out this literal interpretation. In Acts 1:6-7, Jesus reaffirmed that the kingdom would be restored to Israel in the future: "When the apostles were with Jesus, they kept asking him, 'Lord, are you going to free Israel now and restore our kingdom?' 'The Father sets those dates,' he replied, 'and they are not for you to know.'" Jesus had promised the disciples that in his kingdom they would sit on twelve thrones, judging the twelve tribes of Israel (Matt. 19:28). Understandably, they wanted to know when this great event was on God's time schedule. Notice that Jesus did not correct the disciples' statement that the kingdom would be restored to Israel. He simply pointed out that they were not to be concerned about the timing of that event. Just before his ascension back to heaven, Jesus confirmed to his disciples the fact that the kingdom would be restored to Israel. And the future millennial kingdom of Christ is the only time mentioned in Scripture when the Davidic covenant can be literally, completely fulfilled.

Clearest Reading of Revelation 20:1-6 The premillennial position is the clearest, most natural reading of Revelation 20:1-6. This section, which is the only passage in the Bible that specifically mentions the thousand-year reign of Christ, follows immediately after the second coming of Christ in Revelation 19:11-21. In Revelation 19–20, Christ's coming is clearly *pre=* (before) the Millennium or one-thousand-year reign.

CONCLUSION

Now that we have established premillennialism as the best overall system for understanding the prophecies of the Bible, the rest of this book will focus on the particular details of the future of the world. If you have ever wondered what the future holds for you, for the nations of this world, or even for the entire universe, then the next chapter is for you! Fasten your spiritual seat belt as we take a breathtaking tour of the ten main events on God's prophetic calendar.

[1]Robert G. Clouse, editor, *The Meaning of the Millennium: Four Views* (Downers Grove, Ill.: InterVarsity Press, 1977), 117–18.

Ten Key Events
in Bible Prophecy

41

At any high school, college, or NFL football game, the head coach and players line the sideline of the field. They are right there where the action happens. But being that close, they often lack the big picture of what's really occurring in the game. They lose the overall perspective of how the plays are developing. Therefore, each team has a few coaches up in the press box, high above the field, who communicate with the head coach via headphones. The coaches in the press box give those on the sidelines the broader view of the game. They are able to see the formations the other team is using and how particular players are doing, and thus, they can tell the head coach what to look for on the field.

The same is true in life. Often in the close action of everyday life, God's people lose the overall perspective. The only view we have is the view from the sidelines or on the field. We need to get the bigger picture to understand where it's all headed. The purpose of this chapter is to present the press box view of the end times—the big picture, the overview—as we survey the ten main events of the end times.

THE RAPTURE OF THE CHURCH (When the Trumpet Sounds)

The next great event on God's prophetic timetable is the rapture of the church. The Rapture is that future event when Jesus Christ will descend from heaven to resurrect the bodies of departed believers and transform the bodies of living believers into his glorious presence in an instant and then escort them to heaven to live with him forever. The Rapture is the blessed hope of the church.

Whenever someone mentions the Rapture, another is certain to point out that the word *Rapture* never occurs in the Bible. While this is true, the concept of the Rapture is clearly present. The words "caught up" in 1 Thessalonians 4:17 translate from a Greek word that means "to snatch, to seize suddenly, or to transport from one place to another." It is also used of rescuing someone from a threatening danger (Acts 23:10; Jude 1:23). The translation of this Greek word is *rapturo*. That's where we get the English word *Rapture* to describe this future event of being caught up to meet Jesus Christ in the clouds.

The Truth of the Rapture There are three main passages on the Rapture in the New Testament:

- *Don't be troubled. You trust God, now trust in me. There are many rooms in my Father's home, and I am going to prepare a place for you. If this were not so, I would tell you plainly. When everything is ready, I will come and get you, so that you will always be with me where I am. (John 14:1-3)*

- *Let me tell you a wonderful secret God has revealed to us. Not all of us will die, but we will all be transformed. It will happen in a moment, in the blinking of an eye, when the last trumpet is blown. For when the trumpet sounds, the Christians who have died will be raised with transformed bodies. And then we who are living will be transformed so that we will never die. For our perishable earthly bodies must be transformed into heavenly bodies that will never die.*

  When this happens—when our perishable earthly bodies have been transformed into heavenly bodies that will never die—then at last the Scriptures will come true: "Death is swallowed up in victory. O death, where is your victory? O death, where is your sting?" (1 Cor. 15:51-55)

- *Brothers and sisters, I want you to know what will happen to the Christians who have died so you will not be full of sorrow like people who have no hope. For since we believe that Jesus died and was raised to life again, we also believe that when Jesus comes, God will bring back with Jesus all the Christians who have died.*

  I can tell you this directly from the Lord: We who are still living when the Lord returns will not rise to meet him ahead of those who are in their graves. For the Lord himself will come down from heaven with a commanding shout, with the call of the archangel, and with the trumpet call of God. First, all the Christians who have died will rise from their graves. Then, to-

gether with them, we who are still alive and remain on the earth will be caught up in the clouds to meet the Lord in the air and remain with him forever. So comfort and encourage each other with these words. (1 Thess. 4:13-18)

While all three of these texts are of equal importance, we will focus on 1 Thessalonians 4:13-18 in this section. There are seven key points in this passage that reveal the truth of the Rapture.

THE REALIZATION (Verses 13-14) At the outset Paul makes it clear that he wants us to understand the Rapture. Notice these important words: "I want you to know." The Lord wants every believer to know the truth of the Rapture. In the King James Version, verse 13 begins, "I would not have you to be ignorant, brethren." Someone once said that the fastest growing denomination in America is the "church of the ignorant brethren." But the Lord doesn't want us to be ignorant about the truth of the Rapture.

The first thing the Lord wants us to realize about the Rapture is that our believing loved ones who have passed away will not miss out on this event. When Jesus comes, he will bring the perfected spirits of departed believers with him. This truth can bring us comfort and hope and soften our grieving when loved ones pass away. When believers pass away, it is not good-bye; it is more like good night. We will see them again at the Rapture.

THE REVELATION (Verse 15A) Paul also wants us to know without any doubt that what he is saying is directly from the Lord ("I can tell you this directly from the Lord"). What Paul recorded was divinely revealed. It's not something he made up on his own.

THE RETURN (Verses 15B-16B) At the Rapture the Lord himself will come again in the clouds. He will return accompanied by three things: a commanding shout, the call of the archangel, and the trumpet call of God.

This commanding shout is the last of three great cries or commands of the Savior: (1) the cry from the cemetery when Lazarus was raised (John 11:43-44); (2) the cry from the cross when the dead came to life (Matt. 27:50-53); and (3) the cry from the clouds when the dead are raised at his coming (1 Thess. 4:16). Notice that at each of these cries, the dead are resurrected.

THE RESURRECTION (Verse 16B) When Christ comes down from heaven, the first thing that will happen is that the bodies of deceased believers will be raised or resurrected and reunited with their perfected spirits, which will have returned with the Lord. These resurrected bodies will be glorified, incorruptible bodies fit for the heavenly realm (1 Cor. 15:35-56; 2 Cor. 5:1-5; Phil. 3:20-21).

45

THE REMOVAL (Verse 17A) When the dead have been raised, living believers will immediately be transformed into the presence of the calling Christ without ever tasting physical death. As 1 Corinthians 15:51 says, "Not all of us will die, but we will all be transformed." The King James Version translates this verse, "We shall not all sleep, but we shall all be changed." This verse often appears on the door of church nurseries. It's certainly true of many children in the nursery, but, thanks be to God, it will be true of millions of God's children when Jesus returns from heaven. Millions of believers will never face the sting of death but will be removed, raptured, directly into the presence of the Lord in the clouds. This translation will take place in the amount of time it takes to blink one's eye (1 Cor. 15:52).

THE REUNION (Verse 17) The dead in Christ and the living saints will all be raptured together and will meet the Lord in the air. What a glorious reunion as all the saints of this age meet the dear Savior.

THE REASSURANCE (Verse 18) One practical application of the Rapture is that it brings comfort and hope to all of God's people when a believing loved one or friend goes home to be with the Lord. These words have certainly been read at thousands of funerals throughout the centuries and have brought the comfort, hope, and encouragement of the Lord to broken, bereaved hearts.

The Timing of the Rapture All premillennialists believe in the Rapture. But there is wide disagreement about the timing of this event in relation to the Tribulation period. Will the church go through any or all of the Tribulation before the Rapture occurs? In the minds of most

COMPLETE BOOK OF BIBLE PROPHECY

believers, this is the big question about the Rapture, and it is clearly the issue most often debated about the Rapture.

There are five main positions on the timing of the Rapture:

1. The Pre-Tribulation Rapture—the Rapture will occur before the Tribulation period begins.
2. The Mid-Tribulation Rapture—the Rapture will occur at the midpoint of the Tribulation.
3. The Post-Tribulation Rapture—the Rapture will occur at the end of the Tribulation, right before the second coming of Christ to earth.
4. The Partial Rapture—faithful, devoted believers will be raptured before the Tribulation, but the rest of the believers will be left to go through the purging of the Tribulation.
5. The Pre-Wrath Rapture—the Rapture will occur about three-fourths (five and one-quarter years) of the way through the Tribulation, when the wrath of God begins to be poured out on the earth at the seventh seal (Rev. 6:17).

VARIOUS VIEWS OF THE TIMING OF THE RAPTURE

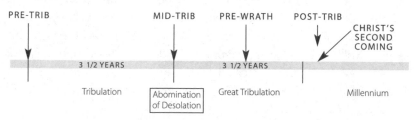

Three Reasons for a Pre-Trib Rapture Rather than pointing out all the strengths and weaknesses of each view, I will present three key reasons why I believe the Bible teaches the Pre-Trib Rapture position.

First, the Bible promises that God's people are exempt from the coming wrath of the Tribulation period (1 Thess. 1:10; 5:9; Rev. 3:10). The nature of the entire Tribulation period is one of pounding judgment against a rebellious world. The judgment of God begins with the first seal (Rev. 6:1-2) and continues all the way until the Second Coming. To say that God confines his wrath to the very end of the Tribulation as the pre-Wrath view maintains, one must overlook the fact that the Lamb opens all of the seal judgments (Rev. 6:1-17; 8:1). They are the wrath of God against sinful humanity, and they are opened at the very beginning of the Tribulation. The very nature of the entire Tribulation period demands that Christ's bride be exempt from this time of trouble.

The rescue of Lot and his family from Sodom (Gen. 18–19) clearly shows that it is against God's character to destroy the righteous with the wicked when he pours out his judgment. The taking of Enoch to heaven before the Flood (Gen. 5:24) and the story of Noah are two other illustrations of this principle.

In Revelation 3:10-11, the Lord's promise of deliverance from the Tribulation period is very specific: "Because you have obeyed my command to persevere, I will protect you from the great time of testing that will come upon the whole world to test those who belong to this world. Look, I am coming quickly." Notice two important things about this promise. First, the Lord says he will keep his people not just from the testing but from the very "time" of worldwide testing. What is the time of worldwide testing? In the context of Revelation, it is clearly the Tribulation period of chapters 6–19. Second, notice the means of this protection in verse 11: "Look, I am coming quickly." Putting these two points together, it is clear that the Lord will protect his people from the time of worldwide testing by coming for them.

The second reason for a pre-Trib Rapture is that, from humanity's viewpoint, it could occur at any moment, and believers should constantly anticipate it (1 Cor. 1:7; 16:22; Phil. 3:20; 4:5; 1 Thess. 1:9-10; Titus 2:13; Heb. 9:28; Jude 1:21). Only the pre-Trib position allows for an imminent and signless coming of Christ for his bride. Only those who believe in a pre-Trib Rapture can honestly say, "Jesus may come today! Glad day! Glad day!" For mid-Tribbers, the Rapture must be at least three and one-half years away; for pre-Wrathers, it must be at least five and one-quarter years away; for post-Tribbers, it is at least seven years down the road.

Christ's coming at any moment is a truth that fills us with hope, anticipation, and motivation to godly living. Believers should live with the hope that Jesus may come today!

A third reason for a pre-Trib Rapture is that the key New Testament passages that deal with the Tribulation period consistently fail to mention the presence of the church. The main portion of the Bible that describes the Tribulation period is Revelation 6–19, and in this section there is a strange silence concerning the church. In Revelation 1–5, the church is specifically mentioned nineteen times, but in Revelation

6–19, the church of Jesus Christ is absent from the earth. In fact, the only place you find the church in Revelation 6–19 is in heaven, as the twenty-four elders, who are seated on thrones, dressed in white, and crowned with crowns worship the Lamb (Rev. 4:4, 10; 5:5-6, 8-14). Where are these elders? Are they on earth getting ready for the Tribulation? No! They are in heaven worshiping him who sits on the throne and the Lamb. They have already been caught up to heaven before the first judgment of the Tribulation, found in Revelation 6:1, begins.

The church will be raptured to heaven before the Tribulation period begins. Keep looking up!

THE JUDGMENT SEAT OF CHRIST (The Crowning Day)

The first major event that will occur in heaven after the church has been raptured is the judgment seat of Christ. At the judgment seat, all believers from the church age—the time between the Day of Pentecost and the Rapture—will appear individually before God to receive rewards or loss of reward based on their lives, service, and ministry for the Lord.

The Seven Future Judgments The judgment of church-age believers will be the first of seven great future judgments that will occur:

THE JUDGMENT SEAT OF CHRIST (2 Cor. 5:10)   Church-age believers will appear before the judgment seat of Christ in heaven after the Rapture for reward or loss of reward.

OLD TESTAMENT BELIEVERS (Dan. 12:1-3)   All Old Testament believers will be resurrected and rewarded after the Second Coming.

TRIBULATION BELIEVERS (Rev. 20:4-6)   Those who trust Christ during the Tribulation and die for their faith will be resurrected and rewarded at the end of the Tribulation.

JEWS LIVING AT THE SECOND COMING (Ezek. 20:34-38)   All Jews who survive the Tribulation will be judged in the wilderness right after the Second Coming. The saved will enter the kingdom, and the lost will be purged.

THE SHEEP AND THE GOATS (Matt. 25:31-46)   All Gentiles who survive the Tribulation will be judged right after the Second Coming, as Christ sits on his glorious throne. The saved will enter the millennial kingdom, and the lost will be cast into hell.

SATAN AND FALLEN ANGELS (Rev. 20:10)   The final judgment of Satan and the fallen angels (demons) will take place after the millennial kingdom.

THE GREAT WHITE THRONE (Rev. 20:11-15)   The judgment of unsaved people will occur at the end of the Millennium. They will be judged according to their works and cast into the lake of fire.

The Bible is clear that God not only judges us according to our deeds but rewards us as well. Consider these passages: Ps. 58:11; 62:12; Prov. 11:18; Isa. 40:10; 62:11; Matt. 5:12; 6:1-2; 10:41-42; Luke 6:35; 1 Cor. 3:8, 14; Eph. 6:8; Heb. 10:35-36; 11:6, 24-26; 2 John 1:8; Rev. 2:23; 11:18; Rev. 22:12. The judgment for church-age believers will occur at what the Bible calls the "judgment seat of Christ" (2 Cor. 5:10, KJV).

In this section we will examine the judgment seat of Christ under seven main headings: the period (when), the place (where), the participants (who), the purpose (why), the principles (how), the pictures (what), and the preparation (getting ready).

The Period of the Judgment (The *When*)   The judgment seat of Christ will occur in heaven immediately after Christ raptures the church. First Corinthians 4:5 places this judgment right after the Rapture: "When the Lord comes, he will bring our deepest secrets to light and will reveal our private motives. And then God will give to everyone whatever praise is due."

The Place of the Judgment (The *Where*)   In ancient times, a judgment seat, or *bema*, which refers to a raised step or platform, was set up for three major purposes. First, the judgment seat or bema was a court of justice where people came to have their grievances redressed. Paul was hauled before the judgment seat of Gallio in Acts 18:12.

Second, the judgment seat was a place in a military camp where the commander administered discipline and addressed the troops.

Third, the judgment seat was the stand at the athletic games from which judges enforced the rules and distributed rewards. This third picture seems to be the primary backdrop for the judgment seat of Christ in Scripture.

The judgment seat of Christ is the place in heaven after the Rapture where Christ will reward those who have finished the race and have obeyed the rules and will withhold reward from those who have been unfaithful.

The Participants of the Judgment (The *Who*) The judgment seat of Christ is for believers only. In 2 Corinthians 5:10, Paul says, "We must all stand before Christ to be judged." The context clearly indicates that he is referring to himself and other believers. Unbelievers will be judged by God at the Great White Throne Judgment, which we will discuss later in this chapter. Every person reading these words will appear at one of two great judgments. Believers will appear at the judgment seat to be rewarded. Unbelievers will appear at the Great White Throne to be condemned (Rev. 20:11-15).

The Purpose of the Judgment (The *Why*) Before stating the purpose of this judgment, it is important to state clearly what it is not. The purpose of the judgment seat of Christ is not to determine whether believers will enter heaven or hell or to mete out punishment for sin. This ultimate issue was already decided when believers put their faith in Jesus Christ as their Savior from sin. God's Word is clear that his children will never be judged for their sins. John 5:24 says, "I assure you, those who listen to my message and believe in God who sent me have eternal life. They will never be condemned for their sins, but they have already passed from death into life." Romans 8:1 echoes this message: "There is no condemnation for those who belong to Christ Jesus." If we ever have one sin brought against us, Christ's work was incomplete. Our salvation rests wholly on the person and work of Christ in our place.

Having said this, let's turn our focus to the purpose of the judgment seat of Christ, which is twofold: to review and to reward. First, the Lord will review our life. His review will be perfectly fair, impartial, thorough, and gracious. He will review our conduct—that is, how we lived our life after we became a believer. As Romans 14:10-12 says, "Each of us will stand personally before the judgment seat of God. For the Scriptures say, "'As surely as I live,' says the Lord, 'every knee will bow to me and every tongue will confess allegiance to God.' Yes, each of us will have to give a personal account to God." Second Corinthians 5:10 adds, "We must all stand before Christ to be judged. We will each receive whatever we deserve for the good or evil we have done in our bodies."

He will also review our service for him after we became a believer: "There is going to come a time of testing at the judgment day to see what kind of work each builder has done. Everyone's work will be put through the fire to see whether or not it keeps its value" (1 Cor. 3:13).

Our words will also be judged. We will have to give account for every word we have ever spoken: "I tell you this, that you must give an account on judgment day of every idle word you speak" (Matt. 12:36).

Finally, he will review our thoughts and motives. The all-knowing Lord will look at why we did what we did. This will be the most searching aspect of our evaluation. The following passages serve as a warning for us to keep our motives pure:

> • *Take care! Don't do your good deeds publicly, to be admired, because then you will lose the reward from your Father in heaven. When you give a gift to someone in need, don't shout about it as the hypocrites do—blowing trumpets in the synagogues and streets to call attention to their acts of charity! I assure you, they have received all the reward they will ever get. (Matt. 6:1-2)*

> • *Be careful not to jump to conclusions before the Lord returns as to whether or not someone is faithful. When the Lord comes, he will bring our deepest secrets to light and will reveal our private motives. (1 Cor. 4:5)*

> • *Nothing in all creation can hide from him. Everything is naked and exposed before his eyes. This is the God to whom we must explain all that we have done. (Heb. 4:13)*

At the judgment seat, all of our conduct, service, words, thoughts, and motives will be turned inside out and will appear in their true light. We can often fool other people about our service and motives, and they may think we are doing some great thing for God. But we can't fool God. He knows what we do and why we do it, and he bases his reward on the true estimation of our actions and attitudes. Many who we believe will receive great reward may walk away empty-handed and vice versa. Remember the words of Jesus in Matthew 20:16: "Many who are first now will be last then; and those who are last now will be first then."

The second purpose of this judgment is to reward. Jim Elliot, the martyred missionary, once said, "He is no fool who gives what he cannot keep to gain what he cannot lose." Those who have faithfully served the Lord and poured out their lives for him will gain eternal rewards that they can never lose.

While there are undoubtedly many areas of service, conduct, and ministry that will bring reward, the New Testament focuses on five specific rewards or "crowns" that the faithful will receive at the judgment seat. These crowns are representative of the kinds of conduct and service that the Lord will reward:

1. The Incorruptible Crown (1 Cor. 9:24-27): The reward for those who consistently practice self-discipline and self-control
2. The Crown of Righteousness (2 Tim. 4:8): The reward for those who eagerly look for the Lord's coming and live righteous lives in view of this fact
3. The Crown of Life (James 1:12; Rev. 2:10): The reward for those who faithfully endure and persevere under the trials and tests of life
4. The Crown of Rejoicing (1 Thess. 2:19): The reward for those who win people for Christ
5. The Crown of Glory (1 Pet. 5:1-4): The reward for those pastors, elders, and church leaders who lovingly and graciously shepherd and oversee God's people

One question that you may have at this point is, What will we do with these crowns? Will we wear them around the streets of gold to show off? Will we compare them to the number of crowns others have received? Here again, the Bible is clear. After receiving these rewards at the judgment seat in heaven, the redeemed will fall down in front of the throne and worship the Lord, lay their crowns at his feet, and sing his praise for his worth and honor. "They lay their crowns before the throne and say, 'You are worthy, O Lord our God, to receive glory and honor and power. For you created everything, and it is for your pleasure that they exist and were created' " (Rev. 4:10-11). In humble gratitude the redeemed will cast their crowns at the feet of the Redeemer, the only one who is worthy of glory, power, and honor.

In addition to these crowns, the other main reward the faithful will receive is responsibility and authority in the coming kingdom. This present age is training time for reigning time. Believers will occupy various positions of authority in the kingdom based on how we live our life here on earth (see Luke 19:13-26).

The Principles of the Judgment (The *How*)   The next issue we need to consider is the "how" of the judgment seat. How will the Lord judge us when we stand before him someday? The Bible provides five basic principles by which Christ will judge our life.[1]

BELIEVERS WILL BE JUDGED FAIRLY   The Lord will take into account how long we have been saved as well as the opportunities and abilities he has given us. The parable of the workers in the vineyard (Matt. 20:1-16) teaches that those who enter the Lord's service later in life can receive the same reward as the "all-day" workers. The righteous judge will make no mistakes. He bases his rewards on what we did with the resources and time at our disposal.

BELIEVERS WILL BE JUDGED THOROUGHLY   The Lord will virtually turn us inside out at the judgment seat. He will expose every hidden motive, thought, and deed (1 Cor. 4:5). Nothing will escape the scrutinizing eye of the Savior (Heb. 4:13).

BELIEVERS WILL BE JUDGED IMPARTIALLY   The Lord is no respecter of persons. "God does not show favoritism" (Rom. 2:11). "God has no favorites who can get away with evil" (Col. 3:25). The only difference in God's standard of judgment is that those who teach God's Word and lead the Lord's people will be held to a higher degree of accountability (James 3:1; Heb. 13:17).

BELIEVERS WILL BE JUDGED INDIVIDUALLY   Every believer will stand alone before the Lord. "Each of us will stand personally before the judgment seat of God. Yes, each of us will have to give a personal account to God" (Rom. 14:10, 12).

Erwin Lutzer captures something of the drama of this scene: "Imagine staring into the face of Christ. Just the two of you, one-on-one! Your entire life is present before you. In a flash you see what he sees. No hiding. No opportunity to put a better spin on what you did. No attorney to represent you. The look in his eyes says it all. Like it or not, that is precisely where you and I shall be someday."[2]

BELIEVERS WILL BE JUDGED GRACIOUSLY   The fact that we will receive any reward or praise at all is a testimony to God's grace. Jesus is a kind and gracious judge who will reward us all with much more than we could ever imagine (Matt. 20:13-15).

The Pictures of the Judgment (The *What*) The New Testament gives us three descriptive pictures of what this coming judgment will be like:

BUILDING The first picture is that of a building.

> *Because of God's special favor to me, I have laid the foundation like an expert builder. Now others are building on it. But whoever is building on this foundation must be very careful. For no one can lay any other foundation than the one we already have—Jesus Christ. Now anyone who builds on that foundation may use gold, silver, jewels, wood, hay, or straw. But there is going to come a time of testing at the judgment day to see what kind of work each builder has done. Everyone's work will be put through the fire to see whether or not it keeps its value. If the work survives the fire, that builder will receive a reward. But if the work is burned up, the builder will suffer great loss. The builders themselves will be saved, but like someone escaping through a wall of flames. (1 Cor. 3:10-15)*

In this passage Paul refers to leaders who are in the process of building churches. He talks specifically about his own work and the work of others in building the church in Corinth. The main thrust of his message is that many leaders are building churches out of worthless materials that won't last. They may be attracting a following, but there is no real substance in their ministry that will transform lives. Others are constructing their churches out of precious, spiritual materials that will stand forever.

While the main point of this passage is for church leaders, we can certainly apply these principles to our own life as well. We, too, are building our life each day, and God will hold us accountable for how we have constructed our building.

Notice that Paul makes a clear distinction between the foundation of the building and the superstructure. A building is only as solid as its foundation. The foundation of our life is the solid Rock, Jesus Christ. He is the only sure foundation on which we can build our life (Matthew 7:24-27). Our salvation rests solely on the foundation.

However, our reward rests on the superstructure we build on top of that foundation. There is one foundation but many superstructures, and we each select the building materials for our life. We can select our materials from two basic categories: (1) worthless/temporary; and (2) valuable/lasting. The worthless materials are referred to as wood, hay, and straw; they represent our activities and attitudes that are motivated by a desire for self-glory or by any other improper motive. The valuable materials are gold, silver, and jewels, and they symbolize our activities and attitudes that are motivated by the Holy Spirit when we live for God's glory.

When any building is completed, the final step in the process is the inspection by the city inspector. It is the inspector's job to make sure that all the codes have been followed, the proper materials have been used, and the building has been properly constructed. God's Word says that someday the building inspector is coming to inspect our life. What kind of building are you constructing? Are you building your life on the sure foundation of Jesus Christ or on the faulty foundation of possessions, prestige, pleasure, or power? Are you using inferior materials or material that will keep its value when the time of testing comes?

STEWARD The second picture is that of a steward or manager. As believers, everything we have is owned by God. We are simply stewards, managers, or caretakers of the Lord's gifts and property while he is away.

First Corinthians 4:1-2 presents this picture of stewardship: "Look at Apollos and me as mere servants of Christ who have been put in charge of explaining God's secrets. Now, a person who is put in charge as a manager must be faithful."

At the judgment seat, the Lord will evaluate how we used the time, treasure, and talents he graciously entrusted to us (see Matt. 25:14-30). The test will not be how much money or talent we possessed or how long we had to serve, but rather how faithful we were with what we were given. The issue for the manager is faithfulness to his or her master. Those who have been faithful managers will one day receive the master's praise: "Well done, my good and faithful servant" (Matt. 25:21).

ATHLETE The third picture is that of an athlete. First Corinthians 9:24-27 develops this picture.

Remember that in a race everyone runs, but only one person gets the prize. You also must run in such a way that you will win. All athletes practice strict self-control. They do it to win a prize that will fade away, but we do it for an eternal prize. So I run straight to the goal with purpose in every step. I am not like a boxer who misses his punches. I discipline my body like an athlete, training it to do what it should. Otherwise, I fear that after preaching to others I myself might be disqualified.

Paul's main point is very simple: The same commitment and dedication that make a winning athlete will make a winning Christian. If athletes are willing to subject themselves to the suffering and demands of rigorous training to receive an earthly prize that will fade away, how much more should we be willing to sacrifice our life for an incorruptible reward in heaven? Imagine what would happen if we, God's people, put the same time, effort, and resources into our Christian life that we put into sports. People willingly invest thousands of dollars and hours into improving their tennis backhand or their driving accuracy off the tee. What if we were willing to devote the same amount of time and resources into our spiritual race?

As we read in the Bible, we are to live our life with purpose, dedication, self-control, and discipline, giving maximum effort as we diligently pursue the prize (Phil. 3:12-14). Even the apostle Paul trained himself, knowing that he, too, could be disqualified from reward if he lived an undisciplined life.

In addition, we will only receive reward as God's athletes if we obey the rules in God's rule book, the Bible. Second Timothy 2:5 reminds us, "Follow the Lord's rules for doing his work, just as an athlete either follows the rules or is disqualified and wins no prize."

I'll never forget watching Ben Johnson shatter the men's one-hundred-meter record in the 1988 Olympics. I was totally amazed. After the race I heard a sport's commentator say that he thought the record would stand for a hundred years. But it didn't even stand for a hundred hours. Within a couple of days, Ben Johnson had been stripped of his medal because he broke the rules of the games. He was disqualified, his record was deleted, and he was disgraced in front of the entire world.

We must sacrifice our own comfort, discipline ourselves, and follow God's rules if we are to receive the eternal prize from our Savior.

The Preparation for the Judgment (Getting Ready) It doesn't take students very long to realize that the most important day in school is test day. When there is a test, everything is different. The whole mood and atmosphere change. As a student, did you ever notice how quiet the class got and how attentive everyone became when the teacher began to give you the questions for the upcoming test? Knowing the questions ahead of time was great.

The Bible tells us that the great test day for our life as God's child is coming. But like a kind, gracious teacher, God has given us the "test questions" for the judgment seat of Christ beforehand. It's our job to study these test questions so we can be prepared and make an A on the final exam. Here is a list of some of the main areas of our life that will be tested when we stand before the Lord:[3]

- How we treat other believers (Heb. 6:10; Matt. 10:41-42)
- How we employ our God-given talents and abilities (Matt. 25:14-29; Luke 19:11-26; 1 Cor. 12:4; 2 Tim. 1:6; 1 Pet. 4:10)
- How we use our money (Matt. 6:1-4; 1 Tim. 6:17-19)
- How well we accept mistreatment and injustice (Matt. 5:11-12; Mark 10:29-30; Luke 6:27-28, 35; Rom. 8:18; 2 Cor. 4:17; 1 Pet. 4:12-13)
- How we endure suffering and trials (James 1:12; Rev. 2:10)
- How we spend our time (Ps. 90:9-12; Eph. 5:16; Col. 4:5; 1 Pet. 1:17)
- How we run the particular race God has given us (1 Cor. 9:24; Phil. 2:16; 3:13-14; Heb. 12:1)
- How effectively we control our fleshly appetites (1 Cor. 9:25-27)
- How many people we witness to and win for Christ (Prov. 11:30; Dan. 12:3; 1 Thess. 2:19-20)
- How much the doctrine of the Rapture means to us (2 Tim. 4:8)
- How faithful we are to God's Word and to God's people (Acts 20:26-28; 2 Tim. 4:1-2; Heb. 13:17; James 3:1; 1 Pet. 5:1-2; 2 John 1:7-8)
- How hospitable we are to strangers (Matt. 25:35-36; Luke 14:12-14)
- How faithful we are in our vocation (Col. 3:22-24)
- How we use our tongue (Matt. 12:36; James 3:1-12)

The powerful, motivating influence the judgment seat should exert on our everyday life has been beautifully captured by Martha Snell Nicholson.

The Judgment Seat of Christ

When I stand at the Judgment Seat of Christ,
And He shows me His plan for me;
The plan for my life as it might have been,
Had He had His way, and I see—

How I blocked Him here and I checked Him there;
And I would not yield my will—
Will there be grief in the Savior's eyes—
Grief, though He loves me still?

He would have made me rich, and I stand there poor,
Stripped of all but His grace,
While memory runs like a hunted thing
Down the paths I cannot retrace.

Then my desolate heart will well nigh break,
With tears that I cannot shed;
I shall cover my face with my empty hands,
I shall there bow my uncrowned head.

Lord, of the years that are left to me,
I give them to Thy Hand;
Take me and break me, mold me to
The pattern Thou hast planned.

Martha Snell Nicholson

"See, I am coming soon, and my reward is with me, to repay all according to their deeds" (Rev. 22:12).

THE MARRIAGE OF THE LAMB (A Marriage Made in Heaven)

God himself is the author of the marriage relationship. It was the first human institution he created. The Bible consistently mentions weddings and marriages to accentuate their importance in God's plan. There are at least twenty weddings mentioned in the Bible:[4]

1. Adam to Eve (Gen. 2:18-25)
2. Lamech to Adah and Zillah (Gen. 4:19)
3. Isaac to Rebekah (Gen. 24:63-67)
4. Esau to Judith and Basemath (Gen. 26:34-35)
5. Abraham to Keturah (Gen. 25:1)
6. Jacob to Leah and Rachel (Gen. 29:18-30)
7. Joseph to Asenath (Gen. 41:45)
8. Moses to Zipporah (Exod. 2:21)
9. Samson to a Philistine girl (Judg. 14:1-20)
10. Boaz to Ruth (Ruth 4:13)
11. David to Michal (1 Sam. 18:27)
12. David to Abigail (1 Sam. 25:39)
13. David to Bathsheba (2 Sam. 11:27)
14. Solomon to Pharaoh's daughter (1 Kings 3:1)
15. Ahab to Jezebel (1 Kings 16:31)
16. Xerxes to Esther (Esther 2:17)
17. Hosea to Gomer (Hos. 1:2-3)
18. Joseph to Mary (Matt. 1:24)
19. Herod to Herodias (Matt. 14:3-4)
20. A couple from Cana (John 2:1-12)

Some of these weddings pleased God, while others didn't. But the greatest, most pleasing wedding of all time is still to come. The Bible calls it the marriage of the Lamb, when the Lord Jesus Christ is joined to his bride in heaven, the church. It is the next great event in heaven that takes place after the reviewing and rewarding of the saints at the judgment seat of Christ. The main passage in the Bible that describes this joyous event is Revelation 19:7-9:

> *"Let us be glad and rejoice and honor him. For the time has come for the wedding feast of the Lamb, and his bride has prepared herself. She is permitted to wear the finest white linen." (Fine linen represents the good deeds done by the people of God.)*
>
> *And the angel said, "Write this: Blessed are those who are invited to the wedding feast of the Lamb." And he added, "These are true words that come from God."*

God's Word is clear that a day is coming when the church, the bride of Christ, will be joined to her Bridegroom in heaven. In order to better understand the marriage of the Lamb, we need to consider two main points: (1) the participants in the marriage; and (2) the phases of the marriage.

The Participants in the Marriage Modern weddings have several key participants: the minister, the bride, the bridegroom, the bridesmaids, the groomsmen, the families, and the guests. The marriage of the Lamb will have four key participants:

THE HOST OF THE WEDDING—THE FATHER IN HEAVEN The Father is the divine host of the marriage of the Lamb. He is the Father of the Bridegroom. He selected the bride. He prepares the wedding and sends out the invitations. As Jesus taught in a parable:

> *The Kingdom of Heaven can be illustrated by the story of a king who prepared a great wedding feast for his son. Many guests were invited, and when the banquet was ready, he sent his servants to notify everyone that it was time to come. (Matt. 22:2-3)*

THE BRIDEGROOM—JESUS CHRIST The glorious Bridegroom at this ceremony will be Jesus Christ, who loved his bride so much that he laid down his life for her.

> *Jesus asked, "Do wedding guests fast while celebrating with the groom? Someday he will be taken away from them, and then they will fast." (Luke 5:34)*

> *John replied, "God in heaven appoints each person's work. You yourselves know how plainly I told you that I am not the Messiah. I am here to prepare the way for him—that is all. The bride will go where the bridegroom is. A bridegroom's friend rejoices with him. I am the bridegroom's friend, and I am filled with joy at his success." (John 3:27-29)*

THE BRIDE—THE CHURCH The beautiful, spotless bride is the church of Jesus Christ, which has been made holy and clean by the death and resurrection of the Bridegroom.

> *You husbands must love your wives with the same love Christ showed the church. He gave up his life for her to make her holy and clean, washed by baptism and God's word. (Eph. 5:25-26)*

THE GUESTS—OLD TESTAMENT AND TRIBULATION SAINTS

Blessed are those who are invited to the wedding feast of the Lamb. (Rev. 19:9)

The Phases of the Marriage Just as every wedding has certain people who participate in the ceremony, a wedding also has a schedule of events that must occur. A wedding in ancient Israel had four main steps or phases. Each phase of ancient wedding ceremonies has a spiritual parallel to the believer's relationship with Christ.

PHASE 1: THE SELECTION OF THE BRIDE BY THE FATHER Obviously, the first step to any marriage ceremony is the selection of a bride. In ancient Israel the father of the bridegroom made the official selection with input, consultation, and encouragement (no doubt) from the son and his mother.

Scripture declares that before God the Father created the world, he selected a bride for his beloved Son: "Long ago, even before he made the world, God loved us and chose us in Christ to be holy and without fault in his eyes" (Eph. 1:4).

PHASE 2: THE BETROTHAL OF THE BRIDE AND GROOM When the selection had been made, the father of the groom contacted the father of the bride. If the proposed marriage was acceptable, the two families entered into a binding contract of betrothal that spelled out the terms of the marriage, the financial arrangements, etc. The betrothal period was similar to our modern engagement, but as you can imagine, it was much more formal and legally binding.

The two parties solemnized the betrothal agreement by three acts: (1) a solemn oral commitment in the presence of witnesses; (2) a pledge of money; and (3) a written pledge or contract. The betrothal document was a binding contractual agreement between the families and could only be broken by death or divorce.

An important part of the process was the gifts of betrothal. There were three important parts to these gifts. First was the *mohar* or "marriage present," which the bridegroom presented to the bride's father. Second, the bride's father gave the dowry to his daughter, who ultimately gave it to the groom. This gift might include servants, valued possessions, or land. Third, the bridegroom gave a gift to the bride, called the "bridegroom's gift." This gift was often jewelry or clothes.

The betrothed couple were considered to be husband and wife, and any violation of the relationship was considered adultery, which was punishable by death (see Matt. 1:18-20). The betrothal period normally lasted one year for virgins and one month for widows. During this time the families carried out preparations for the wedding and marriage.

Just as a groom's father selected a bride for his son, God has selected believers as the bride of Christ. We have been betrothed to our bridegroom: "I am jealous for you with the jealousy of God himself. For I promised you as a pure bride to one husband, Christ. But I fear that somehow you will be led away from your pure and simple devotion to Christ, just as Eve was deceived by the serpent" (2 Cor. 11:2-3).

The betrothal stage of the ancient marriage beautifully parallels our present experience as believers. Our bridegroom, the Lord Jesus, has paid the price for our purchase as the bride of Christ—he paid the price for our sins to the Father by dying on the cross (1 Pet. 1:18-19). Moreover, as part of our betrothal to Christ, the Father has given every believer in Christ an amazing dowry—the indwelling Holy Spirit (Eph. 1:13-14). Having been betrothed to Christ and given the dowry of the Holy Spirit, our salvation is absolutely secure! The divine bridegroom will never violate his betrothal, and the Father will never take back his dowry.

The church is presently in the betrothal stage of God's schedule for the marriage. We have been selected by the Father and betrothed to Christ and are waiting for him to come and take us to be his bride. We don't know how long the betrothal stage will last. In the meantime as we await our bridegroom, like a virtuous bride, we are to keep ourselves spiritually pure and undefiled:

> You husbands must love your wives with the same love Christ showed the church. He gave up his life for her to make her holy and clean, washed by baptism and God's word. He did this to present her to himself as a glorious church without a spot or wrinkle or any other blemish. Instead, she will be holy and without fault. (Eph. 5:25-27)

PHASE 3: THE MARRIAGE OF THE BRIDE AND GROOM When the betrothal period came to its appointed end, the couple were officially joined as husband and wife at a presentation ceremony. The presentation ceremony would occur when the father of the groom told his son, "Go, Son, and get your bride, and bring her home!" Often, to add to the drama and excitement, this would be done in the evening. The anxious son would leave his father's house and, in a torch-lit procession, would go to the home of his bride. Once there, he would announce that he had come to receive his bride to himself. The marriage ceremony consisted mainly in the "taking" of the bride. The bridegroom literally "took a wife." When the bridegroom entered the bride's home, her father would place her hand in the bridegroom's, "presenting" her to him.

The parallel to the believer's experience is obvious. Someday, at the appointed time, the Father in heaven will tell his Son, "Go, Son, and get your bride, and bring her home!" Christ will come and rapture his bride, and she will be presented to him, glorious and unblemished. At this point the Father will have fulfilled his legal contract when he betrothed us to Christ.

We are still awaiting this presentation phase of the marriage. We are waiting for our bridegroom to come to receive us to himself. We are waiting to hear the midnight cry, "Look, the bridegroom is coming!" (Matt. 25:6).

PHASE 4: THE MARRIAGE SUPPER OR CELEBRATION After the bride was presented to her husband, the groom would lead a joyous procession back to his father's house. A party of young virgins who were waiting to catch the procession as it passed by would join the processional on the journey. These young women were friends of the bride and groom (see Matt. 25:1-13).

Upon returning to the father's house, a feast, to which the groom's father had invited friends and neighbors, was ready (John 2:1-11). During the wedding feast, the bridegroom was the focus of attention. He was king for the time of the feast. A faithful steward or close friend supervised the wedding feast, which usually lasted from one to seven days or even up to fourteen days if the parents were wealthy. To refuse an invitation to the wedding feast was a gross insult to the family (see Matt. 22:1-10).

How does all this apply to us? God's Word tells us that Jesus is coming to take us to his Father's house, where he has been preparing a place for us for two thousand years (John 14:1-3). After the Father presents us to our heavenly Bridegroom, the greatest celebration in history will break loose in heaven for the remainder of the time until the Second Coming. However, I believe the marriage supper or feast will spill over into the millennial kingdom. The length of the wedding feast in ancient times was determined by the wealth of the bridegroom's father. When Christ takes his bride, the heavenly Father, whose wealth is infinite, will throw a party that will last not for seven days but for one thousand years. In fact, Jesus frequently compared the millennial kingdom to a wedding feast (Matt. 8:11; 22:1-14; 25:1-13; Luke 14:16-24).

One of the chief concerns of every bride-to-be is what she is going to wear at her wedding and wedding reception. The bride spends hours looking at dresses, shoes, veils, and all the accessories. The marriage of the Lamb should be no different. Revelation 19:8 reminds us that every believer will be present at the wedding feast, dressed in the finest white linen, which is the good deeds we have done. These good deeds are not works we have done to enter heaven. We cannot earn the garments of righteousness that Christ has provided for us by his death on the cross. However, we are to make ourselves ready for the wedding feast every day by preparing the garment we will wear to this occasion. How we are dressed on that day will depend on the life we have lived for Christ. I once heard Lehman Strauss say, "Has it ever occurred to you that at the marriage of the bride to the Lamb, each of us will be wearing the wedding garment of our own making?" Make sure that you will be beautifully dressed on that day by living for Christ today.

The marriage of the Lamb is a certain event. Someday the Bridegroom will come to take his bride to his Father's house. Make sure you have received your invitation and are living a pure life for your loving groom.

THE TRIBULATION PERIOD (Hell on Earth)

Meanwhile, back on the earth, while the judgment seat of Christ and the marriage of the Lamb are occurring in heaven, the Tribulation period will begin to cast its dark shadow across this planet. To help us better understand this time of hell on earth, let's consider four main points about the coming Tribulation: (1) the time of the Tribulation; (2) the nature of the Tribulation; (3) the purpose of the Tribulation; and (4) the terms of the Tribulation.

The Time of the Tribulation The specific time or duration of the entire Tribulation is specifically given in only one place in the Bible—Daniel 9:27: "He will make a treaty with the people for a period of one set of seven." The "he" in this verse is the coming Antichrist, who will make a seven-year peace treaty with Israel that allows the Jews to offer sacrifices in the rebuilt temple in Jerusalem. The signing of this covenant is the event that commences this one set of seven years that we commonly call the Tribulation or the "seventieth week of Daniel." The event that ends the Tribulation period seven years later is the second coming of Christ (Rev. 19:11-21).

This seven-year time of hell on earth is divided into two equal halves of three and one-half years. The final three and one-half years begins when the Antichrist breaks his covenant or treaty with Israel, invades the land, and sets up an abominable image of himself in the temple in Jerusalem:

> *He will make a treaty with the people for a period of one set of seven, but after half this time, he will put an end to the sacrifices and offerings. Then as a climax to all his terrible deeds, he will set up a sacrilegious object that causes desecration, until the end that has been decreed is poured out on this defiler. (Dan. 9:27)*

The last half of the seven-year period is spoken of frequently in the Bible. It is variously referred to as "42 months" (Rev. 11:2), "1,260 days" (Rev. 11:3; 12:6), "time, times, and half a time" (Dan. 7:25; 12:7), and the "great tribulation" (Matt. 24:21, KJV). During this last half of the Tribulation period, the horrors will intensify, and the Antichrist will rule the world (Rev. 13:5).

The Nature of the Tribulation The nature of the Tribulation can be summed up pretty well in one word—horrible. The Bible graphically describes this time as "the horrors to come" (Matt. 24:8), "a time of greater horror" (Matt. 24:21), and "those horrible days" (Matt. 24:29).

The Tribulation period will be a seven-year period of unparalleled, unbelievable divine judgment, wrath, and fury. There are many important characters, places, and events during the Tribulation period. (Most of these will be covered in other places in this book.) The main thread that runs through this seven-year period is God's judgment, which he pours out in three successive waves, with each wave containing seven parts: seven seal judgments, seven trumpet judgments, and seven bowl judgments.[5]

Scripture compares these judgments several times to birth pangs (Jer. 30:4-7; 1 Thess. 5:3). As the Tribulation progresses, like birth pangs, these judgments will intensify in their severity and frequency. Revelation 6–16 describes these three crashing waves of God's judgment in detail.

THE SEVEN SEAL JUDGMENTS

1. First seal (6:1-2)—White horse: Antichrist
2. Second seal (6:3-4)—Red horse: War
3. Third seal (6:5-6)—Black horse: Famine
4. Fourth seal (6:7-8)—Pale horse: Death and hell
5. Fifth seal (6:9-11)—Martyrs in heaven
6. Sixth seal (6:12-17)—Universal upheaval and devastation
7. Seventh seal (8:1-2)—The seven trumpets

THE SEVEN TRUMPET JUDGMENTS

1. First trumpet (8:7)—Bloody hail and fire: One-third of vegetation destroyed
2. Second trumpet (8:8-9)—Fireball from heaven: One-third of oceans polluted
3. Third trumpet (8:10-11)—Falling star: One-third of fresh water polluted
4. Fourth trumpet (8:12)—Darkness: One-third of sun, moon, and stars darkened
5. Fifth trumpet (9:1-12)—Demonic invasion: Torment
6. Sixth trumpet (9:13-21)—Demonic army: One-third of mankind killed
7. Seventh trumpet (11:15-19)—The kingdom: The announcement of Christ's reign

THE SEVEN BOWL JUDGMENTS

1. First bowl (16:2)—Upon the earth: Sores on the worshipers of the Antichrist
2. Second bowl (16:3)—Upon the seas: Turned to blood
3. Third bowl (16:4-7)—Upon the fresh water: Turned to blood
4. Fourth bowl (16:8-9)—Upon the sun: Intense, scorching heat
5. Fifth bowl (16:10-11)—Upon the Antichrist's kingdom: Darkness and pain
6. Sixth bowl (16:12-16)—Upon the Euphrates River: Armageddon
7. Seventh bowl (16:17-21)—Upon the air: Earthquakes and hail

The Purpose of the Tribulation One obvious question at this point is why God would judge with such severity the world he created. Why is such a time of unspeakable trouble necessary?

Scripture gives at least five reasons for the Tribulation. These five reasons each relate to a specific group or person: Israel, the Gentiles, God, Satan, and believers.

TO PURGE ISRAEL (A Reason Relating to Israel) God will use the Tribulation to bring the Jewish people to their knees. During the Tribulation, God will put the nation of Israel in a vise grip from which there is no earthly hope of deliverance. God will refine the rebellious nation in the fire of the Tribulation period. In Zechariah 13:8-9, we read:

> *Two-thirds of the people in the land will be cut off and die, says the Lord. But a third will be left in the land. I will bring that group through the fire and make them pure, just as gold and silver are refined and purified by fire. They will call on my name, and I will answer them. I will say, "These are my people," and they will say, "The Lord is our God."*

Many of the Jewish people will cry out to God for salvation from their sins. They will implore God to split the heavens and come down to save them:

> *Oh, that you would burst from the heavens and come down! How the mountains would quake in your presence! . . . But we are not godly. We are constant sinners, so your anger is heavy on us. How can people like us be saved? We are all infected and impure with sin. When we proudly display our righteous deeds, we find they are but filthy rags. . . . And yet, Lord, you are our Father. We are the clay, and you are the potter. We are all formed by your hand. Oh, don't be so angry with us, Lord. Please don't remember our sins forever. Look at us, we pray, and see that we are all your people. (Isa. 64:1, 5-6, 8-9)*

God will mercifully answer this prayer of confession and will save a remnant in Israel.

TO PUNISH GENTILE NATIONS (A Reason Relating to the Gentiles)   God will use the Tribulation period to punish the Gentile nations and all unbelievers for rejecting his Son (Isa. 24:1-6).

TO PROVE GOD'S POWER (A Reason Relating to God)   About 3,500 years ago, the pharaoh of Egypt mocked the God of heaven when he asked the question, "Who is the Lord that I should listen to him and let Israel go? I don't know the Lord, and I will not let Israel go" (Exod. 5:2). God heard this brazen challenge, and it's as if he spoke from heaven, saying, "Do you want to know who I am? Let me show you who I am!" In the next eight chapters of Exodus, God took Pharaoh's challenge and proved to Pharaoh, his magicians, and all the people who he was. When God finished with the ten plagues, Pharaoh begged the children of Israel to leave.

In a similar show of foolish bravado, the Antichrist will totally deny the true God and will declare himself to be God. God will once again pour out his plagues to prove his power and vindicate his reputation—only this time it will be on a worldwide scale. God will prove to a rebellious world that he alone is God.

TO PORTRAY SATAN'S TRUE CHARACTER (A Reason Relating to Satan) The Tribulation will also serve a purpose relating to the devil. God will use the Tribulation to fully unmask Satan for what he is—a liar, a thief, and a murderer. When God removes all restraint (2 Thess. 2:7), the nefarious character of Satan will be fully manifest as the world experiences the final firestorm from the dragon. Realizing that his time is short, the devil will pour out his venom with force and violence: "Terror will come on the earth and the sea. For the Devil has come down to you in great anger, and he knows that he has little time" (Rev. 12:12).

TO PURCHASE A GROUP OF BELIEVERS (A Reason Relating To Believers) The Tribulation will be the greatest evangelistic tool in the history of humankind. The Lord will graciously use this terrible time of trouble to draw people to himself in repentance and trust. He will harvest more souls during this time than anyone can count:

> I saw a vast crowd, too great to count, from every nation and
> tribe and people and language, standing in front of the throne

and before the Lamb. They were clothed in white and held palm branches in their hands. And they were shouting with a mighty shout, "Salvation comes from our God on the throne and from the Lamb!" Then one of the twenty-four elders asked me, "Who are these who are clothed in white? Where do they come from?"

And I said to him, "Sir, you are the one who knows."

Then he said to me, "These are the ones coming out of the great tribulation. They washed their robes in the blood of the Lamb and made them white." (Rev. 7:9-10, 13-14)

The Terms of the Tribulation One of the best ways to understand what the Tribulation will be like is to take note of the terms, expressions, and phrases the Bible uses to describe this terrible time. The following is a list of all the significant terms and expressions in the Bible for the coming Tribulation period.

TRIBULATION TERMS AND EXPRESSIONS[6]

TRIBULATION TERMS: OLD TESTAMENT REFERENCES	TRIBULATION TERMS: NEW TESTAMENT REFERENCES
• Birth pangs (Isa. 21:3; 26:17-18; 66:7; Jer. 4:31) • Day of the Lord (Obad. 1:15; Joel 1:15; 2:1, 11, 31; 3:14; Amos 5:18, 20; Isa. 13:9; Zeph. 1:7, 14; Ezek. 13:5; 30:3; Zech. 14:1) • Great and dreadful day of the Lord (Mal. 4:5) • Day of wrath (Zeph. 1:15) • Day of distress (Zeph. 1:15) • Day of the Lord's anger (Zeph. 1:18; 2:2-3) • Day of desolation (Zeph. 1:15) • Day of vengeance (Isa. 34:8) • Time of Jacob's trouble (Jer. 30:7) • Day of darkness and gloom (Zeph. 1:15; Joel 2:2) • Day of the trumpet and alarm (Zeph. 1:16, KJV) • Day when destruction comes from the Almighty (Joel 1:15) • Day of their calamity (Deut. 32:35, KJV; Obad. 1:12-14, KJV) • Tribulation (Deut. 4:30) • One set of seven = [Daniel's] seventieth week (Dan. 9:27) • Time/day of distress, anguish (Dan. 12:1; Zeph. 1:15) • The Lord's anger, time of wrath (Isa. 26:20; Dan. 11:36) • The time of the end (Dan. 12:9) • The fire of his jealousy (Zeph. 1:18)	• The day of the Lord (1 Thess. 5:2, 4) • Time of calamity (Matt. 24:22; Mark 13:20) • Wrath (1 Thess. 5:9, KJV; Rev. 11:18) • The wrath to come (1 Thess. 1:10) • The great day of their wrath (Rev. 6:17) • The wrath of God (Rev. 15:7; 14:10, 19; 16:1) • The wrath of the Lamb (Rev. 6:16) • Time of testing (Rev. 3:10) • Those horrible days (Matt. 24:29; Mark 13:24) • Days/time of greater horror (Mark 13:19) • The great tribulation (Rev. 7:14) • The hour of judgment (Rev. 14:7, KJV) • Sorrows (Matt. 24:8, KJV)

THE SECOND COMING OF CHRIST (The King Is Coming!)

The two climactic events of the Great Tribulation are the campaign of Armageddon and the second coming of Jesus Christ—when Jesus returns to this earth as King of kings and Lord of lords.

There is nothing more clearly stated in the Bible than the fact that Jesus Christ is coming again. The second coming of Christ to this earth—his visible, literal, physical, glorious return—is explicitly referred to 1,845 times in the Bible. It is mentioned in twenty-three of the twenty-seven New Testament books. Three of the remaining four books contain only one chapter (Philemon; 2 John; and 3 John), and Galatians implies the Second Coming in 1:4. There are 260 chapters in the New Testament and 318 references to the second coming of Christ.

The first prophecy ever spoken by a man concerned the Second Coming, when Enoch foretold of the Lord coming to judge the earth (Jude 1:14). Also, the final prophecy ever given deals with the Second Coming (Rev. 22:20).

Christ himself refers to his return twenty-one times in Scripture including these two instances:

> As the lightning lights up the entire sky, so it will be when the Son of Man comes. Just as the gathering of vultures shows there is a carcass nearby, so these signs indicate that the end is near. Immediately after those horrible days end, the sun will be darkened, the moon will not give light, the stars will fall from the sky, and the powers of heaven will be shaken. And then at last, the sign of the coming of the Son of Man will appear in the heavens, and there will be deep mourning among all the nations of the earth. And they will see the Son of Man arrive on the clouds of heaven with power and great glory. (Matt. 24:27-30)

> "Yes, it is as you say. And in the future you will see me, the Son of Man, sitting at God's right hand in the place of power and coming back on the clouds of heaven." (Matt. 26:64)

When Christ ascended to heaven, angels stated that he would come back:

It was not long after he said this that he was taken up into the sky while they were watching, and he disappeared into a cloud. As they were straining their eyes to see him, two white-robed men suddenly stood there among them. They said, "Men of Galilee, why are you standing here staring at the sky? Jesus has been taken away from you into heaven. And someday, just as you saw him go, he will return!" (Acts 1:9-11)

The second coming of Jesus Christ is the climax and consummation of human history. While entire books have been written on this breathtaking event, the focus in this section will be on two important points about the Second Coming: the place and the purpose.

The Place of the Second Coming The Bible is clear that Jesus will return to earth at the same place from which he left—the Mount of Olives. Three key passages help identify this as the place of his return:

1. Zechariah 14:4 addresses the second coming of Christ. "On that day his feet will stand on the Mount of Olives, which faces Jerusalem on the east. And the Mount of Olives will split apart, making a wide valley running from east to west, for half the mountain will move toward the north and half toward the south."
2. Jesus gave his great prophetic discourse, which gave the signs of his coming, from the Mount of Olives in Matthew 24–25.
3. When Jesus ascended to heaven from the Mount of Olives in Acts 1:9-11, the angels said that he would return just as he had left.

The Purpose of the Second Coming The Bible tells us that Christ will return for at least six purposes:

TO CONQUER   Christ is coming to defeat the Antichrist and his armies (Rev. 19:19-21).

TO REGATHER AND RESTORE   The most frequently mentioned promise in the Old Testament is God's promise that he will one day regather and restore the nation of Israel (Isa. 43:5-6; Jer. 30:10; 33:6-9; Ezek. 36:24-38; 37:1-28). The regathering of Israel began in 1948 with the creation of its modern state and will continue until the second coming of Christ. During the Tribulation period, Israel will be scattered for the final time, and then at the Second Coming, Christ will gather the believing Jews together and restore them as his people (Isa. 11:11-16). Christ taught this to his disciples:

> They will see the Son of Man arrive on the clouds of heaven with power and great glory. And he will send forth his angels with the sound of a mighty trumpet blast, and they will gather together his chosen ones from the farthest ends of the earth and heaven. (Matt. 24:30-31)

TO JUDGE THE LIVING   When Christ returns, all Gentiles who survived the Tribulation period will appear before him to determine whether they can enter his kingdom (Matt. 25:31-46). This is the judgment of the "sheep and the goats." In addition, Christ will gather all living Jews in the wilderness to determine who can enter the kingdom (Ezek. 20:33-38).

TO RESURRECT THE DEAD   One of the events that will happen soon after the Second Coming as described in Revelation 19:11-21 is the resurrection and rewarding of Old Testament believers and martyred Tribulation believers, who then will reign with Christ (Rev. 20:4-6; see also Dan. 12:1-4).

TO BIND THE DEVIL (Rev. 20:1-3)   The initial event mentioned after Christ returns to defeat the Antichrist is the binding of Satan in the bottomless pit for one thousand years.

TO ESTABLISH HIMSELF AS KING (Rev. 19:16)   Christ returns as King of kings and Lord of lords! He comes to sit on his glorious throne and reign over the earth (Dan. 2:44; Matt. 19:28; Luke 1:32-33). Charles Wesley wrote:

> Lo, He comes with clouds descending
> Once for favored sinners slain;
> Thousand thousand saints attending
> Swell the triumph of His train:
> Alleluia! Alleluia!
> God appears on earth to reign.

The apostle John described Christ's return as such: "Look! He comes with the clouds of heaven. And everyone will see him—even those who pierced him. And all the nations of the earth will weep because of him. Yes! Amen!" (Rev. 1:7).

THE CAMPAIGN OF ARMAGEDDON (The Mother of All Wars)

Probably the best known word in all of Bible prophecy is Armageddon. It is the word many use to refer to the end of the world. In the summer of 1998, a blockbuster movie about an asteroid the size of Texas on a collision course with earth was titled Armageddon. McDonald's joined forces with the movie company and offered drinks and french fries in Armageddon cups and boxes. As I saw the commercials for this movie and drank my Coke at McDonald's out of a cup with the word Armageddon emblazoned on it, I couldn't help but wonder if the movie producers had any idea what the word *Armageddon* means. I also wondered how many of the millions of moviegoers had a clue about the true meaning of Armageddon. While this word has become synonymous in our culture with the end of the world, it is used in the Bible to refer to a very specific event in the last days.

The word *Armageddon* is found only one time in the Bible. It appears in Revelation 16:16: "And they gathered all the rulers and their armies to a place called *Armageddon* in Hebrew."

The Meaning of the Word *Armageddon* The word *Armageddon* is made up of two Hebrew words: *Har* (mountain) and *Megiddo* (a city in the northern part of ancient Israel). The ancient city of Megiddo was built on a hill, and it is therefore called the hill of Megiddo—Armageddon. The city of Megiddo overlooks a beautiful, large valley known as the valley of Jezreel, the valley of Esdraelon, the plains of Megiddo, and the valley of Taanach. According to Revelation 16:12-16, this is the site where the armies of the earth will gather in the last days and face total defeat by the returning King from heaven (Rev. 19:19-21).

What Armageddon Is Not Armageddon is not a battle. It is common to hear people refer to the "battle" of Armageddon. But technically speaking it is a war or campaign involving a series of battles in the land of Israel.

In addition, Armageddon is not the same as the battle of Gog and

Magog in Ezekiel 38–39. Here are a few of the significant differences between these two events.

DIFFERENCES BETWEEN TWO END-TIMES WARS

GOG AND MAGOG	ARMAGEDDON
Gog leads the invasion	Antichrist leads the invasion
Israel is at peace at the time of the invasion	There is no mention of Israel's peace
Armies gather to plunder Israel	Armies gather to fight against Christ
Occurs at the middle of the Tribulation	Occurs at the end of the Tribulation
Russia and her Islamic allies invade Israel	All nations invade Israel
Occurs so that all the nations will know that the Lord is God	Occurs to destroy the nations

Finally, Armageddon is not the last war on earth. It is common to hear Armageddon associated with the last battle or war on earth. However, the final war in history is the final revolt of Satan in Revelation 20:7-11. This war occurs one thousand years after Armageddon.

What Armageddon Is The campaign or war of Armageddon is the climactic event of the Great Tribulation (the second half of the Tribulation), when all the armies of the earth gather to come against Israel and to eradicate the Jewish people once and for all. After Jerusalem is captured, Jesus Christ returns to destroy the invading armies and to deliver the faithful Jewish remnant in Petra.

The Ten Main Passages That Describe Armageddon
1. Psalm 2
2. Isaiah 34:1-15
3. Isaiah 63:1-6
4. Joel 3:1-17
5. Zechariah 12:1-9
6. Zechariah 14:1-15
7. Malachi 4:1-5
8. Revelation 14:14-20
9. Revelation 16:12-16
10. Revelation 19:19-21

The Location of Armageddon The campaign will be spread out over the entire land of Israel, from Megiddo in the north to Edom, or Bozrah, in the south, spanning two hundred miles from north to south and one hundred miles from east to west. Within this larger area, the Bible focuses on three specific places where the battle will be the most intense.

THE VALLEY OF JEHOSHAPHAT (Joel 3:2, 12)   This is probably another title for the Kidron Valley. This valley is on the east side of Jerusalem and runs between the eastern wall of the city and the Mount of Olives.

THE VALLEY OF ESDRAELON (Rev. 16:16)   Also known as the valley of Jezreel, the valley of Taanach, and the plains of Megiddo, this geographic area is twenty miles long and fourteen miles wide. The ruins of Megiddo overlook this great valley. It is here that the armies of the earth, in alliance with the Antichrist, will gather and meet their doom.

BOZRAH/EDOM (Isa. 34:1-5; 63:1)   Bozrah is a city east of the Jordan River in the ancient nation of Edom (modern nation of Jordan). It is near the city of Petra. After his descent to the Mount of Olives, Christ will lead his army down to Edom to rescue the hiding Jewish remnant there. When he returns from Edom, his clothes will be stained red and his sword drenched with blood (Isa. 34:6; 63:1-3). The wicked people of Bozrah will be slaughtered to such an extent that the mountains will flow with blood, and the land will be soaked in blood (Isa. 34:2-7).

Herman A. Hoyt, in his book *The End Times,* provides a gripping description of the scope of Armageddon:

> *The phenomenal aspect will gather about the Battle of Armageddon with which the Tribulation period will come to a close. The staggering dimensions of this conflict can scarcely be conceived by man. The battlefield will stretch from Megiddo on the north (Zech. 12:11; Rev. 16:16) to Edom on the south (Isa. 34:5-6; 63:1), a distance of sixteen hundred furlongs approximating two hundred miles. It will reach from the Mediterranean Sea on the west to the hills of Moab on the east, a distance of almost one hundred miles. It will include the valley of Jehoshaphat (Joel 3:2, 12) and the plains of Esdraelon. And the center of the entire area will be the city of Jerusalem (Zech. 14:1-2). Into this area the multiplied millions of men, doubtless approaching 400 million, will be crowded for the final holocaust of humanity. The kings with their armies will come from the north and the south, from the east and from the west. There will be an invasion from hell beneath. And entering the scene at the last moment will be an invasion from outer space. In the most dramatic sense this will be the "valley of*

decision" for humanity (Joel 3:14) and the great winepress into which will be poured the fierceness of the wrath of almighty God (Rev. 19:15).[7]

The Seven Key Titles of Armageddon
1. The day of the Lord's vengeance (Isa. 34:8)
2. The winepress of God's wrath (Isa. 63:2; Joel 3:13; Rev. 14:19-20)
3. That great and terrible day of the Lord (Joel 2:31)
4. The harvest (Joel 3:13; Rev. 14:15-16)
5. The day of judgment (Mal. 4:1)
6. The great and dreadful day of the Lord (Mal. 4:5)
7. That great judgment day of God Almighty (Rev. 16:14)

The Seven Key Phases of Armageddon Since Armageddon is a military campaign and not just one single battle, it will play out in several distinct phases outlined in Scripture. As we have seen, the events of Armageddon will transpire over the entire land of Israel in several different locations. Therefore, putting all of the major pieces of Armageddon together in chronological order is a difficult task. The following is a proposed chronology of the key phases of Armageddon as presented in Scripture:

- Phase 1: The Euphrates River dries up to prepare the way for the kings of the east (Rev. 16:12).
- Phase 2: The Antichrist's allies assemble to annihilate the Jews once and for all (Rev. 16:12-16).
- Phase 3: The Antichrist's allies attack Jerusalem, and the city falls (Zech. 14:1-3).
- Phase 4: Jesus Christ returns personally on the Mount of Olives (Zech. 14:4).
- Phase 5: Christ and his armies destroy the armies gathered against Jerusalem in the valley of Jehoshaphat (Joel 3:9-17; Zech. 12:1-9; 14:3).
- Phase 6: Christ descends upon Edom to destroy its inhabitants and to deliver the Jewish remnant hiding in and around the city of Petra (Isa. 34:1-7; 63:1-5; Joel 3:19).
- Phase 7: At Armageddon, the Antichrist will rally the armies that remain to fight against the Lord Jesus and his army (Rev. 16:16; 19:19-21). The armies of the Antichrist will suffer total, cataclysmic defeat at the mighty hand of the King (Ps. 2:9).

The Aftermath of Armageddon Two events will take place as a result of this great war. First, the birds of the air will gather to feed on the putrefying carnage that litters the landscape (Matt. 24:28; Luke 17:37; Rev. 19:17-21).

Next, Jesus will cast the Antichrist and the false prophet alive into the lake of fire (Rev. 19:20).

THE MILLENNIAL KINGDOM (Joy to the World or Satan's Chain and the Saints' Reign)

Humanity has always dreamed of a utopia, a great society, a paradise on earth, a return to the Garden of Eden. But the Bible is clear that sinful humankind can never produce such a society on earth by its own strength and ingenuity. However, when the Lord Jesus returns to this earth in power and glory, God's Word tells us that he will reign on earth as King of kings and Lord of lords for one thousand years. Before Christ begins his reign, he will have Satan bound and cast into the bottomless pit so that Satan can no longer deceive the nations (Rev. 20:1-3). Then Christ will begin his reign of one thousand years. (Notice that the thousand years are referred to five times in Revelation 20:1-6.)

The Key Passages on the Millennium While Revelation 20:1-6 is the only passage in the Bible that records the length of Christ's reign on the earth, it is certainly not the only passage that refers to his kingdom. The Old Testament is literally filled with long passages on the millennial kingdom. Numerous students of Bible prophecy have noted that there is more prophetic material devoted to the subject of the Millennium than to any other single end-times topic. Therefore, it is critical that we gain at least a basic understanding of the millennial kingdom.

For starters, here is a list of ten of the most important Old Testament passages on the coming kingdom:

1. Isaiah 2:1-5
2. Isaiah 11:1-16
3. Isaiah 32:1-20
4. Isaiah 35:1-10
5. Isaiah 60:1-22
6. Jeremiah 31:1-40
7. Jeremiah 33:1-26
8. Ezekiel 37:14-28
9. Amos 9:11-15
10. Zechariah 14:6-21

The Nature or Conditions of the Millennium During the millennial reign of Christ, the earth will experience a return to conditions similar to those of the Garden of Eden. It will literally be heaven on earth as the Lord of heaven comes to live among his people.

The Bible has a lot more to say about the Millennium than most people realize. Here are ten of the most prominent conditions that will prevail on the earth during the reign of Christy.

78 PEACE All wars will cease as the world unifies under the reign of the true King (Isa. 2:4; 9:4-7; 11:6-9; Zech. 9:10).

JOY When Isaac Watts wrote the song "Joy to the World," he did not write it to be a Christmas carol. Rather, he penned this song to announce the glorious second coming of Christ to rule and reign on this earth. Think of some of the words of the song—"Joy to the world! The Lord is come; Let earth receive her king. . . . No more let sins and sorrows grow. . . . He rules the world with truth and grace!" This is a song of the Millennium, when full joy will come to the world (Isa. 9:3-4; 12:3-6; 14:7-8; 25:8-9; 30:29; Jer. 30:18-19; Zeph. 3:14-17; Zech. 8:18-19; 10:6-7).

HOLINESS The word *holy* means to be "set apart" to God for sacred purposes. The kingdom of Christ will be a holy kingdom. Everything in it will be set apart to God for his use. The holiness of the Lord will be manifest in his own person as well as in the citizens of his kingdom. The land, the city, the temple, and the subjects will all be holy unto the Lord (Isa. 4:3-4; 35:8; 52:1; Ezek. 43:7-12; 45:1; Zech. 8:3; 14:20-21).

GLORY The effulgent glory of God will be fully manifest in Christ's kingdom (Isa. 35:2; 40:5; 60:1-9; Ezek. 43:1-5).

JUSTICE AND RIGHTEOUSNESS When the millennial kingdom begins, only believers will inhabit it. However, these believers will still have human bodies with a fallen nature and will be capable of sin. Humanity's sin will be judged by the administration of perfect justice at the hands of the Messiah (Isa. 9:7; 11:5; 32:16; 42:1-4; 65:21-23). He will rule with "a rod of iron," restraining and judging sin so that the prevailing atmosphere in the kingdom will be righteousness (Isa. 11:1-5; 60:21; Jer. 31:23; Ezek. 37:23-24; Zeph. 3:13).

FULL KNOWLEDGE The teaching ministry of the Lord and the indwelling Spirit will bring the subjects of the kingdom into a full knowledge of the Lord's ways (Isa. 11:1-2, 9; 41:19-20; 54:13; Jer. 31:33-34; Hab. 2:14).

ABSENCE OF SICKNESS OR DEFORMITY   Our politicians are constantly working on plans to provide better health care for the citizens of our nation. In the Lord's government, the health plan will be out of this world. The King will be both ruler and healer. Christ will heal all diseases and deformities among his people (Isa. 29:18; 33:24; 35:5-6; 61:1-2). As a result of this health-care plan, people will have extended life spans, like those who lived before the Flood. A person who dies at the age of one hundred in this kingdom will have died very prematurely (Isa. 65:20).

UNIVERSAL WORSHIP OF GOD   All the inhabitants of the earth will join their hearts and voices in praise and worship to God and his Son, Jesus Christ (Isa. 45:23; 52:7-10; 66:17-23; Zeph. 3:9; Zech. 13:2; 14:16; Mal. 1:11; Rev. 5:9-14). This worship during the Millennium will be centered in the rebuilt temple in Jerusalem (Isa. 2:3; 60:13; Ezek. 40–48; Joel 3:18; Hag. 2:7, 9). One important aspect of worship in the Millennium is that animal sacrifices will be reinstituted in the millennial temple (Isa. 56:6-7; 60:7; Ezek. 43:18-27; 45:17-23; Zech. 14:16-21). These sacrifices will not be offered to take away sin. No animal sacrifice can ever take away sin (Heb. 10:1-2). Rather, these sacrifices will serve as a powerful memorial to the one sacrifice for sin forever, the sacrifice of Jesus Christ. They will serve, like the Lord's Supper today, as a perpetual, vivid reminder of the holiness of God, the awfulness of sin, and the horrible death the Savior died in our place.

ECONOMIC PROSPERITY   There won't be any need for rescue missions, welfare programs, food stamps, or relief agencies in the kingdom. The world will flourish under the hand of the King of heaven (Isa. 35:1-2, 7; 30:23-25; 62:8-9; 65:21-23; Jer. 31:5, 12; Ezek. 34:26; 36:29-30; Joel 2:21-27; Amos 9:13-14; Mic. 4:4; Zech. 8:11-12; 9:16-17).

THE PRESENCE OF GOD   The greatest thing about the kingdom is that Christ himself will be there. God's presence will be fully recognized, and the Lord's people will experience fellowship unlike anything they have ever known with him (Ezek. 37:27-28; Zech. 2:10-13). The city of Jerusalem will be called Jehovah Shammah, which means "The Lord Is There" (Ezek. 48:35).

The Seven Key Titles of the Millennium   The title for an event helps shed light on its nature. A title summarizes in a word or brief phrase the essence of the event. For instance, the annual NFL championship game is titled "The Super Bowl." The day the allies invaded the beaches of Normandy was called "D-day." The day the stock market crashed is remembered as "Black Tuesday." Likewise, God has given us seven key biblical titles that capture the essence of the coming kingdom:

1. The Kingdom of Heaven (Matt. 3:2; 8:11)
2. The Kingdom of God (Mark 1:15)
3. The Kingdom (Matt. 19:28)
4. The future world (Heb. 2:5)
5. Wonderful times of refreshment (Acts 3:20)
6. The final restoration of all things (Acts 3:21)
7. A Kingdom that cannot be destroyed (Heb. 12:28)

The Purposes of the Millennium The Millennium will serve at least four important functions in the plan of God.

TO REWARD THE FAITHFUL   During the millennial kingdom, Christ will award the saints positions of authority based on their degree of faithfulness in this life (Luke 19:16-19).

TO REDEEM CREATION   When Adam and Eve sinned in the Garden of Eden, God pronounced a series of five curses. He pronounced these five curses against the serpent, Satan, the woman, the man, and nature (Gen. 3:14-19). From that time until today, the earth has lived under this curse, as evidenced by "thorns and thistles" and the hard work that is required by humans to scratch out food from the ground. The new crop of crabgrass in the lawn each spring is a small, yet vivid reminder of the curse.

Romans 8:19-22 poignantly describes the curse on nature:

> *All creation is waiting eagerly for that future day when God will reveal who his children really are. Against its will, everything on earth was subjected to God's curse. All creation anticipates the day when it will join God's children in glorious freedom from death and decay. For we know that all creation has been groaning as in the pains of childbirth right up to the present time.*

One important function of the Millennium is to reverse God's curse on creation. In the kingdom, all animals will revert back to being plant eaters, as they were originally created (Gen. 1:30). The wolf and lamb will live together in harmony, and a child will be able to play next to a poisonous snake (Isa. 11:6-9). The earth will become amazingly productive and beautiful as even the deserts blossom with flowers (Isa. 35:1-7). The whole earth will be like a huge Garden of Eden.

TO RECOGNIZE THE PROMISES OF GOD God made three great unconditional, unilateral, eternal covenants that will find their fulfillment in the millennial kingdom with the regathered, restored nation of Israel. These three promises are known as the Abrahamic covenant, the Davidic covenant, and the New Covenant.

The Abrahamic covenant (Gen. 12:1-3; 15:18-21) is God's threefold promise to Abraham of descendants, land, and blessing:

1. Descendants—God promised that Abraham's descendants would become a great nation (Gen. 12:1-3; 13:16; 15:5; 17:7; 22:17-18).
2. Land—God promised Abraham that his descendants would be given a piece of land to call their own forever. The land he promised includes the modern-day nation of Israel and parts of modern-day Egypt, Syria, Lebanon, and Iraq (Gen. 15:18-21). This unconditional promise has never been fulfilled in history but will be fulfilled in the Millennium when Christ gives the Jewish people the land God promised Abraham (Isa. 60:21; Ezek. 34:11-16).
3. Blessing—God also promised Abraham that through him and his descendants, all the world would be blessed. Certainly this prophecy has been partially fulfilled in the blessing that has come to all the world through Abraham's greatest descendant, Jesus Christ. However, the final blessing from Abraham through Christ will come during the wonderful conditions that will exist on earth during the Millennium.

God's promise to David (the Davidic covenant) also has three basic parts (2 Samuel 7:12-16):

1. House—this refers to David's dynasty or the royal family;
2. Throne—this refers to David's authority or right to rule; and
3. Kingdom—this refers to David's realm or political kingdom, which is the nation of Israel.

God made an eternal, unconditional promise to David that someone from his house, or dynasty, would sit on his throne and rule over his kingdom forever. This promise will be fulfilled only when Jesus Christ, who is in the line of David, sits on David's throne in Jerusalem, ruling over Israel in the coming kingdom and on into eternity (Ezek. 37:22-25; Amos 9:11-15; Zeph. 3:14-17; Luke 1:30-33, 69).

The New Covenant (Jer. 31:31-34), or God's promise to Israel, also contains a threefold promise:

1. The forgiveness of sins—God will forgive Israel for her sins;
2. The indwelling Spirit—God will place his Spirit in the hearts of the people to personally instruct them in his way (Ezek. 36:24-26); and
3. A new heart—God will give his people a new, clean heart with his law inscribed upon it.

While believers today enjoy all of these benefits as a result of the new covenant in Christ's blood (Matt. 26:28), the specific promises in Jeremiah 31:31-34 will find their ultimate fulfillment for Israel in the millennial kingdom, when the Jews are restored to the land with Christ as their King (notice that the context of the covenant, Jeremiah 31:35-40, is the future kingdom).

TO REAFFIRM THE TOTAL DEPRAVITY OF HUMANITY   God's Word clearly teaches that humanity is sinful both by nature and by practice. The millennial kingdom will be the final, conclusive proof of this fact. During the Millennium, Satan will be bound for one thousand years, and the Lord Jesus himself will be personally present, ruling and reigning on the restored earth. Yet the Bible teaches that in spite of these perfect conditions, a host of people who are born and raised during this time will reject the Lord in their hearts. They will outwardly conform to avoid judgment, but inwardly they will harbor a rebellious heart against the King of kings.

When Satan is released for a brief time at the end of the Millennium, the Bible tells us that he will gather "a mighty host, as numberless as sand along the shore" (Rev. 20:8) to try to destroy Christ, his city, and his people.

The Millennium will prove beyond any doubt that regardless of heredity, circumstances, or environment, humanity is incorrigibly sinful apart from God's saving grace. As Dr. Pentecost notes:

> *The millennial age is designed by God to be the final test of fallen humanity under the most ideal circumstances, surrounded by every enablement to obey the rule of the king, from whom the outward sources of temptation have been removed, so that man may be found and proved to be a failure in even this last testing of fallen humanity.*[8]

THE FINAL REVOLT OF SATAN (Satan's Last Stand)

There's an old saying, "The next time Satan comes along and begins to remind you of your past, remind him of his future." The Bible reveals that Satan's future is very bleak. He is doomed to eternal destruction. However, the Bible tells us that he won't go down without a fight. Revelation 20:1-3, 7-10 records the final demise of Satan:

> *I saw an angel come down from heaven with the key to the bottomless pit and a heavy chain in his hand. He seized the dragon—that old serpent, the Devil, Satan—and bound him in chains for a thousand years. The angel threw him into the bottomless pit, which he then shut and locked so Satan could not deceive the nations anymore until the thousand years were finished. Afterward he would be released again for a little while. When the thousand years end, Satan will be let out of his prison. He will go out to deceive the nations from every corner of the earth, which are called Gog and Magog. He will gather them together for battle—a mighty host, as numberless as sand along the shore. And I saw them as they went up on the broad plain of the earth and surrounded God's people and the beloved city. But fire from heaven came down on the attacking armies and consumed them.*
>
> *Then the Devil, who betrayed them, was thrown into the lake of fire that burns with sulfur, joining the beast and the false prophet. There they will be tormented day and night forever and ever.*

These verses reveal three important stages in the final revolt and destruction of the devil: (1) Satan bound; (2) Satan released; and (3) Satan defeated.

Satan Bound When Christ returns as King to establish his kingdom, the first order of business will be to imprison the false king, the usurper to his throne, the Antichrist. The second order of business will be to seize the power behind the Antichrist, the devil himself. Christ immediately dispatches a powerful angel to bind Satan in the bottomless pit for one thousand years. During Satan's thousand-year prison sentence, Christ will rule the earth with his resurrected and raptured saints in the millennial kingdom (Rev. 20:4-6).

Satan Released At the end of the thousand years, God releases Satan for a brief period of time, allowing Satan one last shot at world dominion. Amazingly, when Satan is released, he finds many people who lived on earth during the reign of Christ who are ready to join in his petty rebellion against the King. The Bible says the number of people he deceives is as numberless as the sand on the seashore. He gathers this insubordinate army together to attack God's people and the beloved city of Jerusalem, where Christ has his earthly throne.

Satan Defeated This must be one of the shortest battles in history. As this massive mob of rebels gathers on the broad plain of the earth and surround the city of Jerusalem, God sends down fire from heaven to destroy them. Immediately following this divine firestorm, Satan is cast into the lake of fire forever, to join the other two members of the false trinity, the Antichrist and the false prophet.

The archenemy of man, who first entered the stage of human history in the Garden of Eden back in Genesis 3, exits the stage into the lake of fire forever in Revelation 20.

THE GREAT WHITE THRONE JUDGMENT (Judgment Day)

In the past few decades, we have seen a steady stream of TV shows that focus on the courtroom: *Perry Mason, L.A. Law, Law and Order, The People's Court,* and *The Practice.* John Grisham has sold millions of books and movie tickets by focusing on the high stakes of courtroom tension. People in our nation were spellbound for months by the O. J. Simpson trial. This is all to say that Americans are enamored with the drama of the courtroom.

The Bible tells us that the ultimate courtroom drama will occur someday in heaven in the courtroom of God, when all those who have rejected him will have their day in court. The Bible calls this episode the Great White Throne Judgment.

The court date at the great white throne is set on God's docket to occur after the millennial kingdom has ended and Satan has been cast into the lake of fire. The scene at this final great judgment is the most awesome picture in all the pages of the Bible. Revelation 20:11-15 graphically describes this mind-numbing event:

I saw a great white throne, and I saw the one who was sitting on it. The earth and sky fled from his presence, but they found no place to hide. I saw the dead, both great and small, standing before God's throne. And the books were opened, including the Book of Life. And the dead were judged according to the things written in the books, according to what they had done. The sea gave up the dead in it, and death and the grave gave up the dead in them. They were all judged according to their deeds. And death and the grave were thrown into the lake of fire. This is the second death—the lake of fire. And anyone whose name was not found recorded in the Book of Life was thrown into the lake of fire.

To better understand the final judgment at the end of time, I will break down the courtroom scene into seven headings: the Courtroom, the Judge, the Defendants, the Summons, the Evidence, the Verdict, and the Sentence.

The Courtroom Most adults have seen a courthouse, and many have been in a courtroom as a juror, witness, or as a party to a lawsuit. The scene is very imposing. Courtrooms almost always have high, vaulted ceilings with massive chandeliers. In the gallery the people sit on dark, hard wooden benches with high, straight backs. The atmosphere is always serious and silent except for a few muted whispers. Suddenly the door from the judge's chambers opens, and the bailiff enters, commanding all present to rise as the black-robed judge enters the courtroom. As the judge takes his seat behind the bar, court is in session. He calls the names of the parties, and the case begins. This is the scene that will someday occur at the bar of God in heaven—only multiplied by infinity.

Every person must wonder sometime during his or her life what it will be like to see "the Supreme Court of the Universe"—to see the Ancient of Days sitting on his great white throne. God's throne is "great" (*mega* in Greek) because it is the highest throne in the universe. It is "white" because it is absolutely pure, holy, and righteous. All of the verdicts handed down from this throne are perfectly right, just, and true. This is God's courtroom—God's throne of justice. It is the supreme court of heaven and earth.

The Judge Notice next who it is who sits on this majestic throne. It is none other than the Lord Jesus Christ himself. The Bible is clear that Jesus Christ is the final judge before whom the unbelieving world will stand. As John 5:22 reminds us, "The Father leaves all judgment to his Son." Acts 17:31 reiterates this same truth: "He has set a day for judging the world with justice by the man he has appointed, and he proved to everyone who this is by raising him from the dead." Second Timothy 4:1 calls Jesus Christ the one who will "judge the living and the dead."

The Defendants Scripture refers to the defendants in this courtroom as "the dead, both great and small" (Rev. 20:12). The context of this passage makes it abundantly clear that these are all the people throughout history who died without faith in Christ.

Notice that both the great and small, and everyone in between, will be present. There is no one too great to escape judgment, and there is no one too insignificant to go unnoticed. Alexander the Great, Julius Caesar, Stalin, and Hitler will be there. So will people whose lives never amounted to anything.

The self-righteous will be there. The terrible sinners will be there. The procrastinators will be there. The religious, unconverted church members will be there. No unsaved person will escape his or her day in God's court.

The Summons When the day of judgment comes, there will be no place to hide. There won't be any high-priced lawyers to get the case postponed or thrown out of court. No one will be able to jump bail. Everyone who is summoned must appear.

The dead will be summoned from all kinds of places: "The sea gave up the dead in it, and death and the grave gave up the dead in them" (Rev. 20:13). In the ancient world, the sea was thought to be the most inaccessible place. No one could venture to the depths of the ocean. They believed that no one buried in the ocean could ever be disturbed. But God wants us to know that even the most mysterious, difficult, out-of-the-way, forbidden places to humanity are fully accessible to him. The day of judgment is sure (Heb. 9:27).

The Evidence At this trial the case presented by the prosecutor will be airtight. There will be only two pieces of evidence admitted; the prosecution will submit only two exhibits:

1. Exhibit A is "the books," opened in Revelation 20:12. These books are God's infallible records containing a detailed, meticulous account of all the works of every unsaved person. God is keeping an inscrutable account of every person's life in his books (see Dan. 7:10). The lost will be doomed because of their sinful deeds recorded in these books: "They were all judged according to their deeds" (Rev. 20:13).
2. Exhibit B contains even more damning evidence. This exhibit is "the Book of Life." It is a huge book, listing all the names of the hopelessly lost sinners who trusted Jesus Christ to save them and pardon them from having to appear at this tribunal. Exhibit B will be consulted to see if the defendant's name appears in the Book of Life. "Anyone whose name was not found recorded in the Book of Life was thrown into the lake of fire" (Rev. 20:15).

The Verdict   After considering the books and the Book of Life, the verdict of guilty will ring through the universe. The gavel of God will fall, and the lost will have no appeal. The verdict will stand for all eternity.

The Sentence   The sentence at this judgment will be the harshest sentence ever imagined—life in hell forever, without parole. Jonathan Edwards wrote these riveting words about the final sentence of the damned:

> *When you look forward you shall see a long forever, a boundless duration before you which will swallow up your thoughts and amaze your soul. And you will absolutely despair of ever having any deliverance, any end, any mitigation, any rest at all. You will know certainly that you must wear out long ages, millions of millions of ages, in wrestling and conflicting with this almighty merciless vengeance. And when you have so done, when so many ages have actually been spent by you in this manner, you will know that all has been a point to what remains, so that your punishment will indeed be infinite. Oh, who can express what the state of a soul in such circumstances is. All that we can possibly say about it is but a very feeble, faint representation of it. 'Tis inexpressible and inconceivable, for who knows the power of God's anger.*[9]

However, the Bible does teach that even in hell there will be degrees of punishment based on the evidence contained in the books. The length of the sentence is the same for all the lost, but the severity of the punishment will be based both on the amount and the nature of the sin

87

that one committed as well as the amount of truth that one refused (Matt. 11:21-23; Luke 12:47-48; Romans 2:5-6).

Warren Wiersbe captures something of the drama of the Great White Throne Judgment:

> *The White Throne Judgment will be nothing like our modern court cases. At the White Throne, there will be a Judge but no jury, a prosecution but no defense, a sentence but no appeal. No one will be able to defend himself or accuse God of unrighteousness. What an awesome scene it will be!*[10]

The good news is that you need not appear at this judgment. The Bible says that Jesus suffered the wrath of God on the cross for you and for me. All you have to do to be excused from this day of judgment and to spend eternity with God in heaven is accept God's free pardon through faith in Jesus Christ. What an offer! What a Savior!

THE CREATION OF THE NEW HEAVEN AND NEW EARTH
(Paradise Regained)

Dr. John Walvoord, one of the most recognized authorities on Bible prophecy, tells a story about a brief conversation he had while walking through an airport in Dallas with the editor of *Eternity* magazine. He and the editor were nearing the gate for their flight when a woman who knew Dr. Walvoord approached him and struck up a conversation. During the conversation, Dr. Walvoord introduced the woman to his friend, and she asked the man, "What do you do?" He responded, "I manage *Eternity*," to which she said, "That must be a big job."

Think of what a big job it must be to really manage eternity. It boggles the mind just to think about it. But the Bible declares that the all-powerful, transcendent Creator manages every molecule without any effort whatsoever. He is the ruler of all eternity!

God's Word reveals that after the millennial kingdom and the Great White Throne Judgment, the same God who created this present heaven and earth will destroy it and create a new heaven and a new earth, ushering in the eternal state.

> *I saw a new heaven and a new earth, for the old heaven and the old earth had disappeared. And the sea was also gone. And I saw*

the holy city, the new Jerusalem, coming down fro
heaven like a beautiful bride prepared for her hus

*I heard a loud shout from the throne, saying, "Look, the home
of God is now among his people! He will live with them, and they
will be his people. God himself will be with them. He will remove
all of their sorrows, and there will be no more death or sorrow or
crying or pain. For the old world and its evils are gone forever."*

*And the one sitting on the throne said, "Look, I am making all
things new!" And then he said to me, "Write this down, for what I
tell you is trustworthy and true." And he also said, "It is finished! I
am the Alpha and the Omega—the Beginning and the End. To all
who are thirsty I will give the springs of the water of life without
charge! All who are victorious will inherit all these blessings, and
I will be their God, and they will be my children. But cowards
who turn away from me, and unbelievers, and the corrupt, and
murderers, and the immoral, and those who practice witchcraft,
and idol worshipers, and all liars—their doom is in the lake that
burns with fire and sulfur. This is the second death." (Rev. 21:1-8)*

Revelation 21–22 emphasizes five key points about the new heaven
and new earth:

The Cremation of the Present Heaven and Earth Before the new
heaven and new earth can be created, the present heaven and earth
must be destroyed. The old heaven and the old earth will disappear.
This event is mentioned several times in the Bible:

> • *In ages past you laid the foundation of the earth, and the heavens
> are the work of your hands. Even they will perish, but you remain
> forever; they will wear out like old clothing. You will change them
> like a garment, and they will fade away. (Ps. 102:25-26)*

> • *The heavens above will melt away and disappear like a rolled-
> up scroll. The stars will fall from the sky, just as withered leaves
> and fruit fall from a tree. (Isa. 34:4)*

> • *Look up to the skies above, and gaze down on the earth
> beneath. For the skies will disappear like smoke, and the earth
> will wear out like a piece of clothing. (Isa. 51:6)*

> • *Heaven and earth will disappear. (Matt. 24:35)*

> • *The day of the Lord will come as unexpectedly as a thief. Then the heavens will pass away with a terrible noise, and everything in them will disappear in fire, and the earth and everything on it will be exposed to judgment. You should look forward to that day and hurry it along—the day when God will set the heavens on fire and the elements will melt away in the flames. (2 Pet. 3:10, 12)*

> • *This world is fading away, along with everything it craves. (1 John 2:17)*

According to Revelation 20:11, this event will occur right before the Great White Throne Judgment: "I saw a great white throne, and I saw the one who was sitting on it. The earth and sky fled from his presence, but they found no place to hide." Just think what it will be like for all the people gathered at the great white throne. Right before God judges and consigns them to hell forever, the last thing they will behold is the entire universe going up in smoke. God will give a final display of his power and show them the futility of all that they craved and cherished on this earth. By his spoken word, God will simultaneously untie or break up every atom in the cosmos, and the entire universe will dissolve and disintegrate in a fiery holocaust (2 Pet. 3:7, 10-13).

The Creation of the New Heaven and New Earth After God destroys the present order, he will put it all back together again. What all the kings men could not do for Humpty Dumpty, God will do for the universe. He will gather all the building blocks of the original creation and make a brand new universe.

The Bible contains only four passages that mention the creation of the new heaven and new earth: Isaiah 65:17; 66:22; 2 Peter 3:13; and Revelation 21:1.

The Conditions of the New Heaven and New Earth The Bible doesn't say a lot about the eternal state, but what it does record is exciting. It is a place of perfection characterized both by what is there and what is not there.

Three Things That Will Be There
1. The Holy City, the new Jerusalem
2. God himself, dwelling among his people
3. Righteousness (2 Pet. 3:13)

Ten Things That Will Not Be There
1. The sea (Rev. 21:1)
2. Death (Rev. 21:4)
3. Sorrow (Rev 21:4)
4. Crying (Rev. 21:4)
5. Pain (Rev. 21:4)
6. Night (Rev. 21:25; 22:5)
7. Sun or moon (Rev. 21:23)
8. The temple (Rev. 21:22)—God himself will be the temple, manifesting his glory throughout the new creation.
9. The curse (Rev. 22:3)
10. Sin (Rev. 21:8; 21:27)—Heaven will be free of this pollution.

The Capital of the New Heaven and New Earth (Rev. 21:9–22:5) As John looks at the new heaven and new earth in his vision, he suddenly sees the new Jerusalem, the Holy City, coming down from God, out of heaven. The city is a cube—1,400 miles long, wide, and deep. It contains 2,744,000,000 cubic feet of space—enough to hold 100 trillion people. John sees this cubed city—the size of a continent—floating through space.

I believe this heavenly city will come down and rest on the new earth and serve as its capital city. The fact that Scripture mentions this city in conjunction with the new earth and that the city has huge foundation stones seem to suggest that it will rest on the new earth (see Heb. 11:10).

What will this city be like? What will be there?

THE GLORY OF GOD The main feature of this city is that it has the glory of God (Rev. 21:11, 23). It is described in terms of light, precious stones, and gold polished to mirror brilliance. The celestial skyline dazzles as the light of God shines on the beauty of the city.

THE WALL OF JASPER The wall is for protection, security, and separation. It emphasizes the eternal security of God's people and the eternal separation of the lost from this city. The wall is 216 feet thick, 1,400 miles high, and made of jasper, which probably refers to a diamond or a gem that looks like ice. The wall looks like a shimmering sheet of ice.

THE TWELVE GATES   The gates of the city, which are always open (Rev. 21:25), provide access and entrance for the Lord's people. Each gate is made from a single pearl.

THE TWELVE FOUNDATION STONES   The foundation stones reveal the permanence of the city (Heb. 11:10). They are inlaid with twelve precious gems: jasper (diamond), sapphire (deep blue), agate (green), emerald (green), onyx (layered stone of red), carnelian (blood red), chrysolite (golden yellow), beryl (sea green), topaz (greenish gold or yellow), chrysoprase (gold green), jacinth (gold violet), and amethyst (purple quartz).

THE STREET   People often talk about the streets of gold in heaven, but actually there is only one street of gold. Everyone will live on Main Street. And that street will be paved with gold polished to mirror brilliance. Gold is so plentiful to the Creator that he uses it to pave his street.

A RIVER   A river of crystal-clear water will run down Main Street from the throne of God.

THE TREE OF LIFE   The tree God excluded humanity from when Adam and Eve were expelled from the Garden of Eden will be available to all of God's people for all of eternity.

As these descriptions show, there will be nothing but the best in this city. There won't be any cinder blocks, shag carpet, or cheap imitations. Only the best materials will be used. The heavenly city described in Revelation 21–22 is the place in John 14:1-3 that Jesus was going to prepare for us. It is the Father's house, in which there are many dwelling places that Jesus has been working on now for two thousand years. What a place it will be!

The Citizens of the New Heaven and New Earth   Hebrews 12:22-24 gives a description of the inhabitants of God's new world:

> *You have come to Mount Zion, to the city of the living God, the heavenly Jerusalem, and to thousands of angels in joyful assembly. You have come to the assembly of God's firstborn children, whose names are written in heaven. You have come to God himself, who is the judge of all people. And you have come to the spirits of the redeemed in heaven who have now been made perfect.*

You have come to Jesus, the one who mediates the new covenant between God and people, and to the sprinkled blood, which graciously forgives instead of crying out for vengeance as the blood of Abel did.

There are three identifiable groups in the new Jerusalem besides God himself and Jesus: angels, church-age believers ("the assembly of God's firstborn children"), and the rest of the people of God from the other ages ("the spirits of the redeemed in heaven who have now been made perfect").

Revelation 21:8 describes eight kinds of people who will not be there:

1. Cowards—those who were ashamed of Christ (Matt. 10:33)
2. Unbelievers
3. The corrupt
4. Murderers (A person who commits murder can be saved by God's grace. King David is a perfect example. This refers to people who practice murder and never seek God's forgiveness.)
5. The immoral (Once again, this refers to those who practice this lifestyle and do not repent.)
6. Those who practice witchcraft
7. Idol worshipers
8. Liars

Of course, the key issue is—will you be there? Will you be a citizen of the new heaven, the new earth, the new Jerusalem? Have you received God's offer of salvation?

CONCLUSION

After this whirlwind tour of the ten main events of Bible prophecy, it is now important to stop and let it all soak into our heart and mind. I would encourage you to go back over this chapter again and again until you have these ten events firmly fixed in your mind. These events form the basic outline for understanding the last days.

May God use this chapter to give us a better understanding of his prophetic program for this world and to lead us to love, worship, and revere him more deeply.

---

[1]These five points were taken from Erwin W. Lutzer, *Your Eternal Reward* (Chicago: Moody Press, 1998), 25–36.

[2]Ibid., 23.

[3]Some of these points were taken from Harold Willmington, *Panorama of Prophecy*, 7–11.

[4]This list was taken from Harold Willmington, *Willmington's Book of Bible Lists* (Wheaton, Ill.: Tyndale House Publishers, 1987), 193–94.

[5]J. Dwight Pentecost, in this book *Things to Come* (Grand Rapids: Zondervan Publishing House, 1958, p. 235), summarizes the nature of the Tribulation with ten descriptive words: wrath, judgment, indignation, trial, trouble, destruction, darkness, desolation, overturning, and punishment.

[6]These lists were adapted from a list of tribulation terms provided to me by Randall Price.

[7]Herman A. Hoyt, *The End Times* (Chicago: Moody Press, 1969), 163.

[8]J. Dwight Pentecost, *Things to Come* (Grand Rapids: Zondervan Publishing House, 1958), 538.

[9]This was taken from a famous sermon by Jonathan Edwards entitled "Sinners in the Hands of an Angry God."

[10]Warren Wiersbe, *The Bible Expository Commentary*, vol. 2 (Wheaton, Ill.: Victor Books, 1989), 621.

Ten Key Places in Bible Prophecy

The study of any nation, empire, or religion quickly reveals that certain places are very significant to the citizens or members of that region or faith. For the United States, places like Washington, D.C., Plymouth Rock, Valley Forge, Gettysburg, Kitty Hawk, Wall Street, and the Alamo are important to our history as a nation.

Places usually take on significance not because of the locale itself but rather because of some great event that occurred or occurs there. The same is true of Bible prophecy. There are certain places that are key because of what has happened there or what the Bible says will transpire there in the future. While there are many such places in Bible prophecy, only ten are most important to give us an overall understanding of the last days.

BABYLON

Revelation 17–18 describes a great city in the end times called Babylon. There are seven clues in these chapters that help identify this great end-times city.

1. Babylon is a literal city (Rev. 17:18).
2. Babylon is a city of worldwide importance and influence, probably the capital city of the world (Rev. 17:15, 18).
3. Babylon and the Antichrist are very closely connected with one another. Revelation pictures the woman (Babylon) riding on the Beast (Antichrist).
4. Babylon is a center of false religion (Rev. 17:4-5; 18:1-2).
5. Babylon is the center of world commerce (Rev. 18:9-19). These two systems, religion and commerce, will share the same geographical location under Antichrist's domain.[1]
6. Babylon persecutes the Lord's people (Rev. 17:6; 18:20, 24).

7. Babylon will be destroyed suddenly and completely at the end of the Tribulation, never to rise again (Rev. 18:8-10, 21-24).

Putting these clues together reveals that Babylon will be the great religious, economic capital of the Antichrist's kingdom in the last days. But what city does Babylon represent?

This great harlot of the last days has been identified with the Roman Catholic church and the Vatican, apostate Christendom, New York City, Jerusalem, and Rome. The most likely view, however, is that Babylon, the literal city on the Euphrates in modern-day Iraq, will be rebuilt in the last days. There are seven main points that favor this identification of Babylon in Revelation 17–18.

The City's Name The great city described as the last-days capital of the Antichrist is specifically called "Babylon" six times in Revelation (14:8; 16:19; 17:5; 18:2, 10, 21). While it is possible that the name Babylon is a code name for Rome, New York, Jerusalem, or some other city, since there is no indication in the text that it is to be taken figuratively or symbolically, it seems best to take it as a literal Babylon.

The City's Mention With the exception of Jerusalem, no other city is mentioned more than Babylon in the Bible. Scripture refers to Babylon about 290 times and presents this city as the epitome of evil and rebellion against God. The following passages seem to imply that Babylon is Satan's capital city on earth:

- Babylon is the city where man first began to worship himself in organized rebellion against God (Gen. 11:1-9).
- Babylon was the capital city of the first world ruler, Nimrod (Gen. 10:8-10).
- Nebuchadnezzar, king of Babylon, destroyed the city of Jerusalem and the temple in 586 B.C.
- Babylon was the capital city of the first of four Gentile world empires to rule over Jerusalem.

Since Babylon was the capital city of the first world ruler and is pictured as Satan's capital city on earth throughout Scripture, it makes sense that in the end times, Satan will once again raise up this city as the capital of the final world ruler. In his excellent book *The Rise of Babylon*, Charles Dyer writes:

Throughout history, Babylon has represented the height of rebellion and opposition to God's plans and purposes, so God allows Babylon to continue during the final days. It is almost as though he "calls her out" for a final duel. But this time, the conflict between God and Babylon ends decisively. The city of Babylon will be destroyed.[2]

The City's Specifications Babylon fits the criteria for the city described in Revelation 17–18. As Robert Thomas notes:

Furthermore, Babylon on the Euphrates has a location that fits this description politically, geographically, and in all the qualities of accessibility, commercial facilities, remoteness of interferences of church and state, and yet centrality in regard to the trade of the whole world.[3]

The City's Location Revelation mentions the Euphrates River by name twice (9:14; 16:12). In Revelation 9:14, the text states that four fallen angels are being held at the Euphrates River, awaiting their appointed time to lead forth a host of demons to destroy one-third of humankind. In Revelation 16:12, the sixth bowl judgment dries up the Euphrates River to prepare the way for the kings of the east. These references to the Euphrates point to the fact that something important and evil is occurring there. The rebuilt city of Babylon on the Euphrates, functioning as a religious and political center for Antichrist, is a good explanation for Revelation's emphasis on this river.

The City's Wickedness Zechariah 5:5-11 records an incredible vision that pertains to the city of Babylon in the last days:

The angel who was talking with me came forward and said, "Look up! Something is appearing in the sky."

"What is it?" I asked.

He replied, "It is a basket for measuring grain, and it is filled with the sins of everyone throughout the land."

When the heavy lead cover was lifted off the basket, there was a woman sitting inside it. The angel said, "The woman's name is Wickedness," and he pushed her back into the basket and closed the heavy lid again.

Then I looked up and saw two women flying toward us, with wings gliding on the wind. Their wings were like those of a stork, and they picked up the basket and flew with it into the sky. "Where are they taking the basket?" I asked the angel. He replied, "To the land of Babylonia, where they will build a temple for the basket. And when the temple is ready, they will set the basket there on its pedestal."

99

Around 520 B.C., twenty years after the fall of Babylon to the Medo-Persians, the prophet Zechariah wrote about the evil he saw returning to this city in the future. In this vision Zechariah sees a woman named Wickedness carried away in a basket in the last days to the land of Babylon, where a temple will be built for her.

The parallels between Zechariah 5:5-11 and Revelation 17–18 are striking.

PARALLELS BETWEEN ZECHARIAH AND REVELATION

ZECHARIAH 5:5-11	REVELATION 17–18
Woman sitting in a basket	Woman sitting on the Beast, sevenhills, and many waters (17:3, 9, 15)
Emphasis on commerce (a basket for measuring grain)	Emphasis on commerce (merchant of grain—18:13)
Woman's name is Wickedness	Woman's name is Babylon the Great, Mother of All Prostitutes and obscenities in the World
Focus on false worship	Focus on false worship (18:1-3)
Woman is taken to Babylon	Woman is called Babylon

God's Word teaches that in the end times, wickedness will again rear its ugly head in the same place where it began—Babylon. The prostitute in Revelation fulfills the prophecy of Zechariah 5:5-11, as Babylon is established in the last days as the city that embodies evil.

The City's Destruction Since the city of Babylon was never destroyed suddenly and completely as is predicted in Isaiah 13 and Jeremiah 50–51, these passages must refer to a future city of Babylon that will be totally destroyed on the Day of the Lord.

The City's Description Jeremiah 50–51 clearly describes the geographical city of Babylon on the Euphrates. The many parallels between this passage and the future Babylon described in Revelation 17–18 indicate that they are both describing the same city.

PARALLELS BETWEEN JEREMIAH 50–51 AND REVELATION 17–18[4]

DESCRIPTION	JEREMIAH 50–51	REVELATION 17–18
Compared to a golden cup	51:7	17:3-4; 18:6
Dwelling on many waters	51:13	17:1
Involved with nations	51:7	17:2
Named the same	50:1	18:10
Destroyed suddenly	51:8	18:8
Destroyed by fire	51:30	17:16
Never again to be inhabited	50:39	18:21
Punished according to her works	50:29	18:6
Fall illustrated	51:63-64	18:21
God's people flee	51:6, 45	18:4
Heaven to rejoice	51:48	18:20

The city of Babylon will be rebuilt in the last days to serve as the religious and commercial capital for the Antichrist's empire. Wickedness will return to this place for its final stand. Then, at the end of the Tribulation, in the seventh bowl judgment, God will put it in Antichrist's heart to destroy the great city of Babylon with fire (Rev. 17:16-17; 18:8). Babylon will fall, never to rise again!

The rise of Iraq in recent years on the world political and economic scene is not an accident. In spite of the Gulf war and tremendous worldwide pressure, Iraq remains a formidable foe. The current rebuilding and rise of Babylon may be a key part of God's plan for the last days.

BOZRAH/PETRA

God's Word reveals that at the midpoint of the Tribulation, the Antichrist will break his covenant of peace with the Jewish people. At that time he will invade Jerusalem and set up the abomination of desolation in the temple (Matt. 24:15). When this happens the Bible says that one-third of the Jewish people will flee into the hills, where God will supernaturally protect them for three and a half years from the ravages of the Antichrist and Satan (Rev. 12:6, 14).

Scripture seems to indicate that this last-days hiding place for the Jewish remnant will be the city of Petra in the southern part of modern Jordan. There are four main reasons that support this view.

Specifically Micah 2:12-13 says:

> *Someday, O Israel, I will gather the few of you who are left. I will bring you together again like sheep in a fold, like a flock in its pasture. Yes, your land will again be filled with noisy crowds!*

Your leader will break out and lead you out of exile. He will bring you through the gates of your cities of captivity, back to your own land. Your king will lead you; the Lord himself will guide you.

In Hebrew, the word *fold* is the word *Bozrah*, which means sheepfold. This passage predicts that someday Israel's king will lead his people from exile in Bozrah. The ancient city of Bozrah was located in the region of Mount Seir in Edom. The exact location of Bozrah is still disputed. It may be the present Arab village of Buseira, or it may be the city known today as Petra. It seems most logical to identify the future city of refuge for the Jewish people as the city of Petra. Arnold Fruchtenbaum notes:

Petra is located in a basin within Mount Seir, and is totally surrounded by mountains and cliffs. The only way in and out of the city is through a narrow passageway, called the "Sig," which means a cleft, fissure, gorge, or crack. The Sig extends for about a mile and can only be negotiated by foot or by horseback. The cliffs along this narrow passageway tower over the Sig at heights of up to six hundred feet. This makes the city easy to defend, and its surrounding high cliffs give added meaning and confirmation to Isaiah 33:16. Only two or three abreast can enter through this passage at any one time giving this city an even greater defensibility. The name "Bozrah" means sheepfold. An ancient sheepfold had a narrow entrance so that the shepherd could count his sheep. Once inside the fold, the sheep had more room to move around. Petra is shaped like a giant sheepfold with its narrow passageway opening up to a spacious circle surrounded by cliffs.[5]

Militarily Bozrah, in ancient Edom, is one of the first places Christ goes when he returns to earth. When he comes from there, he is dripping with the blood of his enemies (Isa. 34:5-10; 63:1-6). But why does Scripture emphasize the fact that Christ will go to Petra when he returns? The best answer is that he goes there as part of the campaign of Armageddon to rescue the Jewish remnant who has been hiding there for three and one-half years.

Politically The only nation in the Middle East that will escape the direct control of the Antichrist is the modern nation of Jordan. Daniel

11:41 says, "He will enter the glorious land of Israel, and many nations will fall, but Moab, Edom, and the best part of Ammon will escape."

This makes the area of Petra, which lies in ancient Edom, a perfect place of refuge from the Antichrist during the Tribulation period.

Geographically Scripture says that the Lord will prepare a city of refuge for the Jewish remnant during the last half of the Tribulation. It will be a place that God will prepare, which means it will be adequate as a place of refuge. Scripture also consistently describes this place as being in the hills or the wilderness (Matt. 24:16; Rev. 12:6, 14).

The city of Petra fits all of these criteria. It is adequate to hold what may be one million Jewish people; it is in the hills, in the wilderness; and it is accessible to the fleeing remnant.

EGYPT

There are approximately 250 verses in the Old Testament that, at the time they were given, were prophecies of events yet to take place in Egypt.[6] This point alone makes Egypt an important place in Bible prophecy.

There are five main passages that deal with Egypt in prophecy: Isaiah 11:15-16; 19:1-25; Jeremiah 46:2-28; Ezekiel 29–32; and Daniel 11:40-43. These passages describe three main periods in Egypt's history: the present age, the Tribulation, and the millennial kingdom.

Egypt in the Present Age During this present age, the Bible says that Egypt will never again be a major international power. Egypt will remain an unimportant, minor kingdom. "It will be the lowliest of all the nations, never again great enough to rise above its neighbors" (Ezek. 29:15).

This has been true in Egypt's history. After Persia's rise to power, Egypt never again became a major, independent, international power. Egypt was successively ruled over by Greece, Rome, the Saracens, the Mamluks, the Turks, and the British. Until 1922, Egypt remained under the sovereignty of a foreign power. The existence of the sovereign nation of Egypt today is in preparation for her significant role in the last days.

Egypt in the Tribulation Scripture has much to say about the nation of Egypt during the Tribulation:

> • Egypt, the "king of the south," will lead a great North African confederacy against Israel at the middle of the Tribulation (Dan. 11:40). This

confederacy will include Libya and Sudan. Egypt will also be joined by
Russia, the "king of the north," in this invasion (Dan. 11:40; Ezek. 38:1-23).
• Egypt's army will be destroyed by God (Isa. 19:16; Ezek. 38–39).
• After Egypt's army is destroyed by God, Egypt will be easy prey for the
Antichrist. He will conquer and plunder Egypt (Dan. 11:41-43).
• Egypt will become a wasteland and a wilderness (Isa. 19:16-17; Joel 3:19).
• Many in Egypt will turn to the Lord for salvation (Isa. 19:22).

Egypt in the Millennium The Bible also has much to say about Egypt
during the Millennium:

• Egypt will institute true worship of God. An altar to the Lord will be built
there, and the people will offer sacrifices and offerings to the Lord
(Isa. 19:18-21).
• People from Egypt will go up to Jerusalem to celebrate the feasts of the
Lord (Zech. 14:16-19).
• The Lord will build a highway between Egypt, Israel, and Assyria (Iraq)
(Isa. 11:15-16; 19:23-25).

Imagine Egypt, Israel, and Iraq as friendly, harmonious neighbors.
The idea today seems preposterous. As Wilbur Smith says:

*This is the only place in the Old Testament in which God assigns
to two Gentiles nations a place in a trinity of nations that
includes Israel, giving to each a third. Someone has aptly said,
here we have the promise of blessing upon the three great divi-
sions of the human race, the Semitic, Japhetic, and Hamitic. . . .
The peaceful relationship prevailing among these three nations
promised for the end of the age is the very reverse of the conditions now prevailing there.*[7]

God's future dealings with Egypt are among the most beautiful dem-
onstrations of his grace. No nation has as long a history of rejection of
divine revelation as Egypt. From the times of Abraham, Joseph, and
Moses, Egypt has consistently rejected the true God. But in his infinite
mercy and grace, God will make himself known to the Egyptians, will
bless them, and will bring them into harmony with their neighbors.

JERUSALEM

There are 802 references to Jerusalem in the Bible. Of these, 489 were
prophetic at the time they were uttered. Another way to understand
this city's significance is to note that two-thirds of the books of the Old

Testament and almost half the books of the New Testament mention Jerusalem.[8] In Bible prophecy, Jerusalem is clearly the city at the center. Jerusalem is not only at the center of Bible prophecy; it is also the center of a storm cloud of controversy and attention in the world today. It is difficult to find a newspaper, major periodical, or news program that doesn't mention the nation of Israel and the controversy over Jerusalem. The peace process in the Middle East focuses on Jerusalem. It's amazing that this one small piece of ground could capture so much attention. The only explanation is supernatural.

Randall Price aptly summarizes the importance of Jerusalem in Bible prophecy:

> *Whether perceived or not, Jerusalem is at the center stage because of God's prophetic plan for the future. . . . There can be no question that today Jerusalem is at the center of controversy as the stage is being set for the final conflict. . . . Jerusalem is the city at the center. It is at the center of mankind's hope and God's purposes. God loves it, Satan hates it, Jesus wept over it, the Holy Spirit descended in it, the nations are drawn to it, and Christ will return and reign in it. Indeed the destiny of the world is tied to the future of Jerusalem.*[9]

The importance of Jerusalem in Bible prophecy is also seen in the many different names for this city. Jewish rabbis say that there are sixty different names for Jerusalem in the Bible. While some believe this is an exaggeration, the fact remains that the Bible refers to this city under many different names and titles. Here is just a sample of some of the better known names and titles for Jerusalem:

- Zion
- City of David
- Ariel (Isa. 29:1-2)
- The Holy City (Isa. 48:2; 52:1)
- City of our God (Ps. 48:1, 8)
- The Throne of the Lord (Jer. 3:17)
- City of the Great King (Ps. 48:2; Matt. 5:35)

Since prophecy mentions Jerusalem so frequently, this section will group the major prophecies concerning this city under four main headings: (1) Jerusalem in the Tribulation; (2) Jerusalem during the Millennium; (3) Jerusalem after the Millennium; and (4) The new Jerusalem.

Jerusalem in the Tribulation The Bible has this to say about Jerusalem during the Tribulation:

- Antichrist will make a seven-year peace treaty with Israel that will bring peace to Jerusalem (Dan. 9:27).
- The Jewish temple will be rebuilt in Jerusalem (Dan. 9:27; Rev. 11:1).
- Antichrist will break the peace treaty at its midpoint and will invade Israel, making Jerusalem his throne (Dan. 11:40-45).
- Antichrist will desecrate the temple, set up the abomination of desolation in the Holy Place, and proclaim himself God (Dan. 9:27; 12:11; Matt. 24:15; 2 Thess. 2:3-4; Rev. 13:11-15).
- Jerusalem and all Israel will suffer terrible persecution (Jer. 30:4-7).
- The two witnesses will be killed by Antichrist, and their bodies will lie in the streets of Jerusalem for three and a half days (Rev. 11:7-11).
- Antichrist will gather his allies together to come against Jerusalem (Zech. 12:1-3).
- Jerusalem will fall at the hands of Antichrist, and half the city will be destroyed (Zech. 14:2).
- Christ will return to the Mount of Olives, just east of Jerusalem (Zech. 14:4).
- In a final desperate move, Antichrist will gather his forces against Christ only to be destroyed in and around the city of Jerusalem (Joel 3:12-13; Rev. 19:19).
- A massive earthquake will split the city of Jerusalem into three parts (Zech. 14:4-5).

Jerusalem during the Millennium During the millennial kingdom, the city of Jerusalem will be the political, religious, and economic capital of the world. Here are seven of the most important descriptions of Jerusalem in the kingdom:

1. The city of holiness (Isa. 33:5; Jer. 31:40)
2. The city of God's presence (Ezek. 48:35)
3. The city of worship—the center of millennial rule (Isa. 60:3; Jer. 3:17; Zech. 8:23)
4. The city of political rule (Ps. 2:6; 110:2; Isa. 2:2-4; 24:23; Mic. 4:7)
5. The city of protection, peace, and safety (Isa. 40:2; 66:20; Jer. 31:6)
6. The city of prosperity—the center of world commerce (Isa. 2:2; 60:11; 66:12; Mic. 4:1)
7. The city of prominence (Isa. 2:2-4; Zech. 14:9-10)

The topography of the city will change drastically. God will literally raise up this city above its present height, and Jerusalem will be a place of magnificent beauty.

Jerusalem after the Millennium After the thousand-year reign, Satan will be released for a brief period of time. Revelation 20:7-10 says that Satan will gather all those who have rejected Christ during the Millennium to attack God's people and the beloved city. This is clearly a reference to Jerusalem, and the attack will be the last one against God's city. For God will send fire from heaven to consume Satan's followers, and Satan will be cast into the lake of fire forever.

The New Jerusalem After the Great White Throne Judgment, God will destroy the present heaven and earth and create a new heaven and a new earth. The capital city of this new creation will be "the Holy City, the new Jerusalem, coming down from God out of heaven like a beautiful bride prepared for her husband" (Rev. 21:2). For all eternity Jerusalem will be the city of God.

MEGIDDO (Armageddon)

Even though it is only mentioned one time in the Bible, Armageddon is clearly one of the key places in Bible prophecy. It is a very significant place for two reasons: First, it is where Antichrist will gather all of his forces in the last days for his final assault on Jerusalem. Second, Armageddon has become the watchword in modern society for the end of the world. This is the only word from Bible prophecy that many people know. For this reason alone, it is important that believers understand what Armageddon means.

The only place this term is found is in Revelation 16:16: "And they gathered all the rulers and their armies to a place called *Armageddon* in Hebrew." The word *Armageddon* is made up of two Hebrew words, *har* (mountain) and *Megiddo* (a city in northern Israel). The ruins of ancient Megiddo are a small mound or hill that overlooks a large, beautiful, fertile valley. The valley is triangular in shape and is fifteen by fifteen by twenty miles in size. This valley is known by several different names.

- The valley of Jezreel
- The plain of Esdraelon (Greek form of the name Jezreel)
- The plain of Megiddo
- The valley of Taanach

It is in this valley, near the mountain of Megiddo, that Antichrist will gather his forces to take on the conquering Christ as he returns from heaven.

THE MOUNT OF OLIVES

The Mount of Olives is a small mountain range on the east side of the city of Jerusalem. The New Bible Dictionary describes it like this: "The Mount of Olives . . . is a small range of four summits, the highest being 830 [meters], which overlooks Jerusalem and the Temple Mount from the [east] across the Kidron Valley and the Pool of Siloam."[10]

The Mount of Olives is an important place in Bible prophecy for two main reasons: First, it is the place where Jesus delivered his great prophetic discourse three days before his death. This sermon, called the Olivet Discourse, gives Jesus' basic outline of the end times. The sermon is found in Matthew 24–25, Mark 13, and Luke 21.

Second, the Mount of Olives is the place where Jesus will return to earth at his second coming. Two passages mark this as the place where his feet will touch down on earth:

> *The Lord will go out to fight against those nations, as he has fought in times past. On that day his feet will stand on the Mount of Olives, which faces Jerusalem on the east. And the Mount of Olives will split apart, making a wide valley running from east to west, for half the mountain will move toward the north and half toward the south. (Zech. 14:3-4)*

> *It was not long after he said this that he was taken up into the sky while they were watching, and he disappeared into a cloud. As they were straining their eyes to see him, two white-robed men suddenly stood there among them. They said, "Men of Galilee, why are you standing here staring at the sky? Jesus has been taken away from you into heaven. And someday, just as you saw him go, he will return!" (Acts 1:9-11)*

PATMOS

The sole significance of Patmos in Bible prophecy is that it is the place where the apostle John received the Revelation of Jesus Christ. It was on this tiny, insignificant island that the glorified Christ appeared to the apostle John and unveiled the future of the world.

The New Testament refers to Patmos only once, in Revelation 1:9: "I am John, your brother. In Jesus we are partners in suffering and in the

Kingdom and in patient endurance. I was exiled to the island of Patmos for preaching the word of God and speaking about Jesus."

Patmos is a rocky, thin, crescent-shaped island in the Aegean Sea. It is thirty miles in circumference, ten miles long, and six miles wide. It is about thirty-five miles southwest of Miletus, off the coast of Asia Minor (modern-day Turkey) and is fifty miles from Ephesus, where John lived before he was banished. Patmos occupied a strategic place in the shipping lanes between Ephesus and Rome.

Modern commentators often describe Patmos as a penal colony. It is sometimes referred to as the first-century Alcatraz. It is also common to hear people say that John was on a chain gang working the mines on Patmos as part of his exile. However, there are no ancient sources that describe Patmos in this way. In fact, to the contrary, they describe an island that was inhabited and flourishing.

Patmos was certainly not a deserted island at the end of the first century. It probably was populated, as a military garrison was stationed there. An inscription from the second century B.C. mentions a gymnasium on the island. A second-century A.D. inscription mentions the presence of a temple to Artemis, or Diana (goddess of the hunt).[11] The present-day Monastery of St. John, near the village of Chora, is built on top of the ancient temple of Artemis. There is further evidence that there may have been temples to Apollo (the god of music, poetry, and prophecy) and Aphrodite (goddess of love and beauty) as well. One inscription even mentions the presence of a hippodrome (stadium for horse and chariot races). The acropolis of the island contained a large administrative center.

John was banished to this island for about eighteen months during the reign of Domitian, probably to limit his spiritual influence on the churches in Asia Minor. John wrote Revelation on Patmos around A.D. 95. Tradition says that when Domitian was assassinated in A.D. 96, John returned to Ephesus and died there.

EUROPE

In the great prophecies of Daniel 2 and 7, the Bible previews the course of world history from the time of Nebuchadnezzar and his kingdom to the second coming of Christ to establish his kingdom. These passages revealed that four great Gentile empires would rule the world in succession from 605 B.C. until the Second Coming. These world empires were Babylon, Medo-Persia, Greece, and Rome. From history we know that these empires did in fact rule the world successively in the exact order predicted by Daniel around 530 B.C.

The problem is that the Bible says Rome, the fourth kingdom, will be the great world power when Christ returns to rule the world (Dan. 7:23-28). How can we explain this apparent discrepancy? The answer is actually quite obvious. The Roman Empire must be reunited in the last days before Christ returns.

It is interesting to consider that the Roman Empire was never really destroyed like its predecessors. It fell apart. Rome was simply divided up, primarily into the nations of modern-day Europe. The Bible predicts that in the last days, the Roman Empire will be reunited or brought back together in a ten-kingdom alliance led by the Antichrist (Dan. 7:8, 23-25). Daniel 2 pictures the final form of this Gentile world power in the ten toes of the image; Daniel 7 pictures it by the seven horns on the fourth beast (see also Rev. 13:1-2; 17:12-14).

The current rise of the European Union seems to be a direct fulfillment of Daniel's prophecy. Europe today even has a unified currency called the Euro and is growing stronger and stronger economically. All that remains is for ten nations in Europe to rise to the top and form a consolidated, common government. When this happens, Rome will live again, and out of this Western confederacy, the Antichrist will rise to rule the world during the Great Tribulation.

RUSSIA

Many people might be surprised to learn that one of the key places mentioned in Bible prophecy is Russia. Scripture predicts that the great Russian bear will rise in the last days to mount a furious invasion of Israel (Ezek. 38–39). The prophet Ezekiel predicted 2,600 years ago that in the last days, Israel would be invaded by a people from the distant north (38:6, 15). Many mistakenly thought that when the Soviet Union dissolved, the bear went into permanent hibernation. But the Russian bear today is much more dangerous than ever before. With her economy in shambles, she is a starving bear. With the great Soviet Union dissolved, Russia is a mother bear robbed of her cubs.

The fulfillment of God's prophecies concerning Russia seems more imminent than ever before. As we track the bear in the end times, we discover that her footprints lead right to the land of Israel. In tracking the bear, I will consider five points: the appearance, the allies, the activity, the annihilation, and the aftermath.

The Appearance The only reference to Russia in Scripture is Ezekiel 38:2, where the Hebrew word *rosh* is found. This word simply means "head," "top," "summit," or "chief." It is a very common word to all Semitic languages. In the Old Testament, it occurs approximately 750 times along with its root and derivatives. The problem is that *rosh* in Ezekiel 38:2 can be translated as either a proper noun or an adjective. Many translations take *rosh* as an adjective and translate it as the word *chief.* The King James Version, the Revised Standard Version, the New American Bible, and the New International Version all adopt this translation.

The better translation is to take *rosh* as a proper noun referring to a specific place. The great Hebrew scholars C. F. Keil and Wilhelm Gesenius both state clearly that *rosh* in Ezekiel 38:2-3 and 39:1 is the name of a geographical location.[12] Also, the Septuagint, the Greek translation of the Old Testament, translates *rosh* as the proper name Ros.

Gesenius says that Ros is undoubtedly the Russians, who are mentioned by the Byzantine writers of the tenth century under the name Ros, dwelling to the north of Taurus on the river Rha (Wolga).[13]

The Allies Russia will be led by a power-crazed madman named Gog (whom I will discuss in the next chapter). A host of allies will join Gog, the leader of Russia. Ezekiel 38:9 refers to "you and all your allies—a vast and awesome horde." Ezekiel 38:1-6 mentions eight specific geographical locations.

GEOGRAPHICAL LOCATIONS IN EZEKIEL 38:1-6

ANCIENT NAME	MODERN NATION
Magog	Central Asia (Islamic southern republics of the former Soviet Union)
Meshech	Turkey
Tubal	Turkey
Persia	Iran
Ethiopia (Cush)	Sudan
Libya (Put)	Libya
Gomer	Turkey
Beth-togarmah	Turkey

From this chart it is clear that Russia will have five key allies: Turkey, Iran, Libya, Sudan, and the nations of central Asia. Amazingly, all of these nations are Muslim nations, and Iran, Libya, and Sudan are three of Israel's most ardent opponents. Many of these nations are either forming or strengthening their ties today. This list of nations reads like the Who's Who of this week's newspaper headlines. It's not too difficult to imagine these nations conspiring together to invade Israel in the near future.

The Activity Ezekiel says that these nations, led by Russia, will come against Israel at a time when the people of Israel are living in peace and prosperity (38:8-12). This probably describes the first half of the Tribulation, when Israel will be living under her peace treaty with Antichrist. Near the middle of the Tribulation, Russia and her Islamic allies will descend upon the nation of Israel like a storm and will cover the land like a cloud (38:9). There are four main reasons why Russia and her allies will invade Israel:[14]

1. To cash in on the wealth of Israel (Ezek. 38:11-12)
2. To control the Middle East
3. To crush Israel (The Islamic nations mentioned in Scripture hate Israel.)
4. To challenge the authority of Antichrist (Dan. 11:40-44)

How is an attack on Israel a challenge to the Antichrist's authority? Because Israel will be under a peace treaty with Antichrist, any attack against her is a direct challenge to Antichrist. However, after God supernaturally destroys the armies that invade Israel, Antichrist will move in to consolidate his empire, and then he will break his covenant with Israel and will invade her himself (Dan. 11:41-44).

The Annihilation When these nations invade the land of Israel, it will look like the biggest mismatch in history. It will make the invasions of Israel in 1967 and 1973 by the Arab nations pale in comparison. When Russia assembles this last-days strike force, it will look like Israel is finished. But God is in control of the entire situation. He will mount up in his fury to destroy these godless invaders: "When Gog invades the land of Israel, says the Sovereign Lord, my fury will rise!" (Ezek. 3:18). God will come to rescue his helpless people, using the following four means to destroy Russia and her allies:

1. A great earthquake (Ezek. 38:19-20)
2. Infighting among the troops of the various nations (Ezek. 38:21)[15]
3. Disease (Ezek. 38:22)
4. Torrential rain, hailstones, fire, and burning sulphur (Ezek. 38:22)[16]

The Aftermath   There are four key events that occur in the aftermath of this invasion.

THE BIRDS AND THE BEASTS (Ezek. 39:4-5, 17-20; See also Rev. 19:17-18) The carnage that results from this slaughter will provide a great feast for the birds of the air and the beasts of the field. God refers to the carnage as a "sacrificial feast" and "my banquet table," to which he invites the birds and the beasts as his guests.

THE BURYING OF THE DEAD (Seven Months) (Ezek. 39:11-12, 14-16) Cleanup squads will assemble to go through the land. They will set up markers wherever they see a human bone. When the grave diggers come behind the cleanup squads, they will see the markers and take the remains to the Valley of Gog's Hordes for burial. The cleansing will be so extensive that a town will be established in the valley near the grave-sites to aid those who are cleansing the land. The name of the town will be Hamonah (horde).

THE BURNING OF THE WEAPONS (Seven Years) (Ezek. 39:9-10)   Since this event occurs at the midpoint of the Tribulation, the Israelites will continue to burn these weapons for the final three and a half years of the Tribulation and on into the kingdom for another three and a half years.

THE BLESSING OF SALVATION   In the midst of his wrath and fury, God will also pour out his grace and mercy. God will use the awesome display of his power against Russia and her allies to bring many Jews and Gentiles to salvation:

> *I will bring you against my land as everyone watches, and my holi-ness will be displayed by what happens to you. Then all the nations will know that I am the Lord. . . . I will make myself known to all the nations of the world. . . . Thus, I will make known my holy name among my people of Israel. I will not let it be desecrated*

*anymore. And the nations, too, will know that I am the Lord, the
Holy One of Israel. Thus, I will demonstrate my glory among the
nations. . . . And from that time on the people of Israel will know
that I am the Lord their God.'" (Ezek. 38:16, 23; 39:7, 21-22)*

Many of those who turn to the true God as a result of this demonstration of his power will undoubtedly be among the vast group of the redeemed in Revelation 7:9-14. This is one of the most amazing prophecies in all of Scripture. And everything seems to be getting ready for its fulfillment in the near future. Russia is a key place to watch as the coming of Christ draws nearer.

THE VALLEY OF JEHOSHAPHAT

The Bible mentions the valley of Jehoshaphat only twice by name (Joel 3:2, 12). It is identified as the final place where God will gather the nations in order to destroy them. The word *Jehoshaphat* means "Yahweh judges," so it is a fitting place for God's judgment to be poured out. Joel 3:14 also calls this place "the valley of decision."

This valley is very significant in Bible prophecy because of what the Bible says will happen there at the end of the Tribulation:

> *"At that time, when I restore the prosperity of Judah and Jerusalem," says the Lord, "I will gather all the armies of the world into the valley of Jehoshaphat. . . . Let the nations be called to arms. Let them march to the valley of Jehoshaphat. There I, the Lord, will sit to pronounce judgment on them all." Thousands upon thousands are waiting in the valley of decision. It is there that the day of the Lord will soon arrive. (Joel 3:1-2, 12, 14)*

While it is clear what will happen in this valley, there is disagreement on its location. There are four main views on the location of this valley:

1. The valley that will be created when the Mount of Olives splits (Zech. 14:3-5)
2. A presently unknown valley
3. The Valley of Berachah (Blessing), south of Bethlehem, where Jehoshaphat gathered his forces after battle (2 Chron. 20:26)
4. The Kidron Valley, east of Jerusalem, between the city and the Mount of Olives

The best option is the fourth one. Zechariah locates the final judgment of the nations near the city of Jerusalem (Zech. 14:1-5). Also, Jewish, Christian, and Muslim traditions locate the place of final judgment for the nations in the Kidron valley.[17]

[1]Robert Thomas, *Revelation 1–7: An Exegetical Commentary* (Chicago: Moody Press, 1992), 313.

[2]Charles Dyer, *The Rise of Babylon* (Wheaton, Ill.: Tyndale House Publishers, 1991), 182.

[3]Robert Thomas, 307.

[4]These points were taken from Dr. Charles Dyer, "Babylon and the Bible," unpublished class notes, Dallas Theological Seminary.

[5]Arnold Fruchtenbaum, *The Footsteps of the Messiah: A Study of the Sequence of Prophetic Events* (Tustin, Calif.: Ariel Ministries, 1982), 203.

[6]Wilbur Smith, *Egypt in Bible Prophecy* (Boston: W. A. Wilde Company, 1957), 6.

[7]Ibid., 241–42.

[8]Randall Price, *Jerusalem in Prophecy: God's Final Stage for the Final Drama* (Eugene, Ore.: Harvest House, 1998), 78–79.

[9]Ibid., 65, 74. Thomas Ice and Timothy Demy (*The Truth about Jerusalem in Bible Prophecy*. Pocket Prophecy Series, Eugene, Oreg.: Harvest House Publishers, 1996, p. 8) also highlight the centrality of this city: "The dynamic story of this glorious city continues today. History proclaims its past. Headlines proclaim its present. Prophecy proclaims its future."

[10]*New Bible Dictionary*, 2d ed., s.v. "Olives, Mount of."

[11]David Aune, *Word Biblical Commentary: Revelation 1-5*, vol. 52 (Dallas: Word Books, 1997), 77.

[12]C. F. Keil, *Ezekiel, Daniel, Commentary on the Old Testament*, trans. James Martin (reprint, Grand Rapids: Eerdmans Publishing Company, 1982), 159, and Wilhelm Gesenius, *Gesenius' Hebrew-Chaldee Lexicon to the Old Testament* (Grand Rapids: Eerdmans Publishing Comany, 1949), 752.

[13]Wilhelm Gesenius, 862.

[14]Three of these four points were taken from Harold Willmington, *The King Is Coming* (Wheaton, Ill.: Tyndale House Publishers, 1981), 155.

[15]In the chaos after the powerful earthquake, the armies of each nation represented will turn against each other. This will be the largest case of death by friendly fire in human history.

[16]The famous Six-Day War occurred in Israel in June 1967. This will be the One-Day War or even the One-Hour War when God supernaturally destroys this Russian-Islamic horde.

[17]*New Bible Dictionary*, 2d ed., s.v. "Jehoshaphat, Valley of."

Ten Key Players
in Bible Prophecy

6

Every athletic event, movie, play, or televison program has its key players or actors. These characters are central to the main plot and determine the final outcome in the last scene or the fourth quarter. While there are many supporting actors in Bible prophecy, there are ten key players or actors who occupy the major roles in the final act of human history.

JESUS CHRIST

To say that Jesus Christ is the key person in Bible prophecy is an infinite understatement. As the supreme figure of all history, he dwarfs all of the other players. He is the King of kings and Lord of lords. He is the one who reveals and the one who is revealed in Bible prophecy. As the angel told John in Revelation 19:10, "The essence of prophecy is to give a clear witness for Jesus."

The clearest and most concise way to capture the centrality of Christ

to Bible prophecy is to list all thirty-five names and titles given to him in
Revelation:

1. Jesus Christ (1:1)
2. Faithful witness (1:5)
3. First to rise from the dead (1:5)
4. Commander of all the rulers of the world (1:5)
5. The Alpha and the Omega (1:8)
6. The beginning and the end (1:8)
7. One who is, who always was, and who is to come, the Almighty One (1:8)
8. Son of Man (1:13)
9. The First and the Last (1:17; 2:8)
10. The living one who died (1:18)
11. The one who holds the seven stars in his right hand (2:1)
12. The one who walks among the seven gold lampstands (2:1)
13. The one who has a sharp two-edged sword (2:12)
14. Son of God (2:18)
15. Whose eyes are bright like flames of fire (2:18)
16. Whose feet are like polished bronze (2:18)
17. The one who has the sevenfold Spirit of God and the seven stars (3:1)
18. The one who is holy and true (3:7)
19. The one who has the key of David (3:7)
20. The Amen (3:14)
21. The faithful and true witness (3:14)
22. The ruler of God's creation (3:14)
23. The Lion of the tribe of Judah (5:5)
24. The heir to David's throne (5:5)
25. The Lamb (twenty-eight times)
26. Sovereign Lord, holy and true (6:10)
27. Their Lord (11:8)
28. A boy who was to rule all nations with an iron rod (12:5)
29. The child (12:5)
30. Lord God Almighty (15:3)
31. King of the nations (15:3)
32. Faithful and True (19:11)
33. The Word of God (19:13)
34. King of kings and Lord of lords (19:16)
35. The bright morning star (22:16)

MICHAEL THE ARCHANGEL

While there are myriads of unfallen angels, only two are designated by
name in the canonical books of Scripture. These two named angels are
Gabriel (Mighty One of God) and Michael (Who Is Like God). They are
given special places of importance in Scripture and appear in both the
Old and New Testaments.

Gabriel is God's leading messenger. Each time Scripture mentions him, he is delivering messages to God's people about God's kingdom program (Dan. 8:15-22; 9:21; Luke 1:19, 26).

Michael, on the other hand, might be characterized as the leader of God's heavenly army that protects his people. Scripture mentions Michael by name five times (Dan. 10:13, 21; 12:1; Jude 1:9; Rev. 12:7).

Michael receives the special designation of archangel (Dan. 10:13; 12:1). Although this title sets him above most of the other angels, it does not necessarily mean that he is the only angel of this classification. There may be other angels of the same class or rank. He is called "one of the archangels" in Daniel 10:13. However, the fact that Scripture singles him out by name five times undoubtedly signifies his elevated status among the unfallen angels. Moreover, since he is able to withstand the power of Satan himself in battle, he may even be of the cherubim class. The cherubim are a class of angels equal in power to Satan (Ezek. 28:14-16; Rev. 12:7).

Michael carries out four specific activities in Scripture. First, Michael disputed with Satan concerning the dead body of Moses (Jude 1:9). Second, Michael helped a lesser-ranked angel get through to answer the prayer of Daniel (Dan. 10:13, 21). When demons opposed a lesser angel in Daniel 10:12-15, Michael went to help the angel. He is called "Michael, your spirit prince" (Dan. 10:21). While other nations also seem to have their angelic princes, both good and evil, Michael is the unique angelic defender of Israel.

Third, Michael will stand up for the people of Israel during the Tribulation (Dan. 12:1).

Fourth, Michael will lead the armies of heaven against the forces of Satan in the invisible heavenly realm (Rev. 12:7). The nature of Michael's protective ministry over Israel is seen in more detail in Revelation 12:7-9. As Satan persecutes the nation of Israel during the Tribulation, a war breaks out in the invisible world between the elect angels and the evil angels as Michael and his army come to deliver the persecuted Jewish remnant:

> *Then there was war in heaven. Michael and the angels under his command fought the dragon and his angels. And the dragon lost the battle and was forced out of heaven. This great dragon—the ancient serpent called the Devil, or Satan, the one deceiving the whole world—was thrown down to the earth with all his angels.*

This battle occurs at the midpoint of the Tribulation because the period of Israel's protection is 1,260 days (Rev. 12:6). This three-and-a-half-year period corresponds to the last half of the Tribulation, when God preserves this Jewish remnant from satanic attack.

Names and Titles for Michael
- One of the archangels (Dan. 10:13)
- Michael, your spirit prince (Dan. 10:21)
- The archangel (Dan. 12:1)
- Michael, one of the mightiest of the angels (Jude 1:9)

THE TWENTY-FOUR ELDERS

Revelation makes twelve references to a group of beings called the twenty-four elders (Rev. 4:4, 10; 5:5, 6, 8, 11, 14; 7:11, 13; 11:16; 14:3; 19:4). The fact that they are mentioned twelve times makes them a collective key player in Bible prophecy.

Their Identity (Who Are They?) There are four main views concerning the identity of the twenty-four elders: (1) angelic beings; (2) Israel; (3) the church; and (4) all of the redeemed—Israel and the church. Seven key clues in Revelation reveal that the twenty-four elders represent the church or body of Christ:

THE TITLE They are called elders *(presbuteros)*, who in Scripture are the representatives of God's people. These elders represent the church.

THE NUMBER The Levitical priesthood in the Old Testament numbered in the thousands (see 1 Chron. 24). Since all of the priests could not worship in the temple at the same time, the priesthood was divided into twenty-four groups, and a representative of each group served in the temple on a rotating basis every two weeks. While the nation of Israel was a kingdom of priests (Exod. 19:6), only Aaron's sons were allowed to enter God's presence. However, *all* believers in the church are priests unto God (1 Pet. 2:5, 9). These twenty-four elders, therefore, are representative of the entire church of Jesus Christ.

THE POSITION They sit on thrones. God promises enthronement with Christ to the church (Rev. 3:21).

THE CROWNS Scripture never pictures angels as wearing crowns, yet church-age believers will receive crowns at the judgment seat of Christ

(Rev. 2:10). The elders cannot be Israel, because Old Testament believers will not be resurrected and rewarded until after the Tribulation is over (Dan. 12:1-3).

THE CLOTHING   The white clothing of the elders is the clothing of the redeemed in the church age (Rev. 3:5, 18; 19:8).

120

THE PRAISE   Only the church can sing the song the elders sing in Revelation 5:9-8.

THE DISTINCTION   Revelation 5:11 clearly distinguishes the elders from the angels.

Their Location (Where Are They?)   From their first appearance in Revelation 4:4, the twenty-four elders are in heaven, judged, rewarded, and enthroned. Since the elders represent the church, this is another indication that the church must be raptured to heaven before the Tribulation.

Their Function (What Are They Doing?)   Simply stated, the elders are worshiping. The most common posture of the elders is flat on their faces before the one who sits on the throne and before the Lamb. If you have ever wondered what the church will be doing in heaven after the Rapture and the judgment seat, this is it. The church will gather around the throne, casting their crowns down at the nail-pierced feet of the Lamb (Rev. 4:10) and singing praises to his name. The elders worship the Lord for four things: (1) creation (Rev. 4:11); (2) redemption (Rev. 5:9-10); (3) reigning (Rev. 11:17); and (4) righteous judgment (Rev. 19:4).

THE TWO WITNESSES
During the Tribulation period, God will raise up two special witnesses, who will minister on his behalf in the midst of the darkness and devastation.

What do we know about these two witnesses? Who are they? What will they do? When will they serve? There are five important points about the two witnesses in Revelation 11:1-12.[1]

The Witnesses Are People   The two witnesses have been interpreted symbolically as the Old and New Testament or the law and the prophets. However, Scripture clearly identifies the two witnesses as people who

• wear sackcloth,
• perform miracles,
• prophesy for God for 1,260 days,
• die and lie in the street for three and a half days,
• come back to life, and
• ascend up to heaven.

Revelation 11:4 gives further evidence that the two witnesses are people. There they are called "the two olive trees" and "the two lampstands
that stand before the Lord of all the earth." As David Jeremiah says:

> *How can these two descriptions help us determine that the wit-
> nesses are real people? If we look at the prophecy of Zechariah we
> see, again, two witnesses: Joshua and Zerubbabel (Zech. 4:1-14).
> God uses the lampstand and the olive trees as a picture of them.
> The lampstand burned brightly and the olive tree produced the
> oil, which was burned by the candelabra. It is a picture of the fact
> that these two witnesses are going to shine in the darkness of the
> Tribulation and that they will be fueled by the holy oil of the
> Spirit of God.*[2]

John Walvoord says this about the comparison of the two witnesses
to olive trees and lampstands in Revelation 11:4:

> *The two witnesses are described as two olive trees and two lamp-
> stands who stand before the God of the earth. This seems to be a
> reference to Zechariah 4, where a lampstand and two olive trees
> are mentioned. . . . The olive oil from the olive trees in Zechariah's
> image provided fuel for the two lampstands. The two witnesses of
> this period of Israel's history, namely Joshua the high priest and
> Zerubbabel, were the leaders of Israel in Zechariah's time. Just as
> the two witnesses were raised up to be lampstands or witnesses
> for God and were empowered by olive oil representing the power
> of the Holy Spirit, so the two witnesses of Revelation 11 will like-
> wise execute their prophetic office. Their ministry does not rise in
> human ability but in the power of God.*[3]

Having concluded that the two witnesses are real people, the next
question is, Are they people who have lived before? Many of the early
Christians, such as Tertullian, Irenaeus, and Hippolytus, believed

the two witnesses will be Enoch and Elijah. Others have held that Moses will be one of the two witnesses along with either Enoch or Elijah. There are several reasons why these men have been identified as the two witnesses.

ENOCH   Two main reasons are given to support Enoch as one of the two witnesses. First, Enoch never died (Gen. 5:23-24), and the Bible says that "it is destined that each person dies only once and after that comes judgment" (Heb. 9:27). Of course, this verse is simply establishing the general truth that all must die. There will be millions of exceptions to this general rule at the Rapture, when all the living saints will be translated to heaven without tasting physical death. Second, Enoch was a prophet of judgment, in the days before the Flood, who announced the coming of the Lord (Jude 1:14-15).

MOSES   Three main reasons favor identifying Moses as one of the two witnesses. First, like Moses, the witnesses will turn the rivers to blood and bring other plagues on the earth (Rev. 11:6). Second, on the Mount of Transfiguration, which pictured the second coming of Christ, Moses and Elijah appeared with Christ (Matt. 17:1-9). Third, Moses was a prophet.

ELIJAH   Four main reasons are given for identifying Elijah as one of the two witnesses. First, like Enoch, he never tasted physical death (2 Kings 2:11). Second, like Moses, he was present at the Transfiguration. Third, Scripture predicts that Elijah will come before the great and dreadful day of the Lord (Mal. 4:5). And fourth, like the two witnesses, Elijah was a prophet.

If I had to select two of these three men from the past who are the most likely candidates for the two witnesses, I suppose Moses and Elijah would be the best. The ministry of the two witnesses is most like the ministry of these two men, and they appeared at the Transfiguration together with Christ. However, the fact that they are not named in Revelation 11 causes me to reject this theory. The fact is that since the Lord doesn't tell us who they are, we really don't know for sure. Therefore, while it is possible that the two witnesses may be two of these great men from the past brought back to the earth, it seems best to view the two witnesses as men who have never lived before, whom God will raise up as his special witnesses in the Tribulation.

The Witnesses Are Prophets Scripture says that the two witnesses "will prophesy during those 1,260 days" (Rev. 11:3). They will burst upon the dark scene of the Tribulation, dressed in sackcloth—the garments of mourning—and will proclaim God's message of salvation and judgment on the sin-wracked world.

The Bible clearly states that the time of the ministry of the two witnesses is 1,260 days, or three and one-half years. But one issue that is debated is whether the two witnesses will minister during the first half of the Tribulation or during the Great Tribulation of the final three and a half years. Three reasons favor placing their ministry during the final half of the Tribulation:

CONTEXT The context of Revelation 11:2-3 strongly favors the last half of the Tribulation as the period of their ministry: "Do not measure the outer courtyard, for it has been turned over to the nations. They will trample the holy city for 42 months. And I will give power to my two witnesses, and they will be clothed in sackcloth and will prophesy during those 1,260 days." In other words, the two witnesses will minister during the same forty-two-month or three-and-a-half-year period that the temple is being trampled by the nations. This period of time is clearly the last half of the Tribulation.

THE SEVENTH TRUMPET The event that immediately follows the description of the two witnesses is the blowing of the seventh trumpet, which heralds the second coming of Christ at the end of the Tribulation (Rev. 11:15-19).

THE FORTY-TWO MONTHS When Revelation uses the time periods of forty-two months or 1,260 days, these references always seem to refer to the last half of the Tribulation. The same is true of the 1,260-day ministry of the two witnesses (11:3).

The Witnesses Are Powerful God will give the two witnesses incredible power. Revelation 11:3, 6 says:

> *"I will give power to my two witnesses."* . . . *They have power to shut the skies so that no rain will fall for as long as they prophesy. And they have power to turn the rivers and oceans to blood, and to send every kind of plague upon the earth as often as they wish.*

Apparently, the two witnesses are the human instruments God uses to call forth the first six trumpet judgments—just like Moses called forth the plagues on Egypt.

The Witnesses Are Persecuted As one can imagine, the whole world will hate the two witnesses. As they bring plague after plague upon the earth, the beast and his followers will view these two witnesses as Public Enemy No. 1 and No. 2. But God will surround them with his supernatural protection for three and a half years. "If anyone tries to harm them, fire flashes from the mouths of the prophets and consumes their enemies. This is how anyone who tries to harm them must die" (Rev. 11:5).

However, when the two witnesses have finished their three-and-one-half-year ministry, God will allow the Antichrist to kill them. The whole world will rejoice over the deaths of these prophets, and their bodies will be seen on worldwide television lying in the streets of Jerusalem. People all over the world will be so ecstatic that they will hold celebrations and send gifts to one another:

> *When they complete their testimony, the beast that comes up out of the bottomless pit will declare war against them. He will conquer them and kill them. And their bodies will lie in the main street of Jerusalem, the city which is called "Sodom" and "Egypt," the city where their Lord was crucified. And for three and a half days, all peoples, tribes, languages, and nations will come to stare at their bodies. No one will be allowed to bury them. All the people who belong to this world will give presents to each other to celebrate the death of the two prophets who had tormented them. (Rev. 11:7-10)*

Interestingly, this is the only mention of any kind of rejoicing or celebration on earth during the entire Tribulation period.

The Witnesses Are Preserved Amazingly, after the dead bodies of the two witnesses have laid rotting in the sun for three and a half days, the Lord will raise the witnesses back to life before a horror-stricken world. Revelation 11:11-12 describes their resurrection: "After three and a half days, the spirit of life from God entered them, and they stood up! And terror struck all who were staring at them. Then a loud voice shouted from heaven, 'Come up here!' And they rose to heaven in a cloud as their enemies watched." John Phillips aptly describes the scene:

> *Picture the scene—the sun-drenched streets of Jerusalem, the holiday crowd flown in from the ends of the earth for a firsthand look at the corpses of these detested men, the troops in the Beast's uniform, the temple police. There they are, devilish men from every kingdom under heaven, come to dance and feast at the triumph of the Beast. And then it happens! As the crowds strain at the police cordon to peer curiously at the two dead bodies, there comes a sudden change. Their color changes from cadaverous hue to the blooming, rosy glow of youth. Those stiff, stark limbs—they bend, they move! Oh, what a sight! They rise! The crowds fall back, break, and form again.*[4]

125

After this, there are only a few days at most remaining before Christ comes back in great power and glory.

THE 144,000

Among the key actors in the end times is a mysterious group of 144,000 people who faithfully serve the Lord. They are listed in Revelation 7:1-8 and are discussed again in Revelation 14:1-5.

The Identity of the 144,000 First, it is important to make clear who the 144,000 are not. They are not the church. The church is already in heaven, as pictured by the twenty-four elders, and they are not the Jehovah's Witnesses.

Who are these 144,000 servants of God? If we take Scripture at face value, then it is obvious that these people are a literal group of 144,000 Jewish men, 12,000 from each of the twelve tribes of Israel, whom God raises up in the Tribulation to serve him.

Students of Bible prophecy have often questioned why the tribe of Dan is omitted from the listing of the tribes in Revelation 7:1-8. A common answer is that the Antichrist will come from the tribe of Dan. However, it is better to explain Dan's omission as due to the fact that Dan was the first of the tribes to practice idolatry (Judg. 18:2, 30-31; 1 Kings

11:26; 12:28-30). Deuteronomy 29:18-21 required that the name of any-one who introduced Israel to idolatry was to be blotted out.

The Characteristics of the 144,000 Revelation mentions five main characteristics of the 144,000 that provide insight into the identity and ministry of these servants of God.

PREPARED   The first thing stated about the 144,000 is their prepara-tion for God's service: " 'Wait! Don't hurt the land or the sea or the trees until we have placed the seal of God on the foreheads of his ser-vants.' And I heard how many were marked with the seal of God. There were 144,000 who were sealed from all the tribes of Israel" (Rev. 7:3-4).

On earth during the Tribulation, the followers of the beast will bear his mark on their right hand or forehead as evidence that they belong to him (Rev. 13:16). During this same time, the Lord will place his identify-ing mark or seal of ownership on the forehead of the 144,000: "I saw the Lamb standing on Mount Zion, and with him were 144,000 who had his name and his Father's name written on their foreheads" (Rev. 14:1). This seal sets them apart and prepares them for God's service. Robert Thomas says:

> It was not uncommon for a soldier or a guild member to receive such a mark as a religious devotee. The mark was a sign of conse-cration to deity. The forehead was chosen because it was the most conspicuous, the most noble, and the part by which a person is usually identified. It will be obvious to whom these slaves belong and whom they serve.[5]

One question many Christians ask is, How will these 144,000 come to faith in Christ at the beginning of the Tribulation if all believers are rap-tured to heaven before the Tribulation begins? Who will preach the gos-pel to them? While we don't know for sure what means God will use to save the 144,000, it may be from Bibles and Christian books and videos that are left behind. Or it is possible that there may be 144,000 "Saul-of-Tarsus Damascus-Road" experiences, where the glorified Christ reveals himself personally to these men to call them to himself (Acts 9:1-9).

PROTECTED   God not only prepares the 144,000 for service, he also protects them with his seal, which is his pledge of security. He seals the 144,000 before the four angels bring God's judgment on the earth (Rev. 7:1-3). Therefore, the 144,000 are exempt from the wrath of God and Satan during the Tribulation (Rev. 9:4; 12:17). In Revelation 14:1-5, John sees the 144,000 at the end of the Tribulation, standing triumphantly on Mount Zion. They have come all the way through the Tribulation and are still standing on earth. God has preserved and protected his sealed servants for seven years through the horror of the Tribulation.

PURE   Revelation 14:4 says that the 144,000 are pure virgins who have not defiled themselves with women (KJV). Many interpret this figuratively as saying that they are spiritually undefiled and pure, separated from the corruption and pollution of false religion. However, the fact that Scripture says that they are not defiled with women seems to point to the fact that these men are celibate servants of God. In light of the exigencies of the Tribulation period, God calls them to abstain from a normal, marital life and to devote themselves totally to his service (see 1 Cor. 7:29-35).

PERSISTENT   The 144,000 are persistent in their life and service for the Lord, even under the most dire of circumstances. During the terrible days of the Tribulation, they constantly follow the Lamb wherever he goes (Rev. 14:4).

PREACHERS   The primary ministry of these Jewish servants is to proclaim the gospel of Christ fearlessly during the Tribulation period. There appears to be a cause-and-effect relationship in Revelation 7 between the 144,000 in verses 1-8 and the innumerable crowd of believers in verses 9-17. The ministry of the 144,000 is the cause that leads to the effect of salvation for millions of people. These sealed servants of God will fulfill Matthew 24:14: "The Good News about the Kingdom will be preached throughout the whole world, so that all nations will hear it; and then, finally, the end will come."

They will be the greatest evangelists the world has ever seen. The chief importance of the 144,000 is that they reveal the heart of God to save people even in the midst of the unspeakable judgment of the Tribulation. To the very end, the Savior graciously continues to seek and save those who are lost (Luke 19:10).

GOG

Near the midpoint of the Tribulation, Russia and her Islamic allies will mount an all-out attack of the land of Israel. The leader of this invasion is called Gog in Ezekiel 38:2. The name Gog only appears in the Bible one time outside of Ezekiel 38–39 and Revelation 20:8, in 1 Chronicles 5:4. However, the Gog there has no relation to the Gog of the end times.

The name Gog appears eleven times in Ezekiel 38–39, more than any other name in the chapter. Therefore, we know that Gog is the most important person in this coalition. Gog is clearly the leading actor in this great drama of the end times.

The name Gog means "high," "supreme," "a height," or "a high mountain." The way the book of Ezekiel uses this name reveals that Gog is a person who comes from the ancient land of Magog, which is the southern part of the former Soviet Union. Gog is probably not a person's name but a kingly title like Pharaoh, Caesar, Czar, or President. Gog is also called a prince.

Some erroneously conclude that Gog is just another title for the Antichrist, but Gog leads a Russian-Islamic invasion force, not the reunited Roman Empire. Daniel 11:40 calls Gog the king of the north, and his invasion into Israel is a direct challenge to the Antichrist's treaty with Israel. Therefore, Gog is not the Antichrist. Gog is the final ruler over Russia, who will lead her and her allies to their doom in Israel during the Tribulation period.

THE JEWISH PEOPLE

The Jewish people play a key role in the last days. The Jewish people in the end times will be divided into at least four groups. To fully understand the role of the Jews in the last days, it is important to look at each of these groups briefly to see what specific roles they play.[6]

Group 1: Apostate Jews These are the Jews of Daniel 9:27, who will enter into a covenant with the Antichrist. They are the ones Jesus spoke about in John 5:43 who would readily receive the ones who "represent only themselves." This group will make up about two-thirds of the nation of Israel and will die in the worldwide persecutions by Antichrist when he betrays his peace covenant with them (Zech. 13:8; 12:17; 14:1-5).

Group 2: 144,000 Jews This group of last-days believers will spread the gospel of Christ during the Tribulation (Rev. 7:1-8; 12:17; 14:1-5).

Group 3: Hebrew Christians Besides the special group of the 144,000, many other Jews will turn to Christ for salvation during the Tribulation. The group of people in Revelation 7:9 must include some believers from Israel.

Group 4: The Faithful Remnant These are Jews who will comprise the majority of the one-third who will survive the Tribulation (Zech. 13:8). Throughout the Tribulation period, they will not believe in Christ as their Messiah, but neither will they accept the Antichrist. They are pictured as a woman who will be divinely protected from the Antichrist during the last half of the Tribulation (Rev. 12:6, 13-17).

Just before Jesus returns to the earth, this remnant will turn to Christ. This is the key prerequisite for the Second Coming. Jesus will not return until the Jewish people and their leaders turn to him for salvation and ask him to come back. Two key passages in Scripture support this view:

> I will pour out a spirit of grace and prayer on the family of David and on all the people of Jerusalem. They will look on me whom they have pierced and mourn for him as for an only son. They will grieve bitterly for him as for a firstborn son who has died. (Zech. 12:10)

> O Jerusalem, Jerusalem, the city that kills the prophets and stones God's messengers! How often I have wanted to gather your children together as a hen protects her chicks beneath her wings, but you wouldn't let me. And now look, your house is left to you, empty and desolate. For I tell you this, you will never see me again until you say, "Bless the one who comes in the name of the Lord!" (Matt. 23:37-39)

After Christ returns, the faithful remnant will enter the millennial kingdom, where God will give them the land promised to Abraham in Genesis 15:18, and Christ will rule over them from his throne in Jerusalem.

SATAN

The next three key players form the unholy trinity of the last days: Satan, Antichrist, and the false prophet. Each of these characters counterfeits one of the persons in the Holy Trinity. Satan is the false Father, Antichrist is the false Christ, and the false prophet is the false counterpart to the Holy Spirit.

THE UNHOLY TRINITY OF THE END TIMES

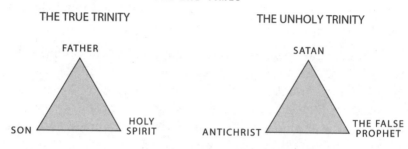

Just as Christ is the great protagonist in Bible prophecy, Satan is the great antagonist. He feverishly, fiendishly opposes God, his work, and his people.

The Primary Activities of Satan in the End Times Satan will involve himself in seven main activities during the last days:

1. He will lead the false, unholy trinity (Rev. 13:2; 16:13).
2. He will be cast out of heaven by Michael at the midpoint of the Tribulation (Rev. 12:7-9).
3. He will persecute the Jewish people (Rev. 12:13-15).
4. He will know that his time is short, so he will pour out his wrath on the earth (Rev. 12:12).
5. He will gather the armies of the world at Armageddon (Rev. 16:13-16).
6. He will continue to deceive the world (Rev. 12:9; 20:8).
7. He will foment and lead the final rebellion against God (Rev. 20:7-10)

Prophetic Names and Titles for the Devil Revelation contains at least eight names or titles for Satan that give us insight into his character:

1. Satan (Rev. 2:9)
2. The Devil (Rev. 2:10; 12:9)
3. A large red dragon (Rev. 12:3)
4. This great dragon (Rev. 12:9)
5. The ancient serpent (Rev. 12:9)
6. The one deceiving the whole world (Rev. 12:9)
7. The Accuser (Rev. 12:10)
8. That old serpent (Rev. 20:2)

THE ANTICHRIST OR BEAST

Other than Jesus Christ, the main person in Bible prophecy and all of human history is the coming world ruler, Antichrist. Dr. Harold Willmington aptly describes the uniqueness of this future world dictator:

> *Since the days of Adam, it has been estimated that approximately 40 billion human beings have been born upon our earth. Four and one-half billion of this number are alive today. However, by any standard of measurement one might employ, the greatest human (apart from the Son of God himself) in matters of ability and achievement is yet to make his appearance upon our planet.*[7]

131

Who is this satanic superman who is yet to burst onto the world scene? What will he do? What will he be like? The following information about Antichrist, presented in a list, will give an overview of the person and work of this last-days world ruler.

His Person Scripture reveals eight attributes or characteristics of the Antichrist's personality:

1. He will be an intellectual genius (Dan. 8:23).
2. He will be an oratorical genius (Dan. 11:36).
3. He will be a political genius (Rev. 17:11-12).
4. He will be a commercial genius (Dan. 11:43; Rev. 13:16-17).
5. He will be a military genius (Rev. 6:2; 13:2).
6. He will be a religious genius (2 Thess. 2:4; Rev. 13:8).
7. He will be a Gentile (Rev. 13:1).
8. He will emerge from a reunited Roman Empire (Dan. 7:8; 9:26).

His Activities Scripture also reveals twenty-six specific activities associated with the Antichrist:

1. He will appear in the time of the end of Israel's history (Dan. 8:17).
2. His manifestation will signal the beginning of the day of the Lord (2 Thess. 2:1-3).
3. His manifestation is currently being hindered by the "one who is holding it back" (2 Thess. 2:3-7).
4. His rise to power will come through peace programs. He will make a covenant of peace with Israel (Dan. 9:27). This event will signal the beginning of the seven-year Tribulation. He will later break that covenant at its midpoint.
5. Near the middle of the Tribulation, the Antichrist will be assassinated or violently killed (Dan 11:45; Rev. 13:3, 12, 14).
6. He will descend into the abyss (Rev. 17:8).
7. He will be raised back to life (Rev. 11:7; 13:3, 12, 14; 17:8).

8. The whole world will be amazed and will follow after him (Rev. 13:3).
9. He will be totally controlled and energized by Satan (Rev. 13:2-5).
10. He will subdue three of the ten kings in the reunited Roman Empire (Dan. 7:24).
11. The remaining seven kings will give all authority to the Beast (Rev. 17:12-13).
12. He will invade the land of Israel and desecrate the rebuilt temple (Dan. 9:27; 11:41; 12:11; Matt. 24:15; Rev. 11:2).
13. He will mercilessly pursue and persecute the Jewish people (Dan. 7:21, 25; Rev. 12:6).
14. He will set himself up in the temple as God (2 Thess. 2:4).
15. He will be worshiped as God for three and a half years (Rev. 13:4-8).
16. His claim to deity will be accompanied by great signs and wonders (2 Thess. 2:9-12)
17. He will speak great blasphemies against God (Dan. 7:8 ; Rev. 13:6)
18. He will rule the world politically, religiously, and economically for three and a half years (Rev. 13:4-8, 16-18).
19. He will be promoted by a second beast who will lead the world in worship of the Antichrist (Rev. 13:11-18).
20. He will require all to receive his mark to buy and sell (Rev. 13:16-18).
21. He will establish his religious, political, and economic capital in Babylon (Rev. 17:1-18).
22. He and the ten kings will destroy Babylon (Rev. 17:16).
23. He will kill the two witnesses (Rev. 11:7).
24. He will gather all the nations against Jerusalem (Zech. 12:1-2; 14:1-3; Rev. 16:16; 19:19).
25. He will fight against Christ when he returns to earth and will suffer total defeat (Rev. 19:19).
26. He will be cast alive into the lake of fire (Dan. 7:11; Rev. 19:20).

His Counterfeit of Christ

The Antichrist will be an amazing parody or counterfeit of the true Christ. Here are a few of the ways he will mimic the ministry of the Son of God.

SIMILARITIES AND DIFFERENCES BETWEEN CHRIST AND THE ANTICHRIST

CHRIST	ANTICHRIST
Miracles, signs, and wonders (Matt. 9:32-33; Mark 6:2)	Miracles, signs, and wonders (Matt. 24:24; 2 Thess. 2:9)
Causes men to worship God (Rev. 1:6)	Causes men to worship Satan (Rev. 13:3-4)
Followers sealed on their forehead (Rev. 7:4; 14:1)	Followers sealed on their forehead or right hand (Rev. 13:16-18)
Violent death (Rev. 13:8)	Violent death (Rev. 13:3)
Crowned with many crowns (Rev. 19:12)	Crowned with ten crowns (Rev. 13:1)
Worthy name (Rev. 19:16)	Blasphemous names (Rev. 13:1)
Resurrection (Matt. 28:6)	Resurrection (Rev. 13:3, 14)
Second coming (Rev. 19:1-21)	Second coming (Rev. 17:8)
One-thousand-year worldwide kingdom (Rev. 20:4-6)	Three-and-a-half-year worldwide kingdom (Rev. 13:5-8)
Part of a holy trinity (Father, Son, Holy Spirit)	Part of an unholy trinity (Satan, Antichrist, false prophet)
Has the power and throne of God (Rev. 12:5)	Has the power and throne of Satan (Rev. 13:2)

His Foreshadowers The Antichrist's personality and attributes will not be new to this earth. Many men in history have been types or pictures of what the coming Antichrist will be like. The following is a brief list:

- Nimrod (Gen. 10–11)—established the first worldwide, organized rebellion against God; first world ruler
- Pharaoh—oppressed God's people and openly defied God
- Nebuchadnezzar—boastful and proud; erected an image that people had to worship or die; destroyed the temple in Jerusalem
- Alexander the Great—mighty world conqueror; declared himself God
- The Roman caesars—ruled the world; promoted emperor worship
- Antiochus Epiphanes—the most pronounced, clearest type of Antichrist (Dan. 8:15-23)

Ten Ways in Which Antiochus Parallels Antichrist
1. Both persecute the Jewish people.
2. Both demand worship.
3. Both establish an image in the temple (abomination of desolation).
4. Both impose an alien belief system on the Jews.
5. Both have a relationship to the Roman Empire.
6. Both have a religious leader who aids them—Antiochus had a priest named Menelaus; Antichrist will have the false prophet (Rev. 13:11-18).
7. Both are opposed by a faithful remnant.
8. Both are reported dead but appear alive again (Compare 2 Maccabees 5:5 with Rev. 13:3, 12, 14).[8]
9. Both are active in the Middle East for about seven years.
10. Both are defeated by the advent of a great deliverer—Antiochus was defeated by Judas Maccabees; Antichrist will be defeated by Jesus Christ.

His Names and Titles Scripture gives the coming world ruler many different names and titles. As A. W. Pink notes, "Across the varied scenes depicted by prophecy there falls the shadow of a figure at once commanding and ominous. Under many different names, like the aliases of a criminal, his character and movements are set before us."[9]

Here are the top ten aliases for the coming world dictator:

The Top Ten Names and Titles for the Coming World Ruler
1. The small or little horn (Dan. 7:8)
2. A fierce king, a master of intrigue (Dan. 8:23)
3. This defiler (Dan. 9:27)
4. The king (Dan. 11:36)
5. A worthless shepherd (Zech. 11:15)
6. The man of lawlessness (2 Thess. 2:3)

7. The one who brings destruction (2 Thess. 2:3)
8. Antichrist (1 John 2:18, 22; 4:3; 2 John 1:7).
9. A rider on a white horse (Rev. 6:2)
10. The Beast (Rev. 13:1-9; 17:3, 8)

THE FALSE PROPHET OR SECOND BEAST

There have always been false prophets and false teachers. One of Satan's chief methods of operation is to counterfeit and corrupt the true message of God through his false messengers. This strategy of Satan will increase dramatically in the end times. The Bible says that in the last days of planet earth, there will be many false prophets who will perform great signs and wonders and spew out deceiving lies (Matt. 24:24).

In this mass of deception, one false prophet will rise high above all the rest in his ability to capture the world's attention. He is the false prophet of Revelation 13:11, and he is the final person in the unholy trinity of the end times. The false prophet is the satanic counterfeit of the Holy Spirit. And just as the ministry of the Holy Spirit is to give glory to Christ and to point people to him in trust and worship, the chief ministry of the false prophet will be to glorify the Antichrist and to lead people to trust and worship him. The Antichrist, or first beast in Revelation 13:1-8, will be primarily a military and political figure, whereas the second beast will be a religious figure. He will be a kind of satanic John the Baptist, preparing the way for the coming of the Antichrist. The false prophet will be the chief propagandist for the Beast, his right-hand man, his closest colleague and companion, and he will lead the world in the false worship of its emperor.

The New Testament mentions the Antichrist and the false prophet together in four passages:

1. Revelation 13:1-18—they share a common goal
2. Revelation 16:13—they share a common agenda for the world
3. Revelation 19:20—they share a common sentence
4. Revelation 20:10—they share a common destiny

The first beast, who comes up out of the sea (Rev. 13:1), is clearly a Gentile. The sea in Revelation is a picture of the Gentile nations. It is possible that the second beast who comes up out of the earth (Rev. 13:11) may be a Jewish apostate.

There are three key facts about the false prophet emphasized in

Revelation 13:11-18: his deceptive appearance, his devilish authority, and his deadly activity.

His Deceptive Appearance (Rev. 13:11) "I saw another beast come up out of the earth. He had two horns like those of a lamb, and he spoke with the voice of a dragon." This is total deception! Here is a man who is described as a wild beast, a lamb, and dragon. He has the nature of a wild beast. He is hostile to God's flock. He ravages God's people. But he has the appearance of a lamb. He looks gentle, tender, mild, and harmless. In addition, he has the voice of a dragon. He is the voice of hell itself, belching forth the fiery lies of Satan. When he speaks, he becomes Satan's mouthpiece. John Phillips summarizes the deceptive appearance and deadly approach of the false prophet:

135

> *The role of the false prophet will be to make the new religion appealing and palatable to men. No doubt it will combine all the features of the religious systems of men, will appeal to man's total personality, and will take full advantage of his carnal appetite. The dynamic appeal of the false prophet will lie in his skill in combining political expediency with religious passion, self-interest with benevolent philanthropy, lofty sentiment with blatant sophistry, moral platitude with unbridled self-indulgence. His arguments will be subtle, convincing, and appealing. His oratory will be hypnotic, for he will be able to move the masses to tears or whip them into a frenzy. He will control the communication media of the world and will skillfully organize mass publicity to promote his ends. He will be the master of every promotional device and public relations gimmick. He will manage the truth with guile beyond words, bending it, twisting it, and distorting it. Public opinion will be his to command. He will mold world thought and shape human opinion like so much potter's clay. His deadly appeal will lie in the fact that what he says will sound so right, so sensible, so exactly what unregenerate men have always wanted to hear.[10]*

His Devilish Authority (Rev. 13:12) The second beast will exercise "all the authority of the first beast." His power comes from the same source as does that of the first beast—Satan himself.

His Deadly Activity (Rev. 13:13-18) Six deadly activities of the false prophet are delineated in this section. These activities reveal how he will use his influence and experience during the days of the Great Tribulation.

1. He will bring down fire from heaven and perform other miracles (verses 13-14). He will mimic the miracles of the two witnesses just like Egyptian magicians counterfeited the miracles of Moses (Exod. 7:11-13, 22; 8:7; Rev. 11:4-6).
2. He will erect an image to the Antichrist for all the world to worship (verse 14). This image or abomination of desolation will undoubtedly be placed in the temple in Jerusalem (Matt. 24:15). Like the image of Nebuchadnezzar on the plain of Dura in Daniel 3, all will have to bow to this image or die.
3. He will raise the Antichrist from the dead (verse 14). While this is not stated explicitly in the text, it is strongly implied. Revelation 13 mentions the death and resurrection of the Antichrist three times (verses 3, 12, 14). Since the false prophet is a miracle worker who deceives the world, it is probable that Satan will use the false prophet as his human instrument to raise the Antichrist back to life.
4. He will give life to the image of the beast (verse 15).
5. He will force everyone to take the mark of the beast (verse 16).
6. He will control world commerce on behalf of the beast (verse 17).

[1] These five points were taken from David Jeremiah's Study Guide *Escape the Coming Night: Messages from the Book of Revelation*, vol. 2 (Dallas: Word, 1997), 121–25.

[2] Ibid., 122.

[3] John Walvoord, *The Revelation of Jesus Christ* (Chicago: Moody Press, 1966), 179–180.

[4] John Phillips, *Exploring Revelation* (Neptune, N.J.: Loizeaux Brothers, 1991), 150.

[5] Robert L. Thomas, *Revelation 1–7: An Exegetical Commentary* (Chicago: Moody Press, 1992), 473.

[6] Arnold Fruchtenbaum, *Footsteps of the Messiah* (Tustin, Calif.: Ariel Ministries, 1982), 198.

[7] Harold Willmington, *The King Is Coming* (Wheaton, Ill.: Tyndale House Publishers, 1981), 81.

[8] Second Maccabees is a book of the Apocrypha, which is a record of the history of the Jewish people during the intertestamental period (that is, the time between the Old and New Testaments).

[9] Arthur W. Pink, *The Antichrist* (Grand Rapids: Kregel Publications, 1988), 9.

[10] John Phillips, 171.

Six Key Things Bible Prophecy Can Do for You

Every key passage on the coming of Christ contains a practical application closely associated with it. Prophecy was not given just to stir our imagination or capture our attention. God intended prophecy to change our attitudes and actions to be more in line with his Word and his character. Charles Dyer emphasizes this purpose of Bible prophecy:

> *God gave prophecy to change our hearts, not to fill our heads with knowledge. God never predicted future events just to satisfy our curiosity about the future. Every time God announces events*

that are future, he includes with his predictions practical appli-cations to life. God's pronouncements about the future carry with them specific advice for the "here and now."[1]

There are at least six life-changing effects or influences that understanding Bible prophecy can have on our heart.

BIBLE PROPHECY HAS A CONVERTING INFLUENCE ON SEEKING HEARTS

No person knows how much time he or she has left on this earth, either personally or prophetically. Personally, all of us—at one point or another—become painfully aware of our mortality. We have no guarantee we will see tomorrow. Prophetically, Christ may come at any moment to take his bride, the church, to heaven, and all unbelievers will be left behind to endure the horrors of the Tribulation period.

With this in mind, the most important question for every reader to face is whether he or she has a personal relationship with Jesus Christ as Savior. The message of salvation through Jesus Christ is a message that contains both bad news and good news.

The bad news is that the Bible declares that all people, including you and me, are sinful and, therefore, are separated from the holy God of the universe (Isa. 59:2; Rom. 3:23). God is holy and cannot simply overlook sin. A just payment for the debt of sin must be made. But we are spiritually bankrupt and have no resources within ourselves to pay the huge debt we owe.

The Good News, the gospel, is that Jesus Christ has come and satisfied our sin debt. He bore our judgment and paid the price for our sins. He died on the cross for our sins and was raised to life on the third day to prove conclusively that the work of salvation had been fully accomplished. Colossians 2:14 says, "He canceled the record that contained the charges against us. He took it and destroyed it by nailing it to Christ's cross." First Peter 3:18 says, "Christ also suffered when he died for our sins once for all time. He never sinned, but he died for sinners that he might bring us safely home to God."

The salvation that Christ accomplished for us is available to all through faith in Jesus Christ. Salvation from sin is a free gift, which God offers to sinful people who deserve judgment. Won't you receive the gift today? Place your faith and trust in Christ, and in him alone, for your eternal salvation. "Believe on the Lord Jesus and you will be saved" (Acts 16:31). Now that you know what is coming upon this world in the last days and how many of these signs seem to be lining up just as the Bible predicts, respond to the invitation before it is too late.

BIBLE PROPHECY HAS A CARING INFLUENCE ON SOUL-WINNING HEARTS

No believer in Jesus Christ can study Bible prophecy without being gripped by the awesome power and wrath of God. Understanding the Bible brings us face-to-face with what is at stake for those who don't know Christ as their Savior. We are reminded in 2 Corinthians 5:20 of our calling during this present age: "We are Christ's ambassadors, and God is using us to speak to you. We urge you, as though Christ himself were here pleading with you, 'Be reconciled to God!'" Those who have already responded to the message of God's grace and forgiveness through Christ know where this world is headed, and we are Christ's ambassadors, representing him and his interests to a perishing world.

BIBLE PROPHECY HAS A CLEANSING INFLUENCE ON SINNING HEARTS

The Word of God is clear that a proper understanding of Bible prophecy should produce a life of holiness and purity. "We are already God's children, and we can't even imagine what we will be like when Christ returns. But we do know that when he comes we will be like him, for we will see him as he really is. And all who believe this will keep themselves pure, just as Christ is pure" (1 John 3:2-3). Focusing the mind and heart on prophecy, especially Christ's coming, is a fail-safe formula for maintaining personal purity. Note the certainty: "And all who believe this will keep themselves pure." Here is a perfect prescription for living a life of holiness—focusing on the coming of Christ. However, his coming must be a reality to us. It is one thing for us to hold right doctrine about Christ's coming. It is another thing for the doctrine to hold us!

In 1988 a book was published entitled *88 Reasons Why Christ Will Return in 1988*. In the book the author stated that he had conclusive proof that Christ would rapture the church to heaven in early October,

1988. A friend of mine who was a pastor in eastern Oklahoma called me in the summer of 1988 to ask me some questions about the book. In our conversation he told me that the book had caused quite a furor among many people in his church and other churches in the area. Of course, the Bible clearly declares that setting dates concerning the coming of Christ is futile and foolish (Matt. 24:36; Luke 21:8). However, this erroneous book caused many people to reexamine their lives just in case the date was right.

Obviously, the book was totally incorrect, but the point is that when people began to consider the fact that Christ might return soon, it transformed their lives. The Bible declares that we are to *always* be looking for Christ's coming—not just when someone sets an arbitrary date. "We should live in this evil world with self-control, right conduct, and devotion to God, while we look forward to that wonderful event when the glory of our great God and Savior, Jesus Christ, will be revealed" (Titus 2:12-13).

Romans 13:11-14 mentions prophecy and purity together:

> *Another reason for right living is that you know how late it is; time is running out. Wake up, for the coming of our salvation is nearer now than when we first believed. The night is almost gone; the day of salvation will soon be here. So don't live in darkness. Get rid of your evil deeds. Shed them like dirty clothes. Clothe yourselves with the armor of right living, as those who live in the light. We should be decent and true in everything we do, so that everyone can approve of our behavior. Don't participate in wild parties and getting drunk, or in adultery and immoral living, or in fighting and jealousy. But let the Lord Jesus Christ take control of you, and don't think of ways to indulge your evil desires.*

Second Peter 3:10-14 also presents the practical, cleansing effect of prophecy:

> *The day of the Lord will come as unexpectedly as a thief. Then the heavens will pass away with a terrible noise, and everything in them will disappear in fire, and the earth and everything on it will be exposed to judgment.*
>
> *Since everything around us is going to melt away, what holy,*

140

godly lives you should be living! You should look forward to that day and hurry it along—the day when God will set the heavens on fire and the elements will melt away in the flames. But we are looking forward to the new heavens and new earth he has promised, a world where everyone is right with God.

And so, dear friends, while you are waiting for these things to happen, make every effort to live a pure and blameless life. And be at peace with God.

When anyone says that studying Bible prophecy is not practical, they reveal that they don't understand what the Bible says about the personal impact of prophecy. In an immoral, sinful society like ours, what could be more practical than personal purity?

BIBLE PROPHECY HAS A CALMING INFLUENCE ON STIRRING HEARTS

Another practical effect of Bible prophecy is that it has a calming influence on us when our heart gets troubled and stirred up. In John 14:1-4, Jesus said:

Don't be troubled. You trust God, now trust in me. There are many rooms in my Father's home, and I am going to prepare a place for you. If this were not so, I would tell you plainly. When everything is ready, I will come and get you, so that you will always be with me where I am. And you know where I am going and how to get there.

The word *troubled* means "to be stirred up, disturbed, unsettled, or thrown into confusion." There are many things in our world today that disturb and unsettle us: the moral decay in our society, crime, economic uncertainty, terrorism, racial unrest, etc. Add to these problems the personal trials and difficulties we all face in our daily life, and we can become quite unsettled. Trouble is the common denominator of all humankind. Often these troubles and difficulties can leave us distraught, distracted, and disturbed. One of the great comforts in times like these is to remember that our Lord will someday return to take us to be with himself.

John 14:1-3 emphasizes three main points to calm our troubled heart—a person, a place, and a promise. The person is our Lord, the place is the heavenly city (the new Jerusalem), and the promise is that he will come again to take us to be with him forever.

BIBLE PROPHECY HAS A COMFORTING INFLUENCE ON SORROWING HEARTS

Every person who is reading these words either has faced or will face the grief of losing a close friend or loved one to death. When death strikes, pious platitudes do little to bring lasting comfort to friends and family. The only real, lasting comfort when death takes someone we love is the hope that we will see that person again in heaven. God's Word tells us with certainty that we are not to sorrow as people who have no hope because we will be reunited with our saved loved ones and friends at the Rapture.

> *Brothers and sisters, I want you to know what will happen to the Christians who have died so you will not be full of sorrow like people who have no hope. For since we believe that Jesus died and was raised to life again, we also believe that when Jesus comes, God will bring back with Jesus all the Christians who have died.*
>
> *I can tell you this directly from the Lord: We who are still living when the Lord returns will not rise to meet him ahead of those who are in their graves. For the Lord himself will come down from heaven with a commanding shout, with the call of the archangel, and with the trumpet call of God. First, all the Christians who have died will rise from their graves. Then, together with them, we who are still alive and remain on the earth will be caught up in the clouds to meet the Lord in the air and remain with him forever. So comfort and encourage each other with these words. (1 Thess. 4:13-18)*

The truth of the Rapture should transform the way we view death. God has promised that death has lost its sting, that it will be ultimately abolished, and that life will reign. This is not to say that we shouldn't grieve when our friends or loved ones die. For example, Jesus wept at the tomb of Lazarus (John 11:35). Stephen's friends wept loudly over his battered body (Acts 8:2). However, the Bible declares that our weeping is not the weeping of despair. We are to find deep solace, hope, and comfort for our sorrowing heart in the truth of God's Word about the future for his children.

BIBLE PROPHECY HAS A CONTROLLING INFLUENCE
ON SERVING HEARTS

In 1 Corinthians 15:58, after presenting the truth of the coming of Christ for his people, Paul concludes with a strong admonition: "So, my dear brothers and sisters, be strong and steady, always enthusiastic about the Lord's work, for you know that nothing you do for the Lord is ever useless." Here Paul is saying, since you know that Christ will someday come to receive you to himself, let nothing move you; be strong and steady in your Christian service. So many today are unstable and unsettled in Christian work. They are constantly vacillating.

Knowing about Christ's coming and future events should cure the problem of instability and inconsistency in Christian labor. Realizing that Christ could return at any time should make us enthusiastic, energetic, and excited about serving the Lord. The first two questions Saul, who later became Paul, asked when he saw the glorified Christ on the road to Damascus were, "Who are you, sir?" and "What shall I do, Lord?" (Acts 22:8, 10). Many professing Christians today have never moved beyond the first question. Many believers in Christ are spiritually unemployed!

The principle in the Bible is clear: Waiters are workers. When Christ comes, we are to be "dressed for service and well prepared" (Luke 12:35). If the events of Bible prophecy are a reality to us, they will motivate us to work faithfully for our Lord. The Lord intends for our knowledge of Bible prophecy to translate into devoted service to those around us as we await his return.

THE WELCOMING COMMITTEE

Warren Wiersbe tells a story of when he was a young man, preaching on the last days, with all the events of prophecy clearly laid out and perfectly planned. At the end of the service, an older gentleman came up to him and whispered in his ear, "I used to have the Lord's return planned out to the last detail, but years ago I moved from the planning committee to the welcoming committee."

Certainly we want to study Bible prophecy and know about God's plan for the future. That's what this book is all about. But we must be careful not to get too caught up in the planning and forget the welcoming. Are you on the welcoming committee for the Lord's return? Are you living each day to please the Master? May God use our study of the last days to transform our life as we wait for our Savior to return.

[1] Charles Dyer, *World News and Bible Prophecy* (Wheaton, Ill.: Tyndale House Publishers, 1995), 270.

Three Key Passages 8
of Bible Prophecy

Title
Transmission
Approaches
Key Words
Theme
Outline
Framework and Overview

While all the passages that deal with Bible prophecy make a unique contribution, there are three main sections of prophecy that contain the essential keys to understanding the future. These three sections are: (1) the book of Daniel; (2) the Olivet discourse (Matt. 24–25); and (3) the book of Revelation. To gain a basic understanding of Bible prophecy, one must have a general grasp of these three key passages. In this chapter I will present a broad overview of each of these key passages. The format I will use in surveying these parts of Scripture is the old ABCs outline: author, background, and content.

1. THE BOOK OF DANIEL (The Handwriting on the Wall)

The book of Daniel is one of the most beloved and beneficial books in the Word of God. The stories in this book are unparalleled in their drama and suspense. Every child who has ever been to Sunday school knows about the three young Hebrew men in the fiery furnace and Daniel in the lion's den. However, there is much more to this precious book than just children's Bible stories. It is also one of the key passages in the Bible that describes the events of the end times. Let's spend a little time delving deeper into this unforgettable book.

Author The book of Daniel bears the name of its human author—the prophet Daniel. Almost all that we know about the life and times of Daniel comes from this book. His contemporary, Ezekiel, mentions him as one of the godliest men who has ever lived (Ezek. 14:14, 20). Nebuchadnezzar's armies deported Daniel to Babylon in 605 B.C., when he was between fourteen and seventeen years old. He lived the remainder of his life in and around Babylon and died around the age of ninety.

Background In 605 B.C., the Babylonian king Nebuchadnezzar subjugated the nation of Judah. His conquest was God's discipline on the disobedient nation (Deut. 28:47-52; Jer. 25:7-11). God had sent his prophets to warn the people of coming judgment if they did not repent. There was a temporary, superficial revival under King Josiah. But when Josiah was killed in battle, the nation started on an irreversible path of rebellion that ended in their conquest and captivity.

Part of Nebuchadnezzar's policy of conquest was to deport some of the finest, brightest young men of nobility to Babylon to train them in the language, culture, religion, and government of Babylon so they could assist him in the administration of his empire. Daniel, along with many other young men, was deported from Judah to Babylon. Daniel was taken away from the godly influence of his parents, ripped away from his culture, and exposed to overwhelming pagan influences.

One can only imagine what must have been going through the mind of this young Hebrew man when he first laid eyes on the city of Babylon, as he entered the massive Ishtar Gate and was led down the ornate, idol-filled avenues of the city. But even in the midst of this godless environment, Daniel remained true to the God of heaven all of his life.

Content

THEME The theme of Daniel is the absolute transcendence and sovereignty of God over the affairs of people and nations. God is the one who raises up kings and kingdoms and brings them down. God reveals hidden mysteries. God rescues his people from seemingly impossible situations.

The book of Daniel contains seventy-eight occurrences of titles for God. In Daniel God is sovereign, loving, omnipotent (all-powerful), compassionate, omniscient (all-knowing), and righteous. He is the Most High God, the King of heaven, the living God, the Ancient One, the God of gods, the God of heaven, the Commander of heaven's armies, and the Most High. Daniel presents God as Ruler, Revealer, and Redeemer.

PURPOSE The purpose of Daniel can be summarized in two words: prophecy and piety. Daniel reveals the prophetic program for this world in the future and how God's people are to live in a godless society in the present.

As noted before, the Bible always links the study of prophecy with living a godly life. Daniel is no exception. This book contains many of the greatest prophecies in the Bible as well as some of the greatest examples of godly living. Therefore, prophecy and piety are the twin pillars of Daniel.

PROPHECY There are five major prophetic sections of Daniel that reveal God's future program for this world. Each of these five sections contains information about the future that God gave to Daniel either by means of a vision, a heavenly visitor, or, in some cases, both. The prophetic sections of Daniel are as follows:

1. Chapter 2—Dream vision of Nebuchadnezzar (the great statue)
2. Chapter 7—Night vision of Daniel (the four beasts out of the sea)
3. Chapter 8—Vision of Daniel in the fortress of Susa (the ram and the goat)
4. Chapter 9:24-27—Visit by the angel Gabriel (the seventy-sets-of seven prophecy)
5. Chapters 10–12—Final vision of Daniel (the rise and fall of Antichrist)

These five sections cover a lot of ground. They unveil the course and consummation of Gentile world history from the time of Nebuchadnezzar in 605 B.C. to the second coming of Christ. They help us understand where this world has been and where it is going. Daniel takes us on a whirlwind tour in these chapters:

• From the fifth century B.C. to the final century A.D.
• From the first world empire (Babylon) to the final world empire (Christ's kingdom)
• From the commencement of Gentile domination of Israel to its completion
• From Nebuchadnezzar to the new Jerusalem
• From the furnace of fire to the lake of fire
• From Nebuchadnezzar's dream to the nightmare of the Antichrist

PIETY There are also five key sections in Daniel that reveal how we are to live our life in the present, in the midst of a pagan society as we await the events of the last days. Chapters 1, 3, and 6 provide us with the positive examples (Daniel and his three friends) who refused to compromise their standards under the pressures of the world. In addition, chapters 4 and 5 warn against pride and rebellion against God:

1. Daniel 1—Daniel refuses to defile himself with the king's food
2. Daniel 3—Three Hebrew men refuse to bow to the king's image
3. Daniel 4—God humbles Nebuchadnezzar, the proud king

4. Daniel 5—The finger of God dramatically ends Belshazzar's drunken orgy
5. Daniel 6—Daniel continues to pray to God even under the threat of death

OUTLINE   The book of Daniel divides into three broad sections.

I. THE PERSONAL HISTORY OF DANIEL (chapter 1)

II. THE PROPHETIC HISTORY OF THE TIMES OF THE GENTILES (Chapters 2–7)
A. The Statue and the Stone (chapter 2)
B. God or the Golden Image? (chapter 3)
C. Beauty Becomes a Beast (chapter 4)
D. The Handwriting on the Wall (chapter 5)
E. Daniel In and Out of the Lions' Den (chapter 6)
F. The Jungle Book (chapter 7)

III. THE PROPHETIC HISTORY OF ISRAEL DURING THE TIMES OF THE GENTILES (Chapters 8–12)
A. A Preview of Coming Attractions (chapter 8)
B. The Prayer of Daniel (9:1-19)
C. The Seventy-Sets-of-Seven Prophecy (9:20-27)
D. The Final Vision (10:1–12:4)
E. All's Well That Ends Well (12:5-13)

THE STRUCTURE OF DANIEL 2–7   These six chapters form the heart of the book. They are presented in what is known as a chiastic structure, that is, each chapter in this section has a corresponding, parallel chapter as you work your way to and from the middle. The center of this chiasm is Daniel 4–5. The following diagram represents this structure:

Chiastic Structure of Daniel 2–7
• Daniel 2—World empires symbolized by four metals of a statue
• Daniel 3—Three young men delivered from the fiery furnace
• Daniel 4—Nebuchadnezzar humbled
• Daniel 5—Belshazzar humbled
• Daniel 6—Daniel delivered from the lions' den
• Daniel 7—World empires symbolized by four wild beasts

THE THREE KEY PROPHETIC SECTIONS OF DANIEL   There are three sections in Daniel that are indispensable to a proper understanding of the last days.

The first section is Daniel 2, which records a dream that Nebuchadnezzar had one night. In this dream, he saw a great statue of a man, made of four different metals. As he looked at the statue, a great stone came and smashed the image to pieces. This stone then became a great mountain filling the whole earth. Daniel interpreted this dream for Nebuchadnezzar. He said that the four different metals in the image represented Gentile world empires that would rule the world in succession.

THE METALLIC MAN

BODY PART	EMPIRE
Head of gold	Babylon
Chest and arms of silver	Medo-Persia
Belly and thighs of bronze	Greece
Legs of iron	Rome
Feet and toes of iron and clay	Rome II (Ten toes equals a ten-nation confederacy.)

The smiting stone that destroyed the image pictures the second coming of Christ, when he will destroy all those opposed to his rule. The mountain that filled the earth is Messiah's worldwide kingdom, which will replace the kingdoms of humanity.

The second section is Daniel 7, which covers the same ground as Daniel 2, only using different imagery and adding a few new details. H. A. Ironside notes an interesting difference between Daniel 2 and 7:

> *Chapter seven covers practically the same ground as chapter two. It takes in the whole course of the Times of the Gentiles, beginning with Babylon and ending with the overthrow of all derived authority and the establishment of the kingdom of the Son of Man. But the difference between the first and second divisions is this: In what we have already gone over we have been chiefly occupied with prophetic history as viewed from man's standpoint; but in the second half of the book we have the same scenes as viewed in God's unsullied light. In the second chapter, when a Gentile king had a vision of the course of world-empire, he saw the image of a man—a stately and noble figure—that filled him with such admiration that he set up a similar statue to be worshiped as a god. But in this opening chapter of the second division, Daniel, the man of God, has a vision of the same empires, and he sees them as four ravenous wild beasts, of so brutal a character, and so monstrous withal, that no actual creatures known to man could adequately set them forth.*[1]

The following chart represents Daniel's vision recorded in chapter 7:

THE FOUR BEASTS OF DANIEL 7

BEAST	EMPIRE
Lion	Babylon
Bear	Medo-Persia
Leopard	Greece
Terrible beast	Rome

The numerous parallels between these chapters reveal that they cover the same material from two vantage points.

PARALLELS BETWEEN DANIEL 2 AND 7

WORLD EMPIRE	DANIEL 2	DANIEL
Babylon	Head of gold	Lion
Medo-Persia	Chest and arms of silver	Bear
Greece	Belly and thighs of bronze	Leopard
Rome 1	Iron	Terrible beast
Rome II (reunited)	Ten toes	Ten horns
Antichrist		Little horn
God's kingdom	The smiting stone that destroys the image	The Son of Man, who receives the kingdom

The third section, Daniel 9:24-27, is one of the most important prophetic portions in the Bible. It is the indispensable key to all prophecy. It has often been called the "backbone of Bible prophecy," and "God's prophetic time clock."

In Daniel 9:1-23, Daniel confesses his sin and prays for the restoration of the people of Israel from Babylonian captivity. He knows that the seventy years of captivity is over (9:1-2), so he begins to intercede for his people. While Daniel is praying, God sends an immediate answer through his angelic messenger, Gabriel (9:21). Daniel 9:24-27 is God's answer to Daniel's prayer, but in this answer God goes far beyond the restoration of Israel from Babylon to Israel's ultimate and final restoration under Messiah:

> *A period of seventy sets of seven has been decreed for your people and your holy city to put down rebellion, to bring an end to sin, to atone for guilt, to bring in everlasting righteousness, to confirm the prophetic vision, and to anoint the Most Holy Place. Now listen and understand! Seven sets of seven plus sixty-two*

sets of seven will pass from the time the command is given to re-build Jerusalem until the Anointed One comes. Jerusalem will be rebuilt with streets and strong defenses, despite the perilous times.

After this period of sixty-two sets of seven, the Anointed One will be killed, appearing to have accomplished nothing, and a ruler will arise whose armies will destroy the city and the Temple. The end will come with a flood, and war and its miseries are de-creed from that time to the very end. He will make a treaty with the people for a period of one set of seven, but after half this time, he will put an end to the sacrifices and offerings. Then as a cli-max to all his terrible deeds, he will set up a sacrilegious object that causes desecration, until the end that has been decreed is poured out on this defiler.

TEN KEYS TO UNDERSTANDING THE SEVENTY WEEKS

1. The term *sets of seven* or *week* refers to periods or sets of seven years. Daniel had already been thinking in terms of years in 9:1-2.
2. The entire period involved, therefore, is a time of 490 years (seventy sets of seven-year periods, using a 360-day prophetic year).
3. The 490 years concerns the Jewish people and the city of Jerusalem, not the church—"for your people and your holy city" (9:24). The purpose of these 490 years is to accomplish these six divine goals:

   - To put down rebellion
   - To bring an end to sin
   - To atone for guilt
   - To bring in everlasting righteousness
   - To confirm the prophetic vision
   - To anoint the Most Holy Place

Since these goals look to the coming kingdom age, then the 490 years must take us all the way to the Millennium.

4. The divine prophetic clock began ticking on March 5, 444 B.C., when the Persian king Artaxerxes issued a decree allowing the Jews to re-turn under Nehemiah's leadership to rebuild the city of Jerusalem.
5. From the time the countdown began until the coming of Messiah ("the Anointed One") will be sixty-nine sets of seven (seven plus sixty-two) or 483 years. This exact period of time, which is 173,880 days, is the precise number of days that elapsed from March 5, 444

B.C. until March 30, A.D. 33, the day that Jesus rode into Jerusalem for the Triumphal Entry.[2]

6. When Israel rejected Jesus Christ as her Messiah, God temporarily suspended his plan for Israel. Therefore, there is a gap of unspecified duration between the sixty-ninth and seventieth sets of seven. During this gap two specific events are prophesied: (1) Messiah will be killed (this was fulfilled in A.D. 33); and (2) Jerusalem and the temple will be destroyed (this was fulfilled in A.D. 70).

7. God's prophetic clock for Israel stopped at the end of the sixty-ninth set of seven. We are presently living in this period of unspecified duration between the sixty-ninth and seventieth sets of seven, called the church age. The church age will end when Christ comes to rapture his bride to heaven.

8. God's prophetic clock for Israel will begin to run again—after the church has been raptured to heaven—when the Antichrist comes onto the scene and makes a seven-year covenant with Israel (9:27). This is the final or seventieth set of seven, which still remains to be fulfilled.

9. The Antichrist will terminate this covenant after three and a half years and will set an abominable, sacrilegious image of himself in the temple of God in Jerusalem (see also Matt. 24:15; Rev. 13:14-15).

10. At the end of the seven years, God will slay the Antichrist ("this defiler"—9:27; see also 2 Thess. 2:8; Rev. 19:20). This will mark the end of the seventy sets of seven and the beginning of the Millennium, when the six characteristics outlined in 9:24 will be fulfilled.

OVERVIEW OF THE SEVENTY WEEKS (Daniel 9:24-27)

REFERENCE	TIME PERIOD
Daniel 9:24	The entire seventy weeks (490 years)
Daniel 9:25	The first sixty-nine weeks—seven weeks plus sixty-two weeks (483 years)
Daniel 9:26	The time between the sixty-ninth and seventieth weeks (? years)
Daniel 9:27	The seventieth week (seven years)

TIME LINE OF THE SEVENTY-WEEKS PROPHECY

The Antichrist in Daniel One of the key topics in Daniel 7–12 is the person and work of the coming world ruler, the Antichrist. He is the dominant human character in these chapters. He holds a prominent place in each of the final four great prophetic sections of Daniel, as outlined in the chart below.

THE ANTICHRIST IN DANIEL 7–12

CHAPTER	ANTICHRIST'S TITLE
Daniel 7	The small or little horn (7:8, 11)
Daniel 8	A fierce king (8:23); a master of intrigue (8:23)
Daniel 9	A ruler (9:26); this defiler (9:27)
Daniel 11	The king (11:36)

Key Predictive Prophecies in Daniel The book of Daniel contains twenty key, predictive prophecies:

1. The successive rule of four great world empires: Babylon, Medo-Persia, Greece, and Rome (chapters 2 and 7)
2. The reuniting of the Roman Empire in the last days in a ten-kingdom form (2:41-43; 7:24)
3. The appearance of Messiah to rule 483 years after the decree to rebuild Jerusalem (9:25): This prophecy was fulfilled to the day when Christ rode into Jerusalem at the Triumphal Entry.
4. The violent death of Messiah (9:26)
5. The destruction of Jerusalem in A.D. 70 (9:26)
6. The rise of Antichrist to power (7:8, 20; 8:23)
7. The beginning of the seventieth week: Antichrist's seven-year covenant with Israel (9:27)
8. Antichrist's breaking of the covenant at its midpoint (9:27)
9. Antichrist's claim that he is God (11:36)
10. Antichrist's persecution of God's people (7:21)
11. Antichrist's setting up of the abomination of desolation in the last-days temple (9:27; 12:11)
12. The Russian-Islamic invasion of Israel and Antichrist (11:40-45; see also Ezek. 38–39)
13. Antichrist's military conquest and consolidation of his empire (11:38-44)
14. The final doom of Antichrist (7:11, 26; 9:27)
15. The second coming of Christ (2:44-45; 7:13)
16. The resurrection of the dead (12:2)
17. The rewarding of the righteous (12:3, 13)
18. The judgment of the wicked (7:9; 12:2)
19. The establishment of Christ's kingdom (2:44-45; 7:14, 22, 27)
20. A great increase in the knowledge of Bible prophecy in the last days (12:4)

2. The Olivet Discourse (The Outline of the End Times) There's an old saying, "If you want to find out what happened yesterday, read the newspaper; if you want to discover what happened today, watch the six-o'clock news; if you want to know what's going to happen tomorrow, read the Word of God." This statement is absolutely true. And there is no place in the Bible that gives a clearer, more concise overview of what's going to happen tomorrow than the basic outline of the last days Jesus gave in his Olivet discourse.

Author The Olivet discourse is a written record of a sermon or discourse that Jesus preached three days before he died on the cross. The author of this teaching therefore was Jesus himself. The Olivet discourse is found in three places in the Gospels: (1) Matthew 24–25; (2) Mark 13; and (3) Luke 21.

Background

THE PLACE   The Olivet discourse is so named because Jesus preached this sermon from the Mount of Olives, just outside Jerusalem. This mountain is directly east of the city of Jerusalem and overlooks the temple area. Jesus gave this message after spending the day in the temple, denouncing the religious leaders of Israel and pronouncing judgment on that generation (Matt. 21:23–23:36). Interestingly, Christ preached this sermon about the last days and his second coming from the same place to which he will one day return (Zech. 14:1-4; Acts 1:10-11).

THE PEOPLE   Jesus preached this sermon to a select group of his disciples. Mark 13:3 says that Jesus' audience consisted of only four men: Peter, James, John, and Andrew. Imagine what it must have been like to hear the Savior outline the blueprint of the end times in such an intimate setting!

THE PROBLEM   Jesus gave this sermon or discourse in response to his disciples' question about the destruction of the temple and the end of the age. Matthew tells us that before arriving at the Mount of Olives, Jesus and his disciples had been in Jerusalem on the temple grounds. As they left this area, Jesus made a monumental statement: "As Jesus was leaving the Temple grounds, his disciples pointed out to him the various Temple buildings. But he told them, 'Do you see all these buildings? I assure you, they will be so completely demolished that not one stone will be left on top of another!'" (Matt. 24:1-2). As Jesus and the disciples made their way across the Kidron Valley to the Mount of Olives, these words must have been seared into the minds of the disciples. They must have wondered how this could be. When would this happen? When would the end come?

When Jesus and the disciples finally arrived at the Mount of Olives, the four men came to him for some clarification: "Later, Jesus sat on the slopes of the Mount of Olives. His disciples came to him privately and asked, 'When will all this take place? And will there be any sign ahead of time to signal your return and the end of the world?' " (Matt.24:3).

THE PERIOD One of the most important questions about this sermon is, What time period does it cover? There are several possible answers to this question, but the best one is that it covers the second coming of Christ and the time immediately preceding his coming. Jesus established the time frame for this sermon in Matthew 23:39, when he said, "I tell you this, you will never see me again until you say, 'Bless the one who comes in the name of the Lord!' " Jesus was telling his disciples that he was going to leave this world and that he would come again only when the Jewish people would repent and receive him as their Messiah. This statement is very significant since it forms the backdrop for what Jesus says in Matthew 24. Obviously this event, which Jesus prophesied has never occurred in the past, so it must still be future or even in our day.

Another related question often considered about this passage is, How many questions did the disciples ask Jesus? The most common answer is two or possibly three questions: (1) When will all this take place? (When will the temple be destroyed as Jesus stated in Matt. 24:2?); (2) Will there be any sign ahead of time to signal your return? and (3) Will there be any sign of the end of the world?

While it is possible that the disciples had two or three questions in mind, it is best to view these questions as one big question with three parts. Clearly, the disciples' question focuses on the return of Christ and the end of the world. For the disciples, the destruction of the temple, the coming of the Messiah, and the end of the world all comprised one great complex of events (see Zech. 14:1-11).

The period of time addressed in this sermon, therefore, is the seven-year Tribulation period that will occur just before Christ returns.

THE TIME PERIOD OF THE OLIVET DISCOURSE

The Tribulation Period (24:4-28)   The Second Coming (24:29-31)

Content

THEME   Jesus' Olivet discourse is often called "The Mini Apocalypse" because it provides a concise yet comprehensive overview of the end times. It is also called "the eschatological discourse" because it previews the end of the age, or "the prophetic discourse" since it prophesies the future. Christ's sermon gives us the basic blueprint or outline for the end—a checklist of the signs of the times.

There are four keys to properly interpreting the Olivet discourse:

1. Study it in conjunction with the other prophetic books.
2. Notice the Jewish atmosphere ("temple," "Judea," "Sabbath").
3. Remember that the main subject is the second coming of Christ, at the end of the age, and the signs that signal this event. The Olivet discourse contains a specific "checklist" of signs that signal the coming of Christ.
4. Observe the importance of the practical application in Matthew 24:32–25:30. These words call those who read them to be alert and ready for Christ's return.

PURPOSE   The purpose of this sermon was to outline for Israel the events that would lead up to the return of their Messiah to establish his kingdom on earth and to call Israel to faithfulness in view of that coming.

OUTLINE   The Olivet Discourse can be divided into three main sections:

I. THE TRIBULATION (24:4-28): RETRIBUTION
   A. The Events of the First Half of the Tribulation (24:4-8): "The beginning of the horrors to come"
      1. False Christs (24:4-5)
      2. Wars (24:6-7)
      3. Famines (24:7)
      4. Earthquakes (24:7)[3]
   B. The Events of the Second Half of the Tribulation (24:9-28)
      1. The General Description (24:9-14): In these verses Jesus gives a broad overview of the last half of the Tribulation period. Notice that verse 14 takes us all the way to the end of the Tribulation—"and then, finally, the end will come."
         a. Persecution
         b. Hatred
         c. False Prophets
         d. Sin and Lack of Love
         e. Worldwide Preaching of the Gospel

2. The Specific Description (24:15-28): Jesus now backs up to go over some of the more specific events of the the final half of the Tribulation. He begins with the "sacrilegious object that causes desecration"; this will occur at the midpoint of the Tribulation and trigger the Great Tribulation, or the second three and a half years of the Tribulation.

  a. The Abomination of Desolation: This is a reference back to the Old Testament book of Daniel, when Antiochus Epiphanes defiled the temple in Jerusalem by setting up a statue of Zeus or Jupiter in the Holy of Holies and offering a pig on the altar. In an even greater act of blasphemy, the Antichrist will set himself in the rebuilt last-days temple in Jerusalem and will declare himself to be God (2 Thess. 2:4). This wretched act, which will occur at the midpoint of the Tribulation, is the main, specific sign of the coming of Christ and is the act that plunges the world into the Great Tribulation.

  b. Great Tribulation (verse 21—"a time of greater horror"): This is the final three and a half years of the seven-year Tribulation period.

  c. False Prophets and False Christs

  d. Second Coming

  e. Judgment (Corpses and Vultures): When Christ returns, the birds will gather to feed on the putrefying carnage (Rev. 19:17-18).

II. THE TRIUMPH (24:29-35): RETURN
  A. The Signs (24:29-30)
    1. Sun and Moon Darkened
    2. Stars Falling from the Sky
    3. Powers of Heaven Shaken
  B. The Son (24:30)
  C. The Salvation (24:31): The gathering of the elect of Israel at the Second Advent

III. THE TEACHING (24:32–25:46): RESPONSIBILITY
  A. Three Parables concerning Preparedness (24:32-51)
    1. Parable of the Fig Tree (24:32-35): There are two important issues with this parable.
      a. The first concerns the imagery of the fig tree.

> "Now learn a lesson from the fig tree. When its buds become tender and its leaves begin to sprout, you know without being told that summer is near. Just so, when you see the events I've described beginning to happen, you can know his return is very near, right at the door."

Many believe that the picture of the fig tree is a reference to the nation of Israel since this was used to represent Israel in the Old Testament. However, Jesus is probably using a natural illustration that anyone could understand. He is simply saying that just as one can tell summer is near by the blossoming of the fig tree, so those alive in the Tribulation will be able to see that his coming is near when the signs predicted in Matthew 24:4-31 begin to happen.

b. The second issue relates to the meaning of the words *this genera-tion* in 24:34. "I assure you, this generation will not pass from the scene before all these things take place." In the context, "this generation" probably refers to those living during the Tribulation, who will personally witness the events described in Matthew 24:4-31. Jesus emphasized that the same generation that experi-ences the Tribulation will also witness the Second Coming.

2. Parallel of Noah (24:36-41): Verses 39-41 are often mistakenly taken as a reference to the Rapture.

> *People didn't realize what was going to happen until the Flood came and swept them all away. That is the way it will be when the Son of Man comes.*
> *Two men will be working together in the field; one will be taken, the other left. Two women will be grinding flour at the mill; one will be taken, the other left.*

John Walvoord explains the meaning of this passage clearly:

> *Because at the Rapture believers will be taken out of the world, some have confused this with the Rapture of the church. Here, however, the situation is the reverse. The one who is left, is left to enter the kingdom; the one who is taken, is taken in judgment. This is in keeping with the illustration of the time of Noah when the ones taken away are the unbelievers. The word for "shall be taken" in verses 40-41 uses the same word found in John 19:16, where Jesus was taken away to the judgment of the cross.*[4]

3. Principles of Alertness (24:42-51)

B. Three Parables of Warning (25:1-46)

1. Parable of the Ten Virgins (25:1-13)
2. Parable of the Master and His Servants (25:14-30)
3. The Parable of the Sheep and the Goats (25:31-46). All the Gentiles who survived the Tribulation will be gathered before the King on his throne. The righteous will enter the millennial kingdom. The unrighteous will be cast into hell.

THE OLIVET DISCOURSE (the Blueprint of the End Times)

TRIBULATION PERIOD (24:4-28)	CHRIST'S SECOND COMING (24:29-31)

↓

7 YEARS

Matt. 24:4-8	Abomination of Desolation	Matt. 24:9-28
"The beginning of the horrors to come"		"A time of greater horror"
First half of the Tribulation 3 1/2 years		Second half of the Tribulation 3 1/2 years
Initial signs		9-14 General signs
		15-28 Specific signs

3. THE BOOK OF REVELATION (Apocalypse WOW!)

As the final book in the Bible, Revelation holds a special place in the hearts of God's people. It is God's final inspired message to the church.

Revelation is particularly important for two key reasons: First, Revelation looks ahead. It is perfectly fitting and necessary that the last book in the Bible reveals God's prophetic program for the future and tells us how everything is going to come out in the end. And this is exactly what Revelation does. The word *revelation* is a translation of the Greek word *apocalupsis*, which means to unveil, uncover, or disclose something that was hidden. The purpose of this book is to reveal, uncover, or "take the lid off" the future. Revelation is an exciting, breathtaking, enthralling account of the future of this world.

Second, Revelation looks back. Revelation not only looks forward to the future consummation of all things under Christ; it also looks back and brings together all the threads from the first sixty-five books of the Bible. Revelation has been called the "Grand Central Station of the Bible" because it's the place where all the trains of thought throughout the whole Bible come in.

Of the 404 verses in Revelation, 278 allude to the Old Testament. In addition, there may be up to 550 total allusions back to the Old Testament in Revelation. Proportionately, Daniel is the book most frequently alluded to, followed by Isaiah, Ezekiel, and Psalms.

Author The apostle John is the human author of Revelation. Four times the human author of Revelation identifies himself as John (1:1, 4, 9; 22:8). He is clearly the leader of the churches in Asia Minor (Rev. 2–3) and calls himself a prophet (22:9). Moreover, Justin Martyr, Irenaeus, Clement of Alexandria, and Tertullian affirm John's authorship of Revelation.

Background John wrote Revelation around A.D. 95, near the end of the reign of the Roman emperor Domitian (A.D. 81–96). At this period of time, the churches in Asia Minor were facing trouble both from without and within. Externally, Domitian proclaimed himself to be God and had a magnificent temple built in his honor in Ephesus. Emperor worship was furthered under Domitian more than under any other ruler. Therefore, needless to say, Domitian was a virulent opponent of Christianity.

Domitian banished John, the last living apostle, to the tiny island of Patmos because of his influence in the Christian community in and around Ephesus (Asia Minor). At the time of his exile, John was probably about ninety years of age.

Internally, the churches were facing the double onslaught of spiritual apathy and false teachers, who promoted heretical teachings and immoral living.

One Sunday morning (the Lord's Day)—probably while John was thinking and praying about the churches of Asia Minor as they gathered together for worship—the glorified Christ appeared to him (Rev. 1:9-20) with a message for seven of these churches. The seven churches Christ singled out are Ephesus, Smyrna, Pergamum, Thyatira, Sardis, Philadelphia, and Laodicea. Against this dark background of external and internal pressure on the church, Revelation was written to reveal the final outcome of human history to God's people in order to encourage them and exhort them to faithfulness. Even though evil seems to prevail, God is in control of all the events of human history, and Christ will return someday in power and great glory to punish the wicked and establish his kingdom.

After writing down the messages and visions Christ revealed to him, John dispatched the message to each of the seven churches by means of an angel. The word *angel* simply means messenger, and in the context of Revelation 2–3, it is best to see these "angels" as human messengers (probably leaders) from each of the seven churches, who had come to visit John on Patmos.

Content

TITLE   Although Revelation contains its own title in the opening verse, the title of this book is often incorrectly stated in two different ways. First, it is frequently referred to as Revelations (plural). But in 1:1, it is "revelation" (singular). It is one revelation.

Second, it is often called "The Revelation of St. John." This also is not the title of the book. It is specifically titled "The Revelation of Jesus Christ" because this book contains a revelation or unveiling of Jesus Christ.

There are two ways to understand the title "Revelation of Jesus Christ." It can mean "a revelation about Christ" (the revealed one) or "a revelation given by Christ" (the revealer). While it is true that this book does powerfully reveal Christ, it is best to take the expression "of Christ" as meaning a revelation from or given by Christ.

This is the best view for two reasons. First, Revelation pictures Christ as a revealer throughout the book. He speaks to the seven churches, and he opens the scroll and discloses its contents. Second, Revelation 1:1 specifically says that Jesus gave the message to the angels and John just as the Father had revealed it to him.[5] Christ is pictured from the outset as the revealer.

CHRIST IN REVELATION[6]

CHRIST'S ROLE	CHAPTERS
Christ in the church	1–3
Christ in the cosmos	4–18
Christ in conquest	19–20
Christ in consummation	21–22

TRANSMISSION   Revelation 1:1 specifically states the transmission or chain of communication for this book: "This is a revelation from Jesus Christ, which God gave him concerning the events that will happen soon. An angel was sent to God's servant John so that John could share the revelation with God's other servants."

The Father gave the revelation to the Son, and the Son shared it with John, sometimes directly from himself and sometimes using an angel as his intermediary. The main point is that the contents of this book came from God. Like the first sixty-five books of the Bible, Revelation is the inspired Word of God.

God the Father ⟶ Jesus ⟶ Angels ⟶ John ⟶ God's Other Servants

APPROACHES   The vivid imagery and striking symbolism in Revelation have led to very different views on how we should interpret it and what time period it describes. Broadly speaking, there are four main ways that people approach the book of Revelation:

1. Preterist view—views most if not all of the book as being fulfilled in the first century with the fall of Jerusalem in A.D. 70

2. Historicist view—sees Revelation as a panorama of church history from the time of the apostles until the Second Coming
3. Idealist view—envisions Revelation as a depiction of the timeless struggle between good and evil that teaches ideal principles
4. Futurist view—interprets Revelation 4–22 as describing real people and events yet to appear on the world scene

I believe the futurist view is far superior to the others. It is the only view that follows the principles of literal interpretation. Moreover, it makes sense that the final book of God's Word would focus on the future and tell us how everything finally comes out in the end. Ed Hindson summarizes the futurist approach:

163

> *The Apocalypse reveals the future. It is God's road map to help us understand where human history is going. The fact that it points to the time of the end is clear throughout the entire book. It serves as the final consummation of biblical revelation. It takes us from the first century to the last century. From persecution to triumph. From the struggling church to the bride of Christ. From Patmos to paradise.*[7]

KEY WORDS Every book in the Bible contains some key words that occur frequently and reveal the emphasis in the book. Revelation has ten key words that define its focus:

1. And (*kai* in Greek) occurs more than 1,200 times in Revelation. About two out of every three verses in Revelation (271 out of 404) begin with the word *kai* in Greek. While it is also sometimes translated as "but," "even," "both," "also," "then," "yet," or "indeed," it is most often translated as "and." The constant repetition of this word moves the book along at a breathtaking rate. As Ed Hindson notes:

   > *One cannot read this book and mentally stand still. The reader will sense, consciously or unconsciously, that he or she is moving through a series of events that appear like instantaneous flashes on a video screen. These glimpses of the future are intended to keep us moving toward the final consummation of human history. The closing chapters actually fast-forward us into eternity itself!*[8]

2. Great (Greek *megas*—eighty-two times): Revelation is a "great" book!
3. Seven (fifty-four times)
4. Throne (forty-six times)
5. Power/authority (forty times)
6. King (thirty-seven times)
7. Lamb (twenty-nine times)
8. Twelve (twenty-two times)

9. Glory/glorify (nineteen times)
10. Overcome, victorious, conquer (Greek word *nikao*—the sporting goods company Nike borrowed this word from ancient Greece; seventeen times)

THEME Revelation contains three main themes, which are emphasized in the three main sections of the book: (1) The Christ (Rev. 1); (2) The church (Rev. 2–3); and (3) the climax (Rev. 4–22).

While these three themes summarize the message of Revelation, the central theme that permeates the entire book is stated in 1:7: "Look! He comes with the clouds of heaven. And everyone will see him—even those who pierced him. And all the nations of the earth will weep because of him. Yes! Amen!"

The central unifying theme of the book is the second coming of Christ. Even in chapters 2–3, the coming of Christ is mentioned again and again.

OUTLINE Many different outlines have been proposed for Revelation, but the best outline is the threefold outline contained in Revelation 1:19: "Write down what you have seen—both the things that are now happening and the things that will happen later."

I. "WHAT YOU HAVE SEEN" (Chapter 1): THE GLORIFIED CHRIST

II. "THE THINGS THAT ARE NOW HAPPENING" (Chapters 2–3): THE LETTERS TO THE SEVEN CHURCHES
   A. Ephesus (2:1-7)
   B. Smyrna (2:8-11)
   C. Pergamum (2:12-17)
   D. Thyatira (2:18-29)
   E. Sardis (3:1-6)
   F. Philadelphia (3:7-13)
   G. Laodicea (3:14-22)

III. "THE THINGS THAT WILL HAPPEN LATER" (Chapters 4–22)
   A. The Tribulation (chapters 4–19)
      1. Worship in Heaven (chapters 4–5)
      2. The Seal (chapter 6)
      3. The 144,000 Witnesses and the Redeemed (chapter 7)
      4. The Trumpets (chapters 8-9)
      5. The Little Scroll (chapter 10)
      6. The Two Witnesses (chapter 11)
      7. The Woman (Israel) and the Dragon (Satan) (chapter 12)
      8. The Antichrist and the False Prophet (chapter 13)
      9. Announcements (chapter 14)
      10. Prelude to the Bowls (chapter 15)

11. The Bowls (chapter 16)
12. The Fall of Babylon (chapters 17–18)
13. The Second Coming of Christ (chapter 19)
B. The Millennium (chapter 20)
C. The Eternal State (chapters 21–22)

FRAMEWORK AND OVERVIEW   The simplest way to survey Revelation is by using the following framework, which divides Revelation into the four different ages found in this book:

165

THE FOUR AGES IN REVELATION

CHAPTERS	AGE	YEARS
Chapters 1–3	Church age	? Years
Chapters 4-19	Tribulation	Seven years
Chapter 20	Kingdom age	One thousand years
Chapters 21–22	Eternal age	Endless years

Revelation begins with three chapters that deal with the present church age. The focus in these chapters is on the lordship of Christ (chapter 1) and the letters of Christ (chapters 2–3). The churches are pictured as lampstands arranged in a circle that are to emit light in the midst of a dark world. Christ is seen standing in the middle of the lampstands as Lord of the church and walking among the lampstands as the all-knowing Lord, inspecting and evaluating his church (1:12-13; 2:1).

Christ writes seven letters, one to each of the seven churches in Asia Minor. (These seven churches were situated on a circular road that linked them together. Postal workers in that day traveled along this route.) The letters follow this basic pattern with a few exceptions:

• The commission
• The character
• The commendation (Letters to Sardis and Laodicea lack this)
• The condemnation (Letters to Smyrna and Philadelphia lack this)
• The correction
• The call
• The challenge

The seven churches are significant for two main reasons. First, they have a practical significance—they are seven literal, historical churches that existed at the end of the first century in the cities mentioned. Second, they have a perennial significance—they represented all the different kinds of churches that would exist simultaneously throughout church history. (There are seven churches mentioned because seven is the number of completeness or totality.)

These seven churches were not selected because they were the most prominent churches in the area; only two of them, Ephesus and Laodicea, are mentioned elsewhere in the New Testament. Rather, these seven were chosen because their spiritual conditions were representative of churches throughout the world.

Here is a simple overview of the different kinds of churches that will always exist. As you look at this list, you might ask yourself which of these represents the church you attend. What would Christ's message be to your church?

- Ephesus—the lost-love church
- Smyrna—the suffering church
- Pergamum—the compromising church
- Thyatira—the permissive and tolerant church
- Sardis—the dead church
- Philadelphia—the faithful church
- Laodicea—the useless church

Many students of Bible prophecy believe that these seven churches have a prophetic significance. They claim that these churches represent seven successive periods of church history spanning the entire church age from the time of the apostles to the last-days church. While this view is possible, I reject it for three reasons: First, there is nothing in the text of Scripture to indicate that these seven churches represent seven stages of church history. Second, there is no clear-cut way to divide church history into seven distinct stages. Third, this view doesn't fit the facts of church history. For instance, while some may view the church in America today as Laodicean (lukewarm, useless), this certainly doesn't describe poor, persecuted churches in other parts of the world.[9]

The second age is the period of the Tribulation (chapters 4–19). The focus in these chapters is on the three sets of seven judgments that the Lord pours out on the earth. There are seven seal judgments (chapter 6), seven trumpet judgments (chapters 8–9), and seven bowl judgments (chapter 16). These series of judgments will be poured out successively during the Tribulation.

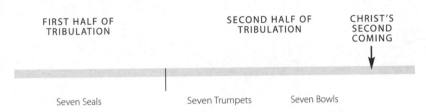

Seven Seals ⟶ Seven Trumpets ⟶ Seven Bowls

The seven seals will be opened during the first half of the Tribulation. The seven trumpets will be blown during the second half of the Tribulation. The seven bowls will be poured out in a very brief period of time near the end of the Tribulation, just before Christ returns.

167

FIRST HALF OF TRIBULATION		SECOND HALF OF TRIBULATION	CHRIST'S SECOND COMING
Seven Seals		Seven Trumpets	Seven Bowls

The third age is the kingdom age (chapter 20). During this time an angel binds Satan and imprisons him in the bottomless pit for a thousand years. In addition, the saints return to earth with Christ to reign with him over his millennial kingdom.

The fourth and last age is the eternal age (chapters 21–22). At this time God will judge those whose names are not found in the Book of Life. He will also destroy the old heaven and the old earth, creating a new heaven and a new earth to take their place. Finally, the new Jerusalem will descend from heaven and come to rest on earth. Here God's people will enjoy eternal life in the presence of their Savior forever.

Revelation 22:20 contains the final words of Jesus Christ to his church: "Yes, I am coming soon!" The only proper response to these words is: "Amen! Come, Lord Jesus!"

[1] H. A. Ironside, H. A. *Ironside Lectures on Daniel the Prophet* (Neptune, N.J.: Loizeaux Brothers, 1911), 117–18.

[2] An excellent discussion of Daniel's seventy weeks is provided by Harold W. Hoehner in *Chronological Aspects of the Life of Christ* (Grand Rapids: Zondervan Pub. House, 1977), 115–39.

[3] Notice the similarity of these events and their chronological order with the seal judgments in Revelation 6:1-7.

[4] John F. Walvoord, *Matthew: Thy Kingdom Come* (Chicago: Moody Press, 1974), 193–94.

[5] Robert L. Thomas, *Revelation 1-7: An Exegetical Commentary* (Chicago: Moody Press, 1992), 52.

[6] Merrill C. Tenney, *Interpreting Revelation* (Grand Rapids: Eerdmans Pub. Co., 1957), 40.

[7] Ed Hindson, *Approaching Armageddon* (Eugene, Oreg.: Harvest House, 1997), 28.

[8] Ibid., 22–23.

[9] For an excellent, thorough discussion of this issue read Robert L. Thomas, *Revelation*, 1505–15.

Fifty Key Questions about Bible Prophecy

9

Question 2: What about Near-Death Experiences?
Question 3: What Is Hell Like?
  Fact 1: Hell Is a Literal Place
  Fact 2 Hell Is Divided into at Least Four Parts
  Fact 3: Hell Is a Place of Memory
  Fact 4: Hell Is a Place of Conscious Torment
  Fact 5: Hell Is a Place of Unquenchable Fire
  Fact 6: Hell is a Place of Separation from God
  Fact 7: Hell Is a Place of Unspeakable Misery, Sorrow, Anger, and Frustration
  Fact 8: Hell Is a Place of Unsatisfied, Raging Thirst
  Fact 9: Hell Is the Only Other Place besides Heaven to Spend Eternity
  Fact 10: Hell Is a Place from Which There Is No Escape
Question 4: Is Punishment in Hell Eternal?
Question 5: Will There Be Degrees of Punishment in Hell?
Question 6: Is Heaven a Real Place?
Question 7: Will We Know Each Other in Heaven?
Question 8: What Will We Do in Heaven?
Question 9: What Kind of Body Will We Have in Heaven?
Question 10: How Can I Be Sure I'll Go to Heaven?

171

People, by nature, are inquisitive. This is certainly true about the last days of planet earth as we know it. Inquiring minds want to know what the future holds. What are the signs that the end is at hand? Who is the Antichrist? What do we know about life after death?

Whether I speak with people at prophecy conferences or talk with people from my home church, I have discovered that people have many of the same, basic questions about Bible prophecy and the last days. Over the past few years, I have collected and compiled the most frequently asked of these questions. While there must be thousands of questions one could ask, I have chosen to include only the top ten questions for five basic areas of Bible prophecy in this chapter. These five broad categories are: (1) general questions about the last days; (2) questions about the Rapture; (3) questions about the Antichrist; (4) questions about the Tribulation, Second Coming, and Millennium; and (5) questions about the afterlife.

Many of the questions in these areas and others have already been answered directly or indirectly in the first eight chapters of this book. But this chapter will focus on answering the specific questions that people like you and I have about the end times.

THE TOP TEN GENERAL QUESTIONS ABOUT THE LAST DAYS

Question 1: Isn't Studying Bible Prophecy All Just Speculation? Bible prophecy has often suffered as much at the hands of its friends as it has at the hands of its foes. Date setting, newspaper exegesis, identifying the Antichrist, and reckless speculation have turned many people off to Bible prophecy. Added to this is the frustration many people feel in wading through all the different views of the end times. Therefore, many of God's children simply write off studying Bible prophecy as an exercise in futility. I have personally heard many people say that when it comes to the last days, no one really has any idea what is going to happen.

While it is certainly true that a small group of overzealous speculators have tainted the legitimate study of Bible prophecy and that there are a number of views of the last days, this should in no way dampen our fervor in studying the end times. Almost every area of Bible study or theology has its quacks, and there are differing views on many subjects in the Bible. But we should not allow this to scare us off from discovering God's truth on any subject he has revealed to us. We should apply the same principles of sound interpretation that we use in other areas of theology and Bible study to the study of prophecy. When we do, we will begin to see and understand the true benefits of studying prophecy, which not only informs us about future events but calls us to be ready for Christ's return. Handling Bible prophecy inappropriately keeps us from discovering these benefits. That is why we need to approach the study of Bible prophecy with an attitude of humility, as well as excitement and expectation.

Question 2: Is America Mentioned in Bible Prophecy? This may be the one question about Bible prophecy that I have been asked more than any other. People here in America want to know if the Bible has anything to say about the future of our nation.

Anyone who has read the Bible would agree that the Bible does not mention America specifically by name. However, this is true of most other modern nations as well. Many students of Bible prophecy believe that America, while not named specifically, is nevertheless referred to in the pages of Scripture. Three main passages of

Scripture are used to support the notion that America is mentioned in Bible prophecy.

The first passage is Isaiah 18:1-7. This passage refers two times to a land "divided by rivers." Many often interpret this statement as a reference to the United States, which is divided by the Mississippi River. The nation in Isaiah 18:1-7 is also called those "who are feared far and wide for their conquests and destruction." This, too, is taken as a reference to the mighty military machine of the U.S. armed forces. The problem with this view is that Isaiah 18:1-2 identifies the nation the rest of the passage describes: "Destruction is certain for the land of Ethiopia, which lies at the headwaters of the Nile. Its winged sailboats glide along the river, and ambassadors are sent in fast boats down the Nile." The nation referred to in this passage is the ancient kingdom of Cush (modern Sudan), not the United States.

The second passage is Ezekiel 38:13: "Sheba and Dedan and the merchants of Tarshish will ask, 'Who are you to rob them of silver and gold? Who are you to drive away their cattle and seize their goods and make them poor?'" Tarshish in ancient times was the farthest region west in the known world; it is the modern nation of Spain. Tarshish could be used in this context to represent all of the Western nations of the last days. Some other translations of Ezekiel 38:13 refer to the "young lions" of Tarshish. Scripture often uses the image of young lions to refer to energetic rulers. Therefore, some view these young lions of Tarshish (the Western powers) as a veiled reference to the United States. While this view is certainly possible, the evidence is too tenuous to make any certain statement about a reference to America.

A third passage cited as referring to the U.S. is Revelation 17–18, where Babylon the great is discussed. Babylon is called "the great city" in Revelation 17:18, which has been identified as New York City. Once again, while some of the description in Revelation 17–18 could be stretched to equate New York City as the Babylon of the end times, it is much better to interpret Babylon as the literal Babylon on the Euphrates or the city of Rome.

Having carefully examined these passages, I have concluded that America is not mentioned in Bible prophecy. However, this raises another interesting question. Why isn't America mentioned in Bible prophecy? What does the prophetic silence about America imply?

First, I believe it is important to recognize that the Bible does not mention most modern nations. Scotland isn't mentioned. India isn't mentioned. Japan isn't mentioned. It shouldn't surprise us that America isn't mentioned either.

Second, some people assume that since America isn't mentioned, she must have undergone a dramatic decline and met her demise. This is the most popular view about America's future. I believe it is very possible that this is true. Consider this fact: If the Rapture were to happen today, the United States would probably lose more people per capita than any other nation in the world. The Islamic nations in the Middle East, for example, would feel almost no affect at all. But the U.S. could become a third-world nation overnight. Millions of home mortgages would go unpaid, the stock market would crash, millions of productive workers would be suddenly removed from the workforce. America may not be mentioned because she will only be a part of the Antichrist's Western confederacy of nations, not a key player on her own.

Question 3: What Is the Number-One Sign That These Are the Last Days?
There are numerous signs of the last days in the Bible. However, the number-one sign or "super sign" of the last days is the current re-gathering of the nation of Israel, which began in 1948. This last-days regathering of Israel is predicted in many places in Scripture (Isa. 43:5-6; Jer. 30:3; Ezek. 34:11-13; 36:34; 37:1-14). Students of Bible prophecy no longer have to say that this will happen someday. It began in 1948 and continues to be fulfilled today.

Israel is the number-one sign of the end times because Israel must exist as a sovereign nation for many prophecies in Scripture to be fulfilled. Here are just five examples:

1. Antichrist will make a seven-year covenant with Israel (Dan. 9:27).
2. Antichrist will invade Israel and desecrate the temple (Dan. 11:40-41; Matt. 24:15-20).
3. Gog and his allies will invade the nation of Israel when it is at peace (Ezek. 38–39).
4. All the nations of the earth will invade Jerusalem (Zech. 12:1-9; 14:1-2).

5. The people of Israel will flee into the wilderness to escape the wrath of Satan (Rev. 12:13-17).

Since so many major prophecies require the existence of the nation of Israel, Israel is the number-one sign of the last days. If you want to know where we are on God's prophetic clock, the best place to look is at the tiny nation of Israel.

John Walvoord highlights the significance of Israel as a sign of the last days:

> *Of the many peculiar phenomena which characterize the present generation, few events can claim equal significance as far as Bible prophecy is concerned with that of the return of Israel to their land. It constitutes a preparation for the end of the age, the setting for the coming of the Lord for his church, and the fulfillment of Israel's prophetic destiny.*[1]

Question 4: Will the Earth Be Destroyed in a Nuclear Holocaust?
According to a *TIME* magazine poll (October 26, 1998), 51 percent of Americans believe that a man-made disaster will wipe out civilization during the next century. Probably the number-one threat on that list would be nuclear weapons.

Ever since the dawn of the nuclear age in the 1940s and humanity's ability to blow up this planet, people have wondered if the world will end in a nuclear nightmare. The recent proliferation of nuclear weapons has escalated this fear. Nations such as Pakistan, North Korea, India, and China now have nuclear weapons, and it's only a matter of time until rogue states such as Iran and Iraq and terrorist organizations have access to "the bomb."

Several passages of Scripture have been used to support the idea that the world will be destroyed by nuclear weapons: Isaiah 24:18-20; Zechariah 14:12; and 2 Peter 3:7, 10-14.

I don't believe the Bible tells us specifically whether nuclear weapons will be used on this earth in the future. Many of the passages cited as referring to a nuclear detonation seem to refer to divine judgment, which comes directly from the hand of God rather than from the hand of man (see Rev. 8:6-12). Nevertheless, however one interprets those passages, the Bible is clear that this world will not be destroyed by man or man-made disaster. The Bible states in Genesis 1:1 that God created the heavens and the earth, and it declares in 2 Peter 3:5-7 that God will someday destroy the present heaven and earth with fire:

> *They deliberately forget that God made the heavens by the word of his command, and he brought the earth up from the water and surrounded it with water. Then he used the water to destroy the world with a mighty flood. And God has also commanded that the heavens and the earth will be consumed by fire on the day of judgment, when ungodly people will perish.*

176

This passage is clear that it is God himself who will "push the button" to destroy this world, not some Middle Eastern madman. The God who created this world is in total control of his creation. There's not a maverick molecule in this vast universe. No man will ever destroy this earth. God has reserved that right for himself.

Question 5: Is the Recent Explosion of Knowledge a Sign of the Last Days? Daniel 12:4 says, "You, Daniel, keep this prophecy a secret; seal up the book until the time of the end. Many will rush here and there, and knowledge will increase." These words have often been cited to prove that in the last days, people will travel at great speeds and there will be a great increase of knowledge. On the basis of this verse, Isaac Newton predicted that the day would come when the volume of knowledge would be so increased that man would be able to travel at speeds up to fifty miles per hour. In response to this suggestion, the atheist Voltaire cast great ridicule on Newton and on the Bible.

Undeniably, knowledge has exploded in the last forty years and continues to expand at a dizzying pace. All the new technology related to the computer industry alone is unbelievable. Consider these figures on the growth of general knowledge in our world:[2]

- From 1500 to 1830 (330 years), knowledge doubled
- From 1830 to 1930 (100 years), knowledge doubled
- From 1930 to 1960 (30 years), knowledge doubled
- From 1960 to 1975 (15 years), knowledge doubled
- From 1975 to 1985 (10 years), knowledge doubled
- From 1985 to 1990 (5 years), knowledge doubled
- Since 1990, knowledge doubles every seventeen months

While these figures are staggering, Daniel 12:4 does not describe a last-days explosion of knowledge in general but a particular kind of knowledge that will increase at this time.

The Bible uses the phrase "many will rush here and there" of movement in search of something, often information (see Amos 8:12; Zech. 4:10). Daniel 12:4 talks about men running to and fro during the last days, studying the book of Daniel to find answers about what in the world is going on. This passage goes on to say that knowledge (literally "*the* knowledge") will increase. In the context of this passage, the knowledge that will increase is the knowledge of God's prophetic program for this world. It is not talking about knowledge in general but knowledge of Bible prophecy. And we see this being fulfilled today, don't we? We understand Daniel's book better today than others did in times past. We have the Olivet discourse of Jesus in Matthew 24–25, the book of Revelation, and 2,500 years of history to help us better understand the prophecies of Daniel. As we get closer to the end, knowledge of the end times will continue to increase. For the final generation during the Tribulation period, the end-times prophecies of Scripture will read like the daily newspaper.

As we approach the end of all things, the book of Daniel is being unsealed, and we are to "rush here and there," searching its pages diligently to gain greater knowledge of God's prophetic program.

Question 6: Will the Temple Be Rebuilt in Jerusalem in the End Times?
God's Word mentions four Jewish temples in the city of Jerusalem: (1) the temple of Solomon; (2) the temple of Zerubbabel and Herod; (3) the Tribulation temple; and (4) the millennial temple.

There are five passages in the Bible that clearly indicate that a temple will exist in Jerusalem during the Tribulation period.

DANIEL 9:27 "He will make a treaty with the people for a period of one set of seven, but after half this time, he will put an end to the sacrifices and offerings." For the Jewish people to offer sacrifices and offerings, the temple must be rebuilt in Jerusalem.

DANIEL 12:11 "From the time the daily sacrifice is taken away and the sacrilegious object that causes desecration is set up to be worshiped, there will be 1,290 days." Once again, if there is to be a daily sacrifice in Israel, it must be in a rebuilt temple.

MATTHEW 24:15 "The time will come when you will see what Daniel the prophet spoke about: the sacrilegious object that causes desecration standing in the Holy Place." The abomination of desolation or sacrilegious idol of Antichrist can only stand in the Holy Place of the temple if a temple exists.

2 THESSALONIANS 2:4 "He will exalt himself and defy every god there is and tear down every object of adoration and worship. He will position himself in the temple of God, claiming that he himself is God." The Antichrist will sit in the rebuilt temple in Jerusalem during the Tribulation, proclaiming himself to be God.

REVELATION 11:1-2 "I was given a measuring stick, and I was told, 'Go and measure the Temple of God and the altar, and count the number of worshipers. But do not measure the outer courtyard, for it has been turned over to the nations. They will trample the holy city for 42 months.'" There will be a future temple that will be trampled underfoot by the Antichrist for the final forty-two months or three and a half years of the Tribulation.

These passages make it abundantly clear that the Jewish people will rebuild the temple in Jerusalem before the coming Tribulation period. Numerous preparations are currently under way in Israel to bring this to fruition. Thomas Ice and Randall Price are experts on the city of Jerusalem and the current efforts in Israel to rebuild the temple. They highlight three current preparations: First, groups in Israel are educating people about the need for rebuilding the temple. The "Society for the Preparation of the Temple" publishes a bi-monthly journal called *Let the Temple Be Built.* Second, 53 of the 103 vessels the Bible says were used in the temple have been or are in the process of being constructed. Third, several groups in Israel are presently preparing men for priestly service in a restored temple in Jerusalem.[3]

Question 7: Do Hidden Bible Codes Tell Us Anything about the End Times? Back in the early 1990s, a Jewish man from Hollywood called me to ask if I knew anything about all the hidden codes in the Old Testament. When I confessed my ignorance on this subject, he offered to send me a video about it. The video contained a teaching session conducted by a Jewish rabbi on the various codes that he claimed lie hidden in the text of the Old Testament. The rabbi's presentation was long, tedious, and boring. So I threw the video away and forgot about Bible codes. Little did I know that a few years later, the whole subject of Bible codes would be such a big issue.

In recent years there has been an explosion of popular books dealing with hidden codes in the Bible. These books have been written by Jewish rabbis, messianic Jews, and Bible prophecy teachers. The basic tenet of these books is that there are hidden codes in the Hebrew text of the Old Testament that can be discovered by using computers to search for the letters of specific words that occur at a specific interval or spacing. The process is referred to as Equidistant Letter Sequencing (ELS) or the "skip process." The sequencer finds a Hebrew letter, skips ten letters, finds another letter, then skips ten more letters, etc., and the hidden word is revealed. The skip can be of any length as long as the skips are equal.

Bible code enthusiasts claim to have found a reference to Hitler, JFK, and many references to *Yeshua* (Jesus) in messianic passages.

While this idea sounds ingenious, the whole notion of Bible codes should be approached with great caution for four main reasons. First, some of the skip distances can be up to one thousand letters. This incredible separation in the letters makes this whole process suspect. Second, using the ELS process, scholars have found 2,328 references to Muhammad, 104 references to Krishna, and 2,729 references to Koresh (as in David Koresh) in the Torah alone (the first five books of the Old Testament).[4]

Third, the uniqueness of these codes to Scripture has yet to be proven. Many excellent biblical scholars strongly contend that these codes are much ado about nothing. The same principles used for finding Bible codes have been used on other books and references, and world figures and world events have been found in these secular writings. Michael Drosnin, author of *The Bible Code,* issued this challenge: When my critics find a message about the assassination of a prime minister encrypted in *Moby Dick,* I will believe them.[5] Accepting that challenge and using the same ELS techniques as Drosnin, Professor Brendan McKay, a mathematician at the Australian National University, searched Melville's *Moby Dick* for encrypted messages. He discovered thirteen predicted assassinations of public figures including Indira Gandhi, Martin Luther King, Sirhan Sirhan, JFK, Abraham Lincoln, and Yitzhak Rabin.

Fourth, even if these hidden codes can be proven, they will not provide any information about the last days. The whole Bible code explosion is an exercise in Monday-morning quarterbacking. We already know all of the information that has been revealed in these codes. We all know about Hitler and JFK, and if a person is a believer, he or she already knows that Jesus is the Messiah.

The only way these codes can possibly be validated is after the fact, and if something is proved after it has already happened, then it is no longer a future event.

Question 8: Is the Moral Decay and Lawlessness of Modern Society a Sign of the Last Days? There is little doubt for most people that our society is declining morally and that the downward slide is picking up speed. The extent and viciousness of crime, the abuse of drugs, the number of unwed mothers (many who are still children themselves), the rate of divorce, the proliferation of pornography, and the open acceptance of homosexuality as an acceptable lifestyle all signal a major moral downgrade in our society.

Most of the passages in the New Testament that discuss the moral and spiritual trends in the last days focus on the spiritual apostasy that will occur in the church, not in society in general. The familiar passage in 2 Timothy 3:1-9 that gives a list of the kinds of behavior that will characterize "the last days" is primarily describing apostasy or a falling away that will take place within the church (notice the context in verses 5 and 8). Apostasy, or departure from the faith within the church, is a clear sign of the last days (1 Tim. 4:1-4; 2 Pet. 3:3-4; Jude 1:18-19). Of course, we can safely assume that spiritual apostasy in the church will translate into moral decline in society as a whole.

The only passage that specifically mentions the increase of lawlessness in society as a whole as a specific sign of the last days is Matthew 24:12: "Sin will be rampant everywhere, and the love of many will grow cold." God's Word is clear that as the end draws near, the sinfulness of humanity will reach a fever pitch, and love for one another will grow cold.

We must be careful, however, in applying this sign of Christ's coming. It is difficult to quantify the sinfulness of man. Sin has always been rampant in our world. At every point in history, people believe it is worse than it's ever been before; no matter how bad things get, they can always get worse. Therefore, we should be careful not to point to every incidence of moral decay in our society as a clear sign of the last days. But we should recognize that as the end draws near, the Bible says that sin as a whole will run rampant in society, and the love people have for one another will grow cold.

181

Question 9: What Should We Do if We Believe Jesus Is Coming Soon?
Believers in the early church were consistently told to be on the lookout for the return of Christ. They were also given clear, practical instruction concerning what they should be doing in light of this event. The most straightforward passage in the New Testament concerning what we should be doing if we believe Jesus is coming soon is 1 Peter 4:7-10:

> *The end of the world is coming soon. Therefore, be earnest and disciplined in your prayers. Most important of all, continue to show deep love for each other, for love covers a multitude of sins. Cheerfully share your home with those who need a meal or a place to stay.*
>
> *God has given gifts to each of you from his great variety of spiritual gifts. Manage them well so that God's generosity can flow through you.*

Notice the word *therefore* in verse 7. Peter is saying to us, "therefore," since the end of the world is coming, here's what you should be doing. This passage emphasizes four things we should do if we believe that the end of the world is coming soon.

KEEP YOUR HEAD CLEAR (Continue to Pray for Others) As we approach the coming apocalypse, more and more people are going to get caught up in the prophetic frenzy. People will be tempted to quit their jobs, to sell all their possessions, and go wait on some mountaintop in their pajamas for Jesus to come. But God's Word tells us that in view of the end of all things, we are to be "earnest." This word means literally "not drunk." In other words, we are to be sober-minded, clearheaded, mentally alert, and disciplined for the purpose of prayer. Believing that Christ could come back today should spur us on to a sober, disciplined prayer life.

KEEP YOUR HEART WARM (Show Love for Others)   The badge of Christianity is love (John 13:34-35). As we see the end approaching, we are to love one another with a "deep love." The word translated "deep" was used in ancient times to denote a horse at full gallop, when its muscles were stretched to the limit. Peter is saying that our love for one another should be stretched out but never to its breaking point.

KEEP YOUR HOME OPEN (Show Hospitality to Strangers)   One of the signs of the second coming of Christ according to Jesus is that "the love of many will grow cold" (Matt. 24:12). In light of this fact, believers are called to show their love in a concrete way by reaching out in Christian love to strangers. The New Testament specifically mentions this beautiful Christian virtue of hospitality six times (Rom. 12:13; 1 Tim. 3:2; 5:9-10; Titus 1:8; Heb. 13:1-3; 1 Pet. 4:9). As this world becomes a colder, more isolated place, we are to keep our home open and show the warmth of Christ to strangers.

KEEP YOUR HANDS BUSY (Use Your Spiritual Gifts in Service for the Lord)
Every believer in Jesus Christ has at least one spiritual gift, that is, a supernatural, divine enablement and empowerment that God has given him or her to serve the body of Christ. As we see the curtain about to rise on the final act of history, the Lord is calling us to keep our hands busy, working in his service, using the gifts he has graciously given to us.

Question 10: How Close Are We to the End?   At every prophecy conference I have ever attended, someone always asks this question. After all, this is the big question, isn't it? How close are we to the end? How much longer will it be until Jesus comes back?

This question reminds me of the man who was sitting downstairs late one night reading, while his wife had already retired to bed. He heard the grandfather clock begin to chime in the hallway and started counting the chimes to see what time it was. The clock chimed nine, ten, eleven, twelve—then thirteen! Upon hearing the thirteenth bell, he got up, ran up the stairs, bolted into the bedroom to wake up his wife, and said, "Honey, wake up, it's later than it's ever been!"

That's the one sure answer to this question I can give. We are closer to the end than we've ever been. However, the ultimate answer to this question is, no one knows for sure how close we are to the end except the Lord. We can point to various signs the Lord has given us, such as the regathering of Israel to her land, the European Community as the possible reuniting of the Roman Empire, the continued heightening of tensions in the Middle East, the unstable conditions in Russia, and the development of a one-world economy that the Antichrist could easily control. And it does appear that these signs point to the imminent return of Christ. So the Rapture must be even nearer. But how near? We really don't know. These signs indicate that the general time of the Second Coming is near. But we still must confess that we don't know the specific day or the hour of his coming for his church. We can confidently say that "Jesus may come today," but we must also admit that he may not come in the next decade. He may not come in my lifetime or yours.

One passage often used to pinpoint the coming of Christ is Matthew 24:34: "'I assure you, this generation will not pass from the scene before all these things take place.'" Some use this verse to prove that once the signs of the last days begin, Christ will return within one generation, which is usually calculated to be about forty years. However, this verse probably means that the generation that personally witnesses the signs in Matthew 24:4-30—that is, the Tribulation period—will not pass away before Christ returns. Thus, Christ could return sixty, seventy, eighty, or more years after these signs begin. Therefore, this verse should not be used to establish a date for the coming of Christ.

For those of us today who see the storm clouds of some of these signs gathering on the horizon, all we can say is that we believe we are in the end times in a general sense.

My grandfather was a pastor who loved the prophetic Scriptures. When Israel became a nation in 1948, he recognized the prophetic significance of this event. My father has told me that my grandfather commented on numerous occasions that he believed Jesus would come in his lifetime. He lived his life believing the end was near and looking for the Rapture. However, the Lord called my grandfather home in 1963 at the age of sixty-three. Was my grandfather wrong? No, he wasn't wrong. He didn't miss the Rapture. He is presently with the Lord, and at the

Rapture he will be resurrected to join the Lord and his saints in the air. The precious hope of the Rapture added unspeakable joy to his life. The point of prophecy in Scripture is that we are to live as if Christ could come at any moment. That's all we can do. We must leave the timing of this event with the Lord.

All I can say when people ask me how close we are to the end is that I earnestly believe that Jesus could come today, and I pray that he will. That's close enough for me!

THE TOP TEN QUESTIONS ABOUT THE RAPTURE

Question 1: Why Is the Rapture Called a "Mystery"? In 1 Corinthians 15:51, the apostle Paul refers to the Rapture as a "mystery" or "wonderful secret." When we think of a mystery, we most often think of a story or event that is difficult to understand or solve. But in the New Testament, a mystery is a truth that is being revealed for the first time, and this is what Paul does in this passage. He reveals the mystery of the Rapture: "Let me tell you a wonderful secret God has revealed to us. Not all of us will die, but we will all be transformed" (1 Cor. 15:51). The mystery of the Rapture is that some people will go to heaven and receive new, glorified bodies without ever dying. They will do an end run on the grave.

This was a completely new truth that God had never disclosed until 1 Corinthians 15:51. If you read the Bible from Genesis 1 to 1 Corinthians 14, you would correctly conclude that the only way to get to heaven in your glorified body would be to die. But in 1 Corinthians 15, that all changes. The Lord unveils this glorious mystery through Paul—that a whole generation of believers will be transformed without tasting the sting of physical death. Millions of believers will be transformed into their new, glorified bodies in the amount of time it takes to blink one's eye. This is the glorious mystery of the Rapture. May we be the generation to experience this breathtaking event!

Question 2: Why Isn't the Word *Rapture* Found in the Bible? A few years ago, I was in a restaurant having lunch with a man who had just started attending our church. He was asking me some questions about the last days, and I was telling him about the Rapture. In the middle of our conversation, a man at the table next to us, who had obviously been listening in on our discussion, told me in no uncertain terms that the Rapture is an unbiblical doctrine because the word *rapture* is not even in the Bible. While he was dead wrong in denying the doctrine of the Rapture, he was absolutely correct in stating that the word *rapture* is not in the English translations of the Bible.

If you were to read all 727,747 words in the King James Version, or any other well-known translation, you would discover that the word *rapture* is not there. However, you also wouldn't find the words *Trinity, Bible,* or *grandfather.* Yet we know that all of these things are very real and true.

In 1 Thessalonians 4:17, the words *caught up* translate the Greek word *harpazo,* which means "to snatch," "to seize," or "to take away." This word was translated in the Latin versions of Scripture as *rapturo,* which was brought over to English as *Rapture.* So while it is true that the word *Rapture* does not occur in most English translations, the concept or doctrine of a "catching up" of living believers to meet the Lord is clearly stated in 1 Corinthians 15:51-55 and 1 Thessalonians 4:17. This doctrine could just as well be called "the catching up of the church," "the snatching away of the church," "the translation of the church," or "the *harpazo* of the church." But since the phrase "rapture of the church" is an excellent description of this event and has become a well-known phrase, there is no reason to change the terminology.

Question 3: Are the Rapture and the Second Coming Identical Events?

Some students of Bible prophecy strongly object to the notion that the Rapture and the second coming of Christ are distinct events separated by seven years. They contend that this is teaching two future comings of Christ, while the Bible only presents one Second Coming.

The only way to resolve this issue is to set what the Bible says about these two events side-by-side to see if it is describing the same occurrence. You be the judge!

Question 4: What Group of People Will Take Part in the Rapture?

The Bible limits the participants in the Rapture to church-age believers. This is why the Rapture is often more specifically called "the rapture of the church." Believers who are alive on earth when the trumpet sounds will be immediately transformed and translated to heaven. Of course, all these living believers will be from the church age. Those who are resurrected at this time are called "the dead in Christ" or "Christians who have died" (1 Thess. 4:16). This also refers only to departed church-age believers. Old Testaments believers are not "in Christ" and are not "Christians."

A COMPARISON BETWEEN THE RAPTURE AND THE SECOND COMING

THE RAPTURE	THE SECOND COMING
Christ comes in the air (1 Thess. 4:16-17)	Christ comes to the earth (Zech. 14:4)
Christ comes for his saints (1 Thess. 4:16-17)	Christ comes with his saints (1 Thess. 3:13; Jude 1:14)
Christ claims his bride	Christ comes with his bride
Not in the Old Testament	Predicted often in the Old Testament
There are no signs—it is imminent (1 Cor. 15:52)	Portended by many signs (Matt. 24:4-29)
A time of blessing and comfort (1 Thess. 4:18)	A time of destruction and judgment (2 Thess. 2:8-12)
Involves believers only (John 14:1-3; 1 Cor. 15:51-55; 1 Thess. 4:13-18)	Involves Israel and the Gentile nations (Matt. 24:1–25:46)
Will occur in a moment—only his own will see him (1 Cor. 15:51-52)	Will be visible to the entire world (Matt. 24:27; Rev. 1:7)
Tribulation begins	Millennium begins
Christ comes as the bright morning star (Rev. 22:16)	Christ comes as the sun of righteousness (Mal. 4:2)

Since this is true, people often wonder what will happen to Old Testament believers. When will they be resurrected and receive their glorified bodies? God has a plan for his Old Testament saints as well. There are two passages in the Old Testament that place the resurrection of Old Testament believers at the end of the Tribulation period. Notice in each of these passages that the resurrection comes after the Tribulation.

> • *Lord, in distress we searched for you. We were bowed beneath the burden of your discipline. We were like a woman about to give birth, writhing and crying out in pain. When we are in your presence, Lord, we, too, writhe in agony, but nothing comes of our suffering. We have done nothing to rescue the world; no one has been born to populate the earth. Yet we have this assurance: Those who belong to God will live; their bodies will rise again! Those who sleep in the earth will rise up and sing for joy! For God's light of life will fall like dew on his people in the place of the dead! (Isa. 26:16-19)*

> • *At that time Michael, the archangel who stands guard over your nation, will arise. Then there will be a time of anguish greater than any since nations first came into existence. But at that time every one of your people whose name is written in the book will be rescued. Many of those whose bodies lie dead and buried will rise up, some to everlasting life and some to shame and everlasting contempt. (Dan. 12:1-2)*

Only church-age believers—that is, those who lived between the Day of Pentecost and the Rapture—will be part of the Rapture before the Tribulation. God has a separate program for Old Testament believers. He will resurrect the Old Testament believers only after the seventy weeks of Daniel 9:24-27 have run their course.

Question 5: What Will Happen at the Rapture to Babies and Young Children Who Have Not Believed? As one could imagine, parents with small children frequently ask this question. Believing parents want to know if their young children, who have not yet trusted Christ, will be left behind at the Rapture. It is important at the outset to note that there is no specific Scripture passage that addresses this subject. Nevertheless, there are three main views on this issue:

VIEW 1: NO CHILDREN WILL BE INCLUDED IN THE RAPTURE Those who hold this view would emphasize that the Rapture is only for believers and that if a person has not personally believed in Christ, he or she is not eligible for the Rapture. They would point out that in the Flood and in the destruction of the inhabitants of Canaan, small children were not excluded from the judgment.

VIEW 2: ALL INFANTS AND YOUNG CHILDREN WILL BE RAPTURED TO HEAVEN BEFORE THE TRIBULATION Those who hold this view would be quick to point out that Scripture strongly implies that when young children die, they go to heaven. Several passages in the Bible seem to support this position: 2 Samuel 12:20-23; Matthew 19:13-15; and Mark 10:13-16. Since all young children or infants who have never put saving faith in Christ go to heaven when they die, many would argue that they will also go to heaven in the Rapture and be exempted from the horrors of the Tribulation. While I agree that infants and small children who die go to heaven to be with Christ, I do not believe that this necessarily means that they will participate in the Rapture. These are two different issues.

VIEW 3: INFANTS AND YOUNG CHILDREN OF BELIEVERS WILL BE RAPTURED TO HEAVEN BEFORE THE TRIBULATION   This is a mediating view between views 1 and 2.

While one should avoid dogmatism on this issue, I believe the third view is the best one for two reasons. First, 1 Corinthians 7:14 reminds us that in a Christian family the children are "set apart for him." It seems inconceivable to me that the Lord would rapture believing parents to heaven and leave their defenseless children alone in the world for the Tribulation period.

Second, I believe there is biblical precedent for this view. When the Lord sent the Flood on the earth during the days of Noah, all the world was destroyed, including unbelieving men, women, and children. But God delivered Noah, his wife, and his three sons and their wives. Likewise, when God destroyed Sodom and Gomorrah, he destroyed all the inhabitants of the cities, including the children of unbelievers. The only ones to escape were Lot and his two daughters. Also, in Egypt, at the first Passover, the blood of the lamb on the doorpost protected the homes of believers, including their young children, from the judgment of God. In each of these cases, believers and their children were delivered from the time of judgment, while unbelievers and their children were not.

While I recognize that Noah's three sons and Lot's two daughters were not infants or small children and may have been believers themselves, I believe that these incidents provide biblical precedent for the idea that when God sends cataclysmic judgment, he rescues both believers and their children but allows unbelievers and their children to face judgment.

I believe that during the Tribulation young children of unbelievers will have the opportunity to believe in Christ as they come of age during this period of judgment. Those who die during the Tribulation before they are old enough to understand the claims of the gospel will be taken to heaven to be with Christ.

Finally, regardless of which view one holds, the one fact we can all rest in is that God is a God of love, compassion, mercy, and justice.

Whatever he does when the Rapture occurs will be wise, righteous, and fair. God loves our children even more than we do. Indeed, they are "precious in his sight."

Question 6: What about Setting Dates for the Rapture? The Bible strictly prohibits date setting for the coming of Christ.

189

- Matthew 24:42: "Be prepared, because you don't know what day your Lord is coming."
- Matthew 24:44: "You also must be ready all the time. For the Son of Man will come when least expected."
- Matthew 25:13: "Stay awake and be prepared, because you do not know the day or hour of my return."
- Acts 1:7: "'The Father sets those dates,' he replied, 'and they are not for you to know.'"

In spite of the clear teaching of Scripture, people continue to set dates for the coming of Christ. Jesus claimed that during his earthly ministry, he did not even know the day of his coming: "No one knows the day or the hour when these things happen, not even the angels in heaven or the Son himself. Only the Father knows" (Matt. 24:36).

Anyone who claims to know the specific time of Christ's coming is claiming that he knows something that the Father didn't even tell the Son while he was on earth. This is the height of arrogance and folly.

Question 7: Who or What Is the "Restrainer" or "The One Who Is Holding It Back" in 2 Thessalonians 2:6-7? Second Thessalonians 2 outlines and describes in broad terms three important ages that take us from the present age to eternity.

1. The present age—the age of restraint
   (before the Rapture)
2. The Tribulation age—the age of rebellion
   (after the Rapture)
3. The messianic age—the age of revelation
   (after the Second Coming)

Amazingly, this present age in which we live is described as the time or age of restraint. There is something or someone who is restraining or holding back the full blast of evil that is to come when the Antichrist is unleashed. Think about it for a moment. If this evil world we live in now is a time of restraint, what in the world will it be like when that restraint is removed? What will this world be like when all restraint against the Antichrist and his wickedness is taken out of the way? It will be like removing a dam from a lake—evil will overflow this world, demolishing everything in its path.

The key question in this discussion is, Who or what is this person or entity who is restraining the appearance of the Antichrist? Down through the centuries, many candidates have been suggested. Here is a list of the most important ones.

190

- The Roman Empire
- The Jewish state
- The apostle Paul
- The preaching of the gospel
- Human government
- Satan
- Elijah
- Some unknown heavenly being
- Michael the archangel
- The Holy Spirit
- The church

St. Augustine was transparent when he said this concerning Paul's passage on the restrainer: "I frankly confess I do not know what he means." I can sympathize with Augustine, but I believe there are four facts that help us identify the restrainer:

1. The Greek word *katecho* ("what is holding him back," "the one who is holding it back"—2 Thess. 2:6-7) means to hold back or restrain.
2. The one who is holding back or restraining is both neuter and masculine: neuter (a principle)—"what is holding him back"; and masculine (a person)—"the one who is holding it back."
3. Whatever it is, it must be removable.
4. It must be powerful enough to hold back the outbreak of evil under Antichrist.

In light of these four facts, only one view on the restrainer's identity is satisfactory. Just ask yourself this one question: Who is able to restrain evil and hold back the appearance of Antichrist? The answer of course is God. In this case, it is God the Holy Spirit who is at work during this age in and through God's people, the church. Therefore, I believe the restrainer in 2 Thessalonians 2:6-7 is not just the Holy Spirit and not just the church. Rather, the one who holds it back is the restraining influence of God the Holy Spirit, who presently restrains evil through the church. There are four reasons for identifying the one who holds it back as the restraining ministry of the Holy Spirit through the church:

1. This restraint requires omnipotent power.
2. This is the only view that adequately explains the change in gender in 2 Thessalonians 2:6-7. In Greek, the word *pneuma* (Spirit) is neuter. But Scripture also consistently refers to the Holy Spirit using the masculine pronoun *he,* especially in John 14–16.
3. Scripture speaks of the Holy Spirit as restraining sin and evil in the world (Gen. 6:3) and in the hearts of believers (Gal. 5:16-17).
4. The church and its mission of proclaiming and portraying the gospel is the primary instrument the Holy Spirit uses in this age to restrain evil. We are the salt of the earth and the light of the world (Matt. 5:13-16). We are the temple of the Holy Spirit both individually and corporately.

The restrainer, then, is the restraining influence and ministry of the Holy Spirit, indwelling and working through his people in this present age. Donald Grey Barnhouse summarizes this view best:

Well, what is keeping the Antichrist from putting in his appearance on the world stage? You are! You and every other member of the body of Christ on earth. The presence of the church of Jesus Christ is the restraining force that refuses to allow the man of lawlessness to be revealed. True, it is the Holy Spirit who is the real restrainer. But as both 1 Corinthians 3:16 and 6:19 teach, the Holy Spirit indwells the believer. The believer's body is the temple of the Spirit of God. Put all believers together then, with the Holy Spirit indwelling each of us, and you have a formidable restraining force.

For when the church is removed at the Rapture, the Holy Spirit goes with the church insofar as his restraining power is concerned. His work in this age of grace will be ended. Henceforth, during the Great Tribulation, the Holy Spirit will still be here on earth, of course—for how can you get rid of God?—but he will not be indwelling believers as he does now. Rather, he will revert to his Old Testament ministry of 'coming upon' special people.[6]

When the Rapture occurs, God will remove the Spirit-indwelt church and its restraining influence, and Satan will put his plan into full swing by bringing his man onto center stage to take control of the world.

Question 8: Are There Any More Prophecies That Must Be Fulfilled before the Rapture Can Occur? When someone speaks about Bible prophecy, it is common to hear him or her say, "There are no more prophecies that must be fulfilled for the Rapture to occur." While this statement is true, it is also misleading because it implies that there were or are some signs that must be fulfilled before the Rapture can take place. The Bible teaches that there are no signs that must take place before the Rapture. The Rapture is a signless, imminent, any-moment event from the human point of view. None of the key Rapture passages in the New Testament mention any signs that must occur for this event to happen. All the signs listed in Scripture—Daniel, Matthew 24–25 (the Olivet discourse), and Revelation—relate to the second coming of Christ to earth, not the Rapture. This is a very important distinction to understand.

As we see the signs in Scripture occurring in our world, we must remember that these are the signs of the approaching Tribulation and second coming of Christ to establish his kingdom. However, the fact that we already see the signs of these events obviously indicates that the Rapture is probably not far away.

Question 9: Will Believers Who Have Been Raptured to Heaven Be Able to Watch the Events of the Tribulation Unfold on Earth? This is a question that every believer has probably asked at one time or another. We are curious about what we will know and be able to see when we get to heaven.

The main passage used to support the idea that departed believers in heaven are watching the events on earth is Hebrews 12:1. Following the inspiring list of the faithful from the past, such as Enoch, Abraham, and Moses, the writer of Hebrews concludes, "Therefore, since we are surrounded by such a huge crowd of witnesses . . ." You may have heard this huge crowd of witnesses described as an audience in a huge heavenly stadium, watching us here on earth. But in this passage, the emphasis is on the fact that we become motivated not because they see us but because we see them. As we look back on the patient endurance and faithfulness of their lives, they are witnesses that motivate us to emulate them.

Moreover, once we get to heaven, I doubt that we will be as interested in watching the events on earth as we might think. Revelation 4–5 pictures the church as the twenty-four elders worshiping the Lord. When we get to heaven, we will be consumed with worshiping the Lamb on the throne, not watching the Tribulation on earth.

Question 10: How Will People Who Are Left Behind Explain the Rapture? When you think about it, the Rapture will be an amazing event. In a split second of time, millions of people will disappear from this earth without a trace (except maybe a pile of clothes). One has to wonder, How in the world will the people who are left behind explain this unparalleled event? The world will be left in total chaos as cars become driverless, planes become pilotless, classrooms become teacherless, and factories, workerless. Missing-persons reports will flood police stations. How will people explain the Rapture?

There will undoubtedly be two main explanations: a natural explanation and a supernatural explanation. The natural explanation will be the most popular. The pundits will flood the airwaves with their theories. *Geraldo Rivera Live* will have numerous guests debating their theories. Conspiracy theories will abound. *Nightline* will have a two-week special to investigate the possible explanations. Who knows what kind of bizarre ideas will surface: a massive UFO abduction, a time warp, a new weapon of mass destruction created by the Russians. People will be at a loss to explain the Rapture, but rest assured, humanity will not be at a loss to try to figure it all out.

The other explanation for the Rapture will be the supernatural one. Many people who have been left behind will suddenly remember what they had been told by a believer about the Rapture. Unsaved church members will remember a sermon on the Rapture. The Rapture may be one of the greatest evangelistic events of all time as millions of people who have heard about this event but never received Christ suddenly realize they have been left behind. While the so-called experts are concocting their theories, thousands of people will realize what has happened and will humbly bow their knee to Christ. These "Tribulation saints" will be persecuted and even martyred for their faith (Rev. 6:9; 7:13-14; 20:4). But when they leave this earth, they will join the mighty company of the redeemed around the throne to worship the Lamb.

THE TOP TEN QUESTIONS ABOUT THE ANTICHRIST

Question 1: Is the Antichrist the Product of a Supernatural Birth?
Scripture presents the Antichrist as a complete parody or counterfeit of the true Christ. Since the Antichrist is such a complete parody of Christ, is it possible that he also is the product of a counterfeit "virgin birth?" Some students of Bible prophecy contend that just as Christ was the product of a human mother and the Holy Spirit, the Antichrist will be the product of a human mother and Satan himself. This was the view of Jerome in the fourth century A.D.

As the counterfeit son, he would have a supernatural origin. He would literally be Satan's son. Hollywood has latched onto this idea in such movies as *The Omen* and *Rosemary's Baby*.

Support for this notion comes primarily from Genesis 3:15, when the Lord cursed the serpent and said, "From now on, you and the woman will be enemies, and your offspring and her offspring will be enemies. He will crush your head, and you will strike his heel." The offspring of the woman in this passage is a clear reference to the coming Messiah or Deliverer, who would crush the head of the serpent once and for all. But notice that there is a reference here to "your offspring," or the offspring of Satan, who would be the arch-adversary of the woman's offspring. For those who hold to a supernatural origin for the Antichrist, Genesis 3:15 is seen as the first prophecy of the coming Messiah as well as the first prophecy of the Antichrist.

While the supernatural origin of the Antichrist is certainly possible, it seems better to view the Antichrist not as Satan's literal son but as a man whom Satan totally controls. The Bible consistently presents the Antichrist as a man.

In 2 Thessalonians 2:9, we read about the person and work of the coming Antichrist: "This evil man will come to do the work of Satan with counterfeit power and signs and miracles." The Antichrist is an "evil man" energized by the power of Satan to do his wicked work.

Revelation 13:4 says that the dragon (Satan) gives his power to the beast (Antichrist). These verses teach that the Antichrist is able to do what he can do not because he is Satan's offspring but because Satan energizes and empowers the Antichrist as his chosen human instrument for world rule.

A man named Adso wrote a book around A.D. 950 called *Letter on the Origin and Life of the Antichrist.* In this work he counters the view held by many in his day that the Antichrist will be born from a virgin. Adso also contends that the Antichrist will be born from the union of a human father and a human mother. Nevertheless, Adso maintains, "he will be conceived wholly in sin, generated in sin, born in sin. The devil will enter the womb of his mother at the very instant of conception. He will be fostered by the power of the devil and protected in his mother's womb."

195

Adso's view, which is the predominant view in church history, seems to be the most consistent with the way the Bible describes the Antichrist. Whether Satan enters the Antichrist at the moment of conception is debatable, but the main point remains—the Antichrist will be fully human and totally possessed by Satan.

Question 2: Is the Antichrist a Jew or a Gentile? This is undoubtedly one of the most asked and debated questions about the coming Antichrist. As far back as the second century A.D., scholars wrote about this issue. Irenaeus (A.D. 120–202) believed that the Antichrist would be a Jew from the tribe of Dan. He based this conclusion on Jeremiah 8:16 and on the fact that Revelation 7:4-8 omits the tribe of Dan from the list of the tribes of Israel. The consistent view of the church during the closing decades of the second century was that the Antichrist would be a Jewish false messiah from the tribe of Dan. This view was also held later by Jerome (A.D. 331–420).

The Scripture most often used to substantiate the Jewish heritage of the Antichrist is the King James Version translation of Daniel 11:37, which says, "Neither shall he regard the God of his fathers. . . ." The entire argument rests on the phrase "the God of his fathers." Those who maintain that the Antichrist is a Jew believe that his rejection of "the God of his fathers" proves his Jewishness. However, this statement could equally apply to a Gentile whose parents were followers of Christianity. Moreover, in most of the more recent translations (ASV, RSV, NASB, and NIV) the word *God* (Elohim) translates as the plural "gods." The New Living Translation translates the verse correctly: "He will have no regard for the gods of his ancestors."

Therefore, whether you follow the KJV translation or one of the newer translations, it is clear that the key verse used by those who believe the Antichrist is a Jew is far from conclusive. In fact, to the contrary, the Bible teaches clearly that the coming Antichrist will be a Gentile. His Gentile origin can be discerned from three main points.[7]

First, Antiochus Epiphanes, who was a Syrian monarch in the second century B.C., is the only historical person specifically identified as a "type" or preview of the person and work of the Antichrist. If the type of the Antichrist is a Gentile, then it follows that the Antichrist will also be a Gentile.

Second, Revelation 13:1 symbolically describes the origin of the beast or Antichrist: "In my vision I saw a beast rising up out of the sea." The word *sea*, when used symbolically in the book of Revelation and the rest of Scripture, is a symbol of the Gentile nations. Revelation 17:15 confirms this interpretation: "The waters . . . represent masses of people of every nation and language."

Third, Scripture presents the Antichrist as the final ruler of Gentile world power. He will sit on the throne over the final form of the final world empire that raises its fist in the face of God. Having a Jew as the last world ruler over Gentile power is not logical. The Antichrist, therefore, will be a Gentile.

Question 3: From What Nation Will the Antichrist Arise? As we have seen, Scripture teaches that the coming world ruler will be a Gentile. But is the Bible more specific? Can we know his nation of origin?

Daniel 9:26 tells us that Antichrist will be of the same nationality as the people who destroyed the Jewish temple in A.D. 70. Of course, we know that the Romans destroyed the temple. Therefore, we know that the Antichrist will be of Roman origin.

Interestingly, the movie *The Omen* begins with the birth of the Antichrist in a dimly lit hospital in Rome. A chilling poem from this same movie reinforces the belief that the coming Antichrist will arise from the Holy Roman Empire.

> *When the Jews return to Zion,*
> *And a comet rips the sky,*
> *And the Holy Roman Empire rises,*
> *Then you and I must die.*

From the eternal sea he rises,
Creating armies on either shore,
Turning man against his brother,
'Til man exists no more.

As we look at our world today, the Jews have returned to Zion, and the Holy Roman Empire is rising before our eyes in the European Community. The rise of Antichrist may not be far behind!

Question 4: Is the Antichrist a Homosexual? In the King James Version, Daniel 11:37 says that the coming Antichrist will show no "regard" for "the desire of women." Many students of Bible prophecy interpret this as meaning that the Antichrist will be a homosexual. Many believe that the Antichrist, as totally controlled by Satan, will live his life in complete disobedience to God in every area of life, including his sexual orientation. Thus, many view the Antichrist as sexually polluted, perverted, and profane.

While this is certainly a possible interpretation of this verse, the verse only says that he will not have a natural desire for women, not that he will have sexual desire for men. The context of this passage seems to indicate that the Antichrist will be so intoxicated with his love for power that it will totally consume all of his passion. Daniel 11:38-39 goes on to explain verse 37:

> *Instead of these, he will worship the god of fortresses—a god his ancestors never knew—and lavish on him gold, silver, precious stones, and costly gifts. Claiming this foreign god's help, he will attack the strongest fortresses. He will honor those who submit to him, appointing them to positions of authority and dividing the land among them as their reward.*

So, while it is certainly possible that the Antichrist will be a homosexual, it seems more likely that he will be someone who is so enraptured with the "god" of military might, conquest, and political power that this obsession will eclipse his normal desire for women.

Question 5: Is the Antichrist a Resurrected Individual from the Past? As we have already observed, the Antichrist is Satan's complete parody or counterfeit of the true Christ. Part of Satan's masterfully deceptive work will be a counterfeit of the greatest event of Christianity—the death and resurrection of Christ. There are several fascinating verses that refer to the death of the Antichrist and his resurrection back to life.

- Revelation 13:3
- Revelation 13:12-14
- Revelation 17:8
- Daniel 11:45

In the early church, a well-accepted theory concerning the identity of the Antichrist was the *Nero redivivus*, that is, that Antichrist would be Nero revived or raised back to life. Nero died by suicide in A.D. 68, and a series of imposters pretending to be Nero returned in A.D. 69 and 80. In A.D. 88 a serious Nero impostor appeared in Parthia.

Another popular theory is that Antichrist will be Judas Iscariot brought back from the grave. There are three main arguments used to support this view. First, Luke 22:3 says that "Satan entered into Judas Iscariot." John 6:70-71 is even stronger: "Jesus said, 'I chose the twelve of you, but one is a devil.' He was speaking of Judas, son of Simon Iscariot, one of the Twelve, who would betray him."

Second, in John 17:12, our Lord refers to Judas Iscariot as "the son of perdition" or "the one headed for destruction." The only other place this title appears in the New Testament is in 2 Thessalonians 2:3, in reference to the Antichrist.

Third, Acts 1:25 states that when Judas died, he went to the place "where he belongs." Some interpret this as meaning that Judas went to a special place when he died to await the time when he would be brought back as the final Antichrist. Those who adhere to this view correlate Acts 1:25 with Revelation 17:8, identifying that special place as the abyss or "bottomless pit." Revelation 17:8 says, "The beast you saw was alive but isn't now. And yet he will soon come up out of the bottomless pit and go to eternal destruction."

While it is certainly possible that the Antichrist could be Nero, Judas Iscariot, or some other nefarious individual from the past brought back to life, the Bible never clearly identifies any person from the past as the future Antichrist. Therefore, without any direct biblical proof, it seems best to view the Antichrist as a future world ruler who will be under the total control of Satan and not a resurrected character from the past.

Question 6: Will the Antichrist Be Killed and Rise from the Dead? This is a follow-up to question 5. As we discovered in answering that question, there are several passages in the book of Revelation that clearly speak of the death and resurrection of the Antichrist. Having concluded from Scripture that the Antichrist is not a resurrected individual from the past, the conclusion is that he will be a future individual who will be violently killed (probably assassinated) and miraculously raised from the dead during the coming Tribulation period.

199

Just think of the overwhelming impact this will have on the world. At the climax of history, a great ruler will experience a healing that closely approximates the death and resurrection of Jesus Christ. Revelation 13:3-4 and 17:8-9 record the worldwide amazement at the resurrection of the beast:

> • *I saw that one of the heads of the beast seemed wounded beyond recovery—but the fatal wound was healed! All the world marveled at this miracle and followed the beast in awe. They worshiped the dragon for giving the beast such power, and they worshiped the beast. "Is there anyone as great as the beast?" they exclaimed. "Who is able to fight against him?" (Rev. 13:3-4)*

> • *The beast you saw was alive but isn't now. And yet he will soon come up out of the bottomless pit and go to eternal destruction. And the people who belong to this world, whose names were not written in the Book of Life from before the world began, will be amazed at the reappearance of this beast who had died. (Revelation 17:8)*

This will be the greatest event in the history of the world as far as the people of this earth are concerned. Imagine the violent death—the assassination, perhaps—of the most charismatic, most effective politician the world has ever seen. The whole world will be in mourning. The collective angst will be profound. It will be similar to the death of JFK in 1963 or of Lady Diana in 1997. The world will watch the funeral procession on every network. CNN will carry the entire event with painstaking detail and commentary. Suddenly, as the decorated hearse arrives at the cemetery and the pallbearers remove the coffin, the most incredible thing the world has ever seen will transpire right in front of the eyes of billions of people—the body rises up out of the coffin, the pallbearers recoil in terror and drop the coffin, and the Antichrist stands up, walks calmly to the nearest microphone, and begins to speak to a totally dumbfounded world. Can't you just picture the news anchors reporting this story?

It is this great event that catapults the Antichrist to worldwide rule. The Bible tells us in Revelation 17:8 that when the Antichrist is violently killed, he goes to the bottomless pit for a period of time and then comes back to life. During this brief period in the bottomless pit, Satan completely energizes the Antichrist. Antichrist probably receives his orders and strategy from Satan, literally selling his soul to the devil, and then comes back to earth with hellish ferocity to establish his world domination over a completely awestruck earth.

Any discussion of this issue always raises at least one other question: Does Satan have the power to raise a dead person back to life? Many who do not believe that he does, think that the Antichrist only appears to die and then fakes a counterfeit resurrection to deceive the world. However, the words used to describe the death of the Antichrist are used in other places to describe a violent death. Revelation 13:3 uses the same word for the death of the Antichrist as Revelation 5:6 does for the death of Jesus Christ, the Lamb of God. Moreover, after the Antichrist dies, Revelation 17:8 says that he goes to the bottomless pit or abyss for a time before he suddenly reappears on earth. This doesn't seem to describe someone who is faking death.

I cannot explain every detail of how this death and resurrection will occur, but I believe that these passages teach that God will permit Satan to perform this marvelous feat to further his nefarious parody of Christ and to further deceive the world.

Question 7: Will Believers in Christ Know Who the Antichrist Is before Being Raptured to Heaven? In recent times people seem to be fascinated with trying to identify the Antichrist. Many interesting names have appeared on lists of Antichrist candidates: Napoleon, various Catholic popes, Benito Mussolini, Adolf Hitler, Henry Kissinger,

Mikhail Gorbachev, Juan Carlos and his son Philippe, Bill Clinton, or any other person one doesn't especially like.

These failed attempts often draw a great deal of attention for a while, but they also highlight the danger of trying to identify the Antichrist. The New Testament teaches that believers will not know who the Antichrist is before being raptured to heaven. Second Thessalonians 2:2-3 says:

> *Please don't be so easily shaken and troubled by those who say that the day of the Lord has already begun. Even if they claim to have had a vision, a revelation, or a letter supposedly from us, don't believe them. Don't be fooled by what they say.*
>
> *For that day will not come until there is a great rebellion against God and the man of lawlessness is revealed—the one who brings destruction.*

Paul wrote the Thessalonian believers to clear up some confusion they had about the coming Day of the Lord or the Tribulation period. Evidently someone had taught these believers that they were already in the Tribulation period, but Paul corrected this false teaching by pointing out that the Day of the Lord can't come until two things happen: (1) a great apostasy or rebellion; and (2) the revelation of the Antichrist or "man of lawlessness." Since the Antichrist will be revealed at the beginning of the Day of the Lord or Tribulation period and the church will be raptured before this time, it doesn't appear that Christians will know the identity of the Antichrist before we are raptured to heaven. If you ever figure out who the Antichrist is, then I've got bad news for you—you've been left behind!

Having said this, I do believe that as we see the last days develop, we may be able to recognize certain individuals who could fit the picture of the Antichrist given in the Bible. However, believers should avoid ever specifically identifying any person as the coming Antichrist. Satan's superman will be unveiled at the beginning of the Day of the Lord, after the church has been translated to glory. We should spend our time and energy looking for Christ, not the Antichrist.

Question 8: What Is the Mark of the Beast (666)? There has probably been more speculation about this subject than almost any other aspect of the last days. As my friend Dr. Harold Willmington says, "There's a lot of sick, sick, sick about 666." The mark of the Beast has been identified as everything from PIN numbers to credit card numbers to social-security numbers to about any other number that the government may assign to people. In the movie *The Omen*, Damien was born on June 6, at 6:00 (666) to symbolize his identification as the coming Antichrist.

Almost everyone, including even the most biblically illiterate person, has heard something about 666 or the mark of the Beast. Revelation 13:16-18 is the key passage on the meaning of 666 or the mark of the Beast:

> *He required everyone—great and small, rich and poor, slave and free—to be given a mark on the right hand or on the forehead. And no one could buy or sell anything without that mark, which was either the name of the Beast or the number representing his name. Wisdom is needed to understand this. Let the one who has understanding solve the number of the Beast, for it is the number of a man. His number is 666.*

This passage provides five key clues[8] as to the interpretation of the mark of the Beast.

1. The name of the Beast
2. The number representing his name
3. The number of the Beast
4. The number of a man
5. The number is 666

When these five clues are followed through their logical progression, the number or mark of the Beast is the number of a man who is the Antichrist or final world ruler. This number is the number of the Antichrist's own name. In a Jewish system of letter values called *gematria*, each letter in the Hebrew alphabet (twenty-two letters in all) is assigned a numerical value as follows: 1, 2, 3, 4, 5, 6, 7, 8, 9, 10, 20, 30, 40, 50, 60, 70, 80, 90, 100, 200, 300, and 400. Therefore, every person's name in Hebrew has a numerical value. As Arnold Fruchtenbaum notes:

> *In this passage whatever the personal name of the Antichrist will be, if his name is spelled out in Hebrew characters, the numerical value of his name will be 666. So this is the number that will be put on the worshipers of the Antichrist. Since the number of dif-*

ferent calculations can equal 666, it is impossible to figure the
name out in advance. But when he does appear, whatever his
personal name will be, it will equal 666. Those who are wise
(verse 18) at that time will be able to point him out in advance.[9]

When the Antichrist appears on the world scene at the beginning of the Tribulation, those who understand God's Word will be able to identify him by the number of his name. Then when he seizes power at the middle of the Tribulation, every person on earth will be faced with a monumental decision. Will they take the mark of the Beast on their right hands or foreheads? Will they swear allegiance to the man who claims to be God? Or will they bow the knee to the true God and lose their right to buy and sell and even face beheading (Rev. 20:4)? The Antichrist's economic policy will be very simple: Worship me or starve. But it will be far better to refuse Antichrist and starve or face beheading, because in receiving his mark, a person will forfeit eternal life. All who take the mark of the Beast will face the eternal judgment of God (Rev. 14:9-10).

Question 9: What Finally Happens to the Antichrist? God's Word is very clear and specific about the demise and doom of the coming Antichrist. Two main passages in the New Testament spell out how he meets his end.

Second Thessalonians 2:8 says: "Then the man of lawlessness will be revealed, whom the Lord Jesus will consume with the breath of his mouth and destroy by the splendor of his coming." This passage reveals that the Lord will destroy the power of the Antichrist simply by his spoken word. All that will be necessary is for him to speak forth the Antichrist's doom, and it will immediately be so.

The Bible further reveals that the Antichrist will be singled out by the Lord when he comes for a uniquely quick and severe judgment.

I saw the beast gathering the kings of the earth and their armies
in order to fight against the one sitting on the horse and his army.
And the beast was captured, and with him the false prophet who
did mighty miracles on behalf of the beast—miracles that
deceived all who had accepted the mark of the beast and who
worshiped his statue. Both the beast and his false prophet were

> *thrown alive into the lake of fire that burns with sulphur. Their entire army was killed by the sharp sword that came out of the mouth of the one riding the white horse. And all the vultures of the sky gorged themselves on the dead bodies. (Revelation 19:19-21)*

204 When the Lord Jesus is revealed in all his glory, he will destroy all the armies gathered at Armageddon with the sharp sword of his word, which proceeds from his mouth. All he will have to do to destroy all of man's military might is simply say, "Drop dead," and the armies of the world will melt before him like wax. However, the Antichrist and his henchman, the false prophet, will not be killed like the others. They will be "thrown alive into the lake of fire that burns with sulphur," where they will be joined one thousand years later by the devil, the head of this false trinity (Rev. 20:10).

This is the final doom of the devil's masterpiece. His false kingdom will be swept away, and the glorious kingdom of Christ will be established. Daniel 7:26-27 is a powerful reminder of the Antichrist's termination and Christ's exaltation:

> *The court will pass judgment, and all his power will be taken away and completely destroyed. Then the sovereignty, power, and greatness of all the kingdoms under heaven will be given to the holy people of the Most High. They will rule forever, and all rulers will serve and obey them.*

Question 10: Is the Antichrist Alive Today? The clearest, most concise answer to this question is, no one knows for sure! Many have speculated about this, but no one really knows.

Jeane Dixon, the pseudoprophet, has prophesied that a child was born in the Middle East at 7:17 A.M. on February 5, 1962, who will lead the entire world.

In her book *My Life and Prophecies,* she relates how she received this prophecy and what it signifies:

> *My eyes once again focused on the baby. By now he had grown to manhood, and a small cross which had formed above his head enlarged and expanded until it covered the earth in all directions.*

Simultaneously, suffering people, of all races, knelt in worshipful adoration, lifting their arms and offering their hearts to the man. For a fleeting moment I felt as though I were one of them, but the channel that emanated from him was not that of the Holy Trinity. I knew within my heart that this revelation was to signify the beginning of wisdom, but whose wisdom and for whom? An overpowering feeling of love surrounded me, but the look I had seen in the man when he was still a babe—a look of serene wisdom and knowledge—made me sense that there was something God allowed me to see without my becoming a part of it.

I also sensed that I was once again safe within the protective arms of my Creator.

I glanced at my bedside clock. It was still early—7:17 A.M.

What does this revelation signify? I am convinced that this revelation indicates a child, born somewhere in the Middle East shortly after 7:00 A.M. on February 5, 1962—possibly a direct descendant of the royal line of Pharaoh Ikhnaton and Queen Nefertiti—will revolutionize the world. There is no doubt that he will fuse multitudes into one all-embracing doctrine. He will form a new "Christianity," based on his "almighty power," but leading man in a different direction far removed from the teaching and life of Christ, the Son.[10]

While no one knows if *the* Antichrist is alive today, including Jeane Dixon, we can be certain that *an* Antichrist is alive in the world at this very moment. Writing late in the first century A.D., the apostle John said that the spirit of Antichrist was already at work undermining and opposing the work of God (1 John 2:18; 4:3). We can be certain that the spirit of Antichrist is alive and well today!

Satan has a man ready in every generation, a satanically prepared vessel, to take center stage and rule the world. The devil doesn't know when the coming of Christ will occur, so he is prepared in every generation with his man to stand against Christ and the establishment of his glorious kingdom. Satan has always had a Nimrod, a Pharaoh, a Nebuchadnezzar, an Alexander the Great, an Antiochus, a Caesar, a Napoleon, a Hitler, a Stalin, and a someone alive today to set up a rival kingdom and to usurp the rightful place of the King of kings.

While no one can say for sure if the Antichrist is alive today, the Bible tells us without any doubt that the Antichrist is going to come, and in fact, he may already be alive and walking on the face of the earth. Make no mistake, Antichrist is coming!

Movies like *The Omen* that preview what the coming of the Antichrist may be like are make-believe horror films. But often the main premise is biblically sound. There is a gripping scene early in this movie. On the morning after the nightmarish fifth birthday party for Damien (the Antichrist), a Catholic priest named Father Brennan pays an unannounced visit to Ambassador Thorn's office. As soon as Father Brennan is alone with Thorn (Damien's father), he blurts out a startling warning to the ambassador: "You must accept Christ as your Savior. You must accept him now!"

The same warning is still applicable today. When the Antichrist appears, most people will still refuse to accept Christ and will instead turn to follow the lawless one. Don't put it off any longer. If you haven't already done so, accept Jesus Christ as your Savior now!

THE TOP TEN QUESTIONS ABOUT THE TRIBULATION, SECOND COMING, AND MILLENNIUM

Question 1: Can People Who Have Rejected the Gospel and Missed the Rapture Still Be Saved During the Tribulation? All premillennialists would agree that people will be saved during the Tribulation period. The salvation of the lost is one of the chief purposes of the Tribulation period: "Anyone who calls on the name of the Lord will be saved. There will be people on Mount Zion in Jerusalem who escape, just as the Lord has said. These will be among the survivors whom the Lord has called" (Joel 2:32).

However, many respected students of Bible prophecy contend that God will preclude anyone who heard the gospel and openly rejected it before the Rapture from ever being saved during the Tribulation. They hold that God will send strong deception upon those who heard the truth and rejected God's offer of mercy. Support for this view is based on 2 Thessalonians 2:9-12.

> *This evil man will come to do the work of Satan with counterfeit power and signs and miracles. He will use every kind of wicked*

deception to fool those who are on their way to destruction because they refuse to believe the truth that would save them. So God will send great deception upon them, and they will believe all these lies. Then they will be condemned for not believing the truth and for enjoying the evil they do.

While this verse could be used to support this position, it does not seem to refer to people who reject the truth before the Rapture but rather those who reject the truth and receive the Antichrist after the Rapture. This entire passage describes what happens during the Tribulation period. It refers to those who witness the deception of the Antichrist, believe his message, and reject the truth. This passage says that God will condemn those who do this.

I believe that many who have rejected the gospel before the Rapture will undoubtedly continue to reject it after the Rapture. However, to say, based on this verse, that no one who has clearly heard the claims of Christ before the Rapture and rejected them can receive God's mercy during the Tribulation is making this verse say much more than the context allows.

God can and will use the horror of the Tribulation period to bring millions of sinners to faith in his Son (Rev. 7:9-14). Among this numberless crowd, there will certainly be some whom our gracious Lord will have given a second opportunity for salvation.

Question 2: Is the "Tribulation" the Same As the "Great Tribulation"?

In chapter 4 of this book, there is a chart with all of the biblical terms for the coming seven-year period, when God will pour out his wrath on this earth. The most commonly used term for this time is the *Tribulation period.* This term is found in Matthew 24:9 in many modern translations. Matthew 24:21 intensifies the term by titling it the "Great Tribulation" ("a time of greater horror," NLT). The relationship between the words *Tribulation* and *Great Tribulation* has confused some people.

God's Word clearly teaches that the future seven-year time of worldwide trouble will be divided into two equal segments of three and one-half years. On this point almost all would agree. However, there are several options concerning how the terms *Tribulation* and *Great Tribulation* relate to this seven-year period of time.

- Option 1: Initial three and a half years = Tribulation; final three and a half years = Great Tribulation
- Option 2: Entire seven years = Tribulation; entire seven years = Great Tribulation
- Option 3: Entire seven years = Tribulation; final three and a half years = Great Tribulation

208   I favor option 3 because the term *Tribulation* in Matthew 24:9 seems to encompass the entire seven-year period. It is an excellent word to describe the overall nature of the final seven years of this age, and it is frequently used that way by most students of Bible prophecy. The term *Great Tribulation* in Matthew 24:21, on the other hand, describes the more specific time that will follow the setting up of the abomination of desolation at the midpoint of the seven-year period. Therefore, it appears that the title *Great Tribulation* describes the intensification of God's wrath during the final three and a half years of the seven-year Tribulation.

Question 3: Are We in the Tribulation Now? On the night before his crucifixion, our Lord reminded his disciples that in this life they would have trouble: "I have told you all this so that you may have peace in me. Here on earth you will have many trials and sorrows" (John 16:33). In Acts 14:22, Luke echoes these same words: "They strengthened the believers. They encouraged them to continue in the faith, reminding them that they must enter into the Kingdom of God through many tribulations." While it is true that we must enter the Kingdom through many tribulations, the Bible makes a clear distinction between the general tribulations that all believers in every age experience and the intense time of worldwide Tribulation the Bible says will conclude this age.

Nevertheless, because of the difficulty of the Christian journey, some have been led to believe that this present age is the Tribulation period. This seems to have been the problem the Thessalonians were having when Paul wrote his second letter to them. Paul addressed this problem in 2 Thessalonians 2:1-3:

> Brothers and sisters, let us tell you about the coming again of our Lord Jesus Christ and how we will be gathered together to meet him. Please don't be so easily shaken and troubled by those who

say that the day of the Lord has already begun. Even if they claim to have had a vision, a revelation, or a letter supposedly from us, don't believe them. Don't be fooled by what they say.

For that day will not come until there is a great rebellion against God and the man of lawlessness is revealed—the one who brings destruction.

209

Paul assured the Thessalonian believers and us that we are not currently in the Tribulation or Day of the Lord. He said that the Tribulation cannot come until two things happen: a great, world-wide rebellion against God and the unveiling of the Antichrist. Since neither of these things has happened, we cannot currently be in the Tribulation period.

Question 4: Is the Army of 200 Million in Revelation 9:16 a Reference to China? Revelation 9:15-16 describes a massive army of 200 million mounted troops, who destroy one-third of all the people on earth. The most common interpretation of this passage is that it describes a great Chinese invasion of Israel during the battle of Armageddon. This conclusion is based on three main points:

1. The army of 200 million is viewed as parallel with the kings from the east in Revelation 16:12, who cross the dried-up Euphrates River and gather at Armageddon.
2. The modern nation of China could amass an army of this magnitude.
3. The description of the weapons used by this army is similar to a scene of modern warfare such as tanks, helicopters, artillery, rocket launchers, and missiles. Revelation 9:17-19 vividly describes the weaponry.

While it is possible that these verses describe the Chinese army, I believe it is better to view this massive army as an armada of demonic invaders. There are five reasons I prefer this view:

1. The unleashing of this army is the sixth trumpet judgment. The fifth trumpet judgment is clearly a demonic invasion of earth, and the fifth and sixth trumpet judgments go together since they are the first two of three "terrors."
2. Fallen angels, like those of the fifth trumpet judgment, lead this armada (Rev. 9:15). Since the leaders are four fallen angels or demons, it makes sense that the troops they are leading are also demons.
3. The fearsome description in Revelation 19:17-19 fits supernatural beings much better than modern warfare.
4. There are other examples in Scripture of supernatural armies of

cavalry. Horses of fire swept Elijah up to heaven (2 Kings 2:11). Horses and chariots of fire protected Elisha at Dothan (2 Kings 6:13-17). Heavenly horses and horsemen from the celestial realm introduce the reign of Christ (Rev. 19:14). The Lord himself will return riding on a white horse (Rev. 19:11). It seems logical that Satan would resist the coming of the kingdom with his own infernal cavalry.

5. The weapons mentioned—fire, sulfur, and smoke—are always supernatural weapons in the Bible and are associated with hell four times in Revelation (14:10-11; 19:20; 20:10; 21:8).

For these reasons, I believe the army of 200 million in Revelation 9:16 is an invasion of earth by demonic cavalry—hellish horsemen riding satanic steeds!

Question 5: Will Anyone Survive the Tribulation? Even a cursory reading of the book of Revelation leaves one wondering how anyone could survive. In the fourth seal judgment, one-fourth of the earth is killed, and in the sixth trumpet judgment, another one-third of the earth is destroyed. That's one-half of the world's population in just two of the Tribulation judgments. Then as the angels pour out the bowls of wrath of Revelation 16 in rapid succession, the total annihilation of the human race looks imminent.

Our Lord knew that people would someday ask this question, so he has already given us his solution to the problem: "That will be a time of greater horror than anything the world has ever seen or will ever see again. In fact, unless that time of calamity is shortened, the entire human race will be destroyed. But it will be shortened for the sake of God's chosen ones" (Matt. 24:21-22). This passage doesn't mean that the Lord will shorten the Tribulation period to make it less than the time he intended. It also doesn't mean that the days will be less than twenty-four hours. These encouraging words simply mean that there will be a termination of this period of time—that is, the Lord will not allow it to go on indefinitely. He will cut it short by ending it at the divinely appointed time. This is another way of saying that if the Tribulation were allowed to go on indefinitely, no one would survive. The Lord ends the Tribulation when he does for the sake of those who have been saved during this time and are undergoing terrible suffering.

The Lord assures us that there will be many people who will survive the horrors of the Tribulation. All of these people will be gathered together for judgment when Christ returns, and the righteous will enter the millennial kingdom, while the lost will be cast into eternal fire (Matt. 25:31-46).

Question 6: Who Are the Armies of Heaven That Return with Christ?
When Jesus Christ returns from heaven to destroy the Antichrist, judge the nations, and establish his glorious kingdom, a great host will ac- company him. This mighty army will follow in his train as he splits the clouds, riding on a milk white stallion. The Bible makes is clear that this mighty army will be made up of both angels and redeemed human beings. Here are a few of the most familiar verses that describe the armies of heaven that return with the conquering Christ:

- "Then the Lord my God will come, and all his holy ones with him" (Zechariah 14:5).
- "When the Son of Man comes in his glory, and all the angels with him, then he will sit upon his glorious throne" (Matt. 25:31).
- "God will provide rest for you who are being persecuted and also for us when the Lord Jesus appears from heaven. He will come with his mighty angels, in flaming fire" (2 Thess. 1:7-8).
- "Look, the Lord is coming with thousands of his holy ones" (Jude 1:14).
- "I saw heaven opened, and a white horse was standing there. And the one sitting on the horse was named Faithful and True. For he judges fairly and then goes to war. The armies of heaven, dressed in pure white linen, followed him on white horses" (Rev. 19:11, 14).

Just imagine what it will be like to follow the King of kings and Lord of lords and to lead the mighty angels who come in flaming fire, as the Lord God Omnipotent comes back to reign.

Question 7: During the Campaign of Armageddon, Will Blood Literally Flow in the Land of Israel As High As a Horse's Bridle for 180 Miles? The most vivid description of the severity and brutality of Armageddon is found in Revelation 14:17-20:

After that, another angel came from the Temple in heaven, and he also had a sharp sickle. Then another angel, who has power to destroy the world with fire, shouted to the angel with the sickle, "Use your sickle now to gather the clusters of grapes from the vines of the earth, for they are fully ripe for judgment." So the angel swung his sickle on the earth and loaded the grapes into the great winepress of God's wrath. And the grapes were trodden in the winepress outside the city, and blood flowed from the winepress in a stream about 180 miles long and as high as a horse's bridle.

Prophecy preachers often use this passage with great effect. They describe in gory, gruesome detail how blood will literally flow four feet deep for 180 miles, which is the entire length of the land of Israel, from Megiddo in the north to Bozrah in the south.

212

Others maintain that this can't be taken literally and hold that the language is hyperbolic or intentionally exaggerated to impress the reader with the massive extent of the slaughter and bloodletting.

While either of these views is possible, I believe that the picture here is drawn from the imagery of the winepress. When the grapes were put into the press, people standing inside it would stomp around on the grapes, forcing the juice out of the grapes and down into a collection vat. However, in Revelation 14:17-20, the winepress is "the great winepress of God's wrath." The Lord is the one who is doing the stomping, but he is stomping on people, not grapes. And what pours out is blood, not juice (see also Isa. 63:2-3; Joel 3:13; Rev. 19:15).

I don't believe that this passage necessarily means that a river of blood will flow four feet deep. The imagery is that the stomping of his judgment is so fierce and intense that the blood from his winepress will splash out as high as a horse's bridle. I don't know how hard one would have to stomp in a winepress to splash grape juice four feet high, but this is a picture of the ferocity of God's judgment. The Lord is saying that at Armageddon he is going to throw all the nations into his great winepress and that his intense, blood-splattering judgment will extend over the entire land of Israel, from Megiddo to Bozrah.

Question 8: What Will Believers Who Return to Earth with Christ Do during the Millennial Kingdom? When Jesus Christ returns to this earth at his second coming, he will bring his saints with him, according to Jude 1:14 and Revelation 19:14. After he defeats the armies of the Antichrist at Armageddon and judges the nations, he will establish his kingdom on earth.

While we will certainly do many things in worshiping and serving our Lord in the kingdom, our function that Scripture emphasizes is ruling and reigning with Christ. The Bible says that all believers from every age will reign with Christ for a thousand years. Consider what these verses say about what you will be doing in the kingdom:

> • *In the end, the holy people of the Most High will be given the kingdom, and they will rule forever and ever. . . . Then the time arrived for the holy people to take over the kingdom. Then the sovereignty, power, and greatness of all the kingdoms under heaven will be given to the holy people of the Most High. They will rule forever, and all rulers will serve and obey them. (Dan. 7:18, 22, 27)*

> • *Don't you know that someday we Christians are going to judge the world? And since you are going to judge the world, can't you decide these little things among yourselves? Don't you realize that we Christians will judge angels? So you should surely be able to resolve ordinary disagreements here on earth. (1 Cor. 6:2-3)*

> • *To all who are victorious, who obey me to the very end, I will give authority over all the nations. They will rule the nations with an iron rod and smash them like clay pots. They will have the same authority I received from my Father, and I will also give them the morning star! (Rev. 2:26-28)*

> • *They came to life again, and they reigned with Christ for a thousand years. . . . They will be priests of God and of Christ and will reign with him a thousand years. (Rev. 20:4, 6)*

What an exciting prospect! We will rule the nations with Christ for a thousand years on earth. We will even judge the angels.

During this present age, God is testing us to determine our future position of authority and responsibility in the kingdom. According to Luke 19:11-26, we will be given rulership in the kingdom over people and angels based on what we did with the treasures and talents God entrusted us with here on earth. Some will be governors over ten cities; some will rule over five cities. We will all reign, but the extent and responsibility of that reign is being determined right now in your life and mine.

Question 9: Is the Battle of Gog and Magog in Revelation 20:7-10 the Same as That in Ezekiel 38–39? Ezekiel 38–39 describes a great Russian-Islamic invasion of Israel during the coming Tribulation. This invasion is often referred to as the Gog and Magog invasion, after the title of its leader. The only other place the words Gog and Magog occur in the Bible is in Revelation 20:8. This repetition has led some to believe that these passages describe the same event. However, I believe these passages describe two separate invasions, separated by more than one thousand years.

There are two important reasons why these two passages should be thought of as distinct from one another. First, Ezekiel 38–39 is set in the context of restoration (chapters 33–39) followed by a description of the millennial temple and sacrifices (chapters 40–48). The invasion in Ezekiel 38–39 is a part of Israel's restoration, which will occur chronologically before Christ officially establishes the millennial kingdom. In Revelation 20:7-10, the events fit chronologically after the Millennium.

Second, the disposal of the bodies and weapons is a problem for those who would equate Gog and Magog in Ezekiel 38–39 and Revelation 20:7-10. Ezekiel 39 states that it requires seven months to bury the bodies of the slain (verses 12, 14) and seven years to burn the weapons of the armies (v. 9). In Revelation 20, the next event after the battle of Gog and Magog is the Great White Throne Judgment (20:11-15). In this judgment all of the unsaved will stand before the bar of God in resurrected bodies to face their sentence. It seems illogical for Israel to spend seven months burying the dead only to have them immediately raised out of the graves to appear before God.

This discussion immediately raises another question. If these two passages are not describing the same invasion, then why does John use the phrase "Gog and Magog" in Revelation 20:8? John probably used this familiar language from Ezekiel 38–39 like we would use the word *Waterloo* today to describe a disastrous defeat. When we say that someone met his "Waterloo," we don't mean that he was literally at the battle of Waterloo in 1815. We are simply using a familiar, stereotyped word that emphasizes the similarity between the two events. John used the words *Gog and Magog* as a shorthand way to describe what is going to happen. In essence, he was saying, "This is going to be just like the Gog and Magog in Ezekiel 38–39. A great confederation of nations will invade Israel and be destroyed by supernatural judgment."

Therefore, in spite of the mention of Gog and Magog in both of these passages, and in spite of the similarities between them, these two invasions are distinct from one another and are separated by one thousand years. The Gog and Magog invasion in Ezekiel 38–39 will occur during the Tribulation period, while the one in Revelation 20:7-10 will occur at the end of the Millennium.

Question 10: How Can the Millennium Be a Literal Thousand Years If God's Kingdom Is Eternal? Revelation 20:1-7 states clearly six times that the reign of Christ on earth after his glorious return will last for one thousand years. However, in several other places in Scripture, it is stated that Christ's kingdom is eternal or forever (Dan. 7:14, 27; Rev. 11:15). This has led many to conclude that the thousand years in Revelation 20:1-7 must not be literal.

The best way to reconcile this apparent inconsistency is to recognize that both of these statements are true: Christ will rule over his kingdom on this present earth for one thousand years, and he will reign forever. The future kingdom of God has two parts or phases. Phase one is the millennial reign of Christ on this earth (Rev. 20:1-7), and phase two is the eternal state (Rev. 22:5). As I once heard it described, "The Millennium is the front porch of eternity."

THE TOP TEN QUESTIONS ABOUT THE AFTERLIFE

Question 1: What Happens to People When They Die? More Americans than ever—81 percent—now say that they believe in life after death. Since the turn of the century, belief in an afterlife among U.S. Catholics, Jews, and those with no religious affiliation has grown significantly. However, as more people profess to believe in life after death, it doesn't seem that most people have much of an idea about what will happen to them when they die.

Death in the Bible means separation, not annihilation. A person who is spiritually dead is a person who is spiritually separated from God. When a person physically dies, he or she does not cease to exist. There is a separation between the material part (body) and the immaterial part (soul/spirit) of the person. When this separation occurs, the body "falls asleep" and is laid to rest. But the immaterial part of the person immediately goes to one of two places, depending on the person's relationship with Christ.

The departed spirit of a believer in Christ goes immediately into the presence of the Lord.

- "Jesus said, 'There was a certain rich man who was splendidly clothed and who lived each day in luxury. At his door lay a diseased beggar named Lazarus. As Lazarus lay there longing for scraps from the rich man's table, the dogs would come and lick his open sores. Finally, the beggar died and was carried by the angels to be with Abraham." (Luke 16:19-22)
- "Yes, we are fully confident, and we would rather be away from these bodies, for then we will be at home with the Lord." (2 Cor. 5:8)
- "To me, living is for Christ, and dying is even better. I'm torn between two desires: Sometimes I want to live, and sometimes I long to go and be with Christ. That would be far better for me." (Phil. 1:21, 23)
- When Christ comes at the Rapture, the perfected spirits of the redeemed will be reunited with their resurrected, glorified bodies. (1 Thess. 4:14-16)

When an unbeliever dies, his or her departed spirit goes immediately into hades to experience conscious, unrelenting torment. In the parable of the rich man and Lazarus in Luke 16:19-31, when the unbelieving rich man died, his soul was transported instantly to hades. "The rich man also died and was buried, and his soul went to the place of the dead. There, in torment, he saw Lazarus in the far distance with Abraham" (Luke 16:22-23). At the great white throne, the bodies of all the lost will be resurrected and joined with their spirits to appear before the Judge of the universe.

Question 2: What about Near-Death Experiences? Some of the best-selling books in the last decade have been about near-death experiences or NDEs. Books like *Embraced by the Light* and *Saved by the Light* have captured the attention of millions of people who want to peer behind the veil of death to get a sneak preview of the afterlife.

Two points about NDEs are important to understand. First, it is critical to note that they are called "near-death" experiences, not "death" or "after-life" experiences. The fact that the person came back from whatever state he or she was in is proof that he or she didn't really die. Therefore, we shouldn't put any stock in what this person purports to tell us about the afterlife. After all, this person was only *near* death, not dead. It's as ridiculous as a woman telling another woman about her "near-pregnancy" experience. The idea is laughable. Everyone knows that you're either pregnant or you're not. Likewise, you're either dead or you're not. As one writer said, near-death experiences "tell us no more about death than someone who has been near Denver but never within city limits can tell us about that town. Both NDEs (near-Denver and near-death experiences) are bereft of certitude. . . . In both cases, more reliable maps are available."[11]

The only people who ever really came back from the dead are the few individuals in Scripture that the Lord or one of his prophets or disciples raised. And none of them wrote a book about their experience or hit the talk-show circuit. Even the apostle Paul, who was caught up to heaven on one occasion, did not reveal the things he saw there (2 Cor. 12:1-5).

Second, the only reliable map for the afterlife is the Bible. The Bible defines death as separation of the spirit from the body (James 2:26). And true physical death occurs only one time for each person (Heb. 9:27). Moreover, much of the idle speculation related from NDEs sounds more occultic and New Age than biblical. If we want to know about the afterlife, we should turn to God's Word and be satisfied with what he has chosen to reveal to us about heaven and hell.

For anyone who wants to know more about the afterlife, I would suggest reading the parable of the rich man and Lazarus in Luke 16:19-31 and the description of heaven in Revelation 21–22.

Question 3: What Is Hell Like? *USA Today* often publishes statistics on its front page that shape the nation. In 1998, it presented interesting statistics on how people answered this question: Is there a hell? Fifty-two percent of adults are certain there's a hell; 27 percent think there might be. The pollsters then asked people what they think hell will be like. Forty-eight percent believe it is a real place where people suffer eternal torment; 46 percent say it is an anguished state of existence rather than an actual place; and 6 percent don't know.

Many have concocted their own theories about hell. The noted theologian Woody Allen once said, "Hell is Manhattan at rush hour. There is no question there's an unseen world. The question is, how far is it from midtown and how late does it stay open."

217

While people might joke about hell, make light of it, and come up with their own theories about whether it even exists at all, the Bible gives us God's terrifying view of hell. And it is no laughing matter. The Bible never gives us a complete, detailed description of what hell is like, but it does provide us with several frightening, sobering facts. Here are ten terrible facts about hell.

FACT 1: HELL IS A LITERAL PLACE   In the parable of the rich man and Lazarus in Luke 16:19-31, hell or hades is pictured as a literal place where the unrighteous rich man immediately went when he died. Eleven of the twelve times the word *gehenna* (hell) occurs in the New Testament, it is found on the lips of the Savior. Make no mistake, Jesus believed in a literal hell. He talked about it more than any other person in the Bible. Jesus is our primary source for what hell is like.

FACT 2: HELL IS DIVIDED INTO AT LEAST FOUR PARTS   There are four different words in the Greek New Testament to describe the under-world. Each of these words describes a unique division of this horrible place:

1. The Abyss or Bottomless Pit (nine times in the Greek New Testament): This is a place where some demons are presently confined who will be released for a period of five months during the Tribulation to afflict the lost (Rev. 9:1-5). It is also the place where Satan will be bound for one thousand years during the millennial kingdom (Rev. 20:1-3).
2. Tartarus (one time in the Greek New Testament—2 Peter 2:4): Tartarus is a permanent place of confinement where the angels who sinned in Genesis 6:1-4 are being held until they are finally cast into the lake of fire (Jude 1:6-7).
3. Hades (ten times in the Greek New Testament): This is the place where the souls of lost people are presently confined while they await the final day of judgment.
4. Gehenna (twelve times in the Greek New Testament): Gehenna is the final place of torment for Satan, demons, and all the lost (Rev. 20:10, 14-15). Gehenna is also called "the lake of fire that burns with sulfur" (Rev. 20:10), "the lake of fire" (Rev. 20:14), and "the second death" (Rev. 20:6, 14). It is called the second death because it is a place of final, eternal separation from God.

FACT 3: HELL IS A PLACE OF MEMORY   In hell there will be continued consciousness and immediate awareness of where one is. In Luke 16:19-31, the rich man knew immediately where he was. There will also be identity—the rich man knew who he was. There will also be memory—the rich man remembered his five brothers and Lazarus.

FACT 4: HELL IS A PLACE OF CONSCIOUS TORMENT   The worst part of hell is that there will be torment and agony. The rich man said, "I am in anguish in these flames" (Luke 16:24). He described Hades as "this place of torment" (16:28).

FACT 5: HELL IS A PLACE OF UNQUENCHABLE FIRE

> • *I, the Son of Man, will send my angels, and they will remove from my Kingdom everything that causes sin and all who do evil, and they will throw them into the furnace and burn them. (Matt. 13:41-42)*

> • *It is better to enter the Kingdom of God half blind than to have two eyes and be thrown into hell, "where the worm never dies and the fire never goes out." (Mark 9:47-48)*

> • *I am in anguish in these flames." (Luke 16:24)*

FACT 6: HELL IS A PLACE OF SEPARATION FROM GOD   "They will be punished with everlasting destruction, forever separated from the Lord and from his glorious power" (2 Thess. 1:9).

FACT 7: HELL IS A PLACE OF UNSPEAKABLE MISERY, SORROW, ANGER, AND FRUSTRATION   "There will be weeping and gnashing of teeth" (Matt. 13:42).

FACT 8: HELL IS A PLACE OF UNSATISFIED, RAGING THIRST   "The rich man shouted, 'Father Abraham, have some pity! Send Lazarus over here to dip the tip of his finger in water and cool my tongue' " (Luke 16:24).

FACT 9: HELL IS THE ONLY OTHER PLACE BESIDES HEAVEN TO SPEND ETERNITY   In other words, there are only two places people go after death—paradise or perdition. There is no in-between place. There is no third choice. The rich man went to hades; Lazarus went to paradise. These are still the only two options today.

FACT 10: HELL IS A PLACE FROM WHICH THERE IS NO ESCAPE   Nothing can change one's fate after death. There is no purgatory, no second chance, no parole for good behavior, and no graduation. As the old saying goes, "As death finds us, eternity keeps us. Hell is truth seen too late."

The lost can never come to heaven, and the saved can never end up in hell. Remember Abraham's words to the rich man in hades: "There is a great chasm separating us. Anyone who wanted to cross over to you from here is stopped at its edge, and no one there can cross over to us" (Luke 16:26). Hell is a place of destiny!

Question 4: Is Punishment in Hell Eternal? The doctrine of hell is undoubtedly the most disturbing subject in the Bible, and the most disturbing truth about hell is its duration. The idea of people being punished for their sins and misdeeds doesn't bother most people. But the notion that hell will last forever is totally repugnant. For this reason many have tried to soften this truth by adopting a kinder, gentler view of hell.

Two erroneous views of the fate of the lost have become popular in recent years. The first of these views is annihilationism, which teaches that all souls are immortal but that the wicked lose their immortality at the final judgment, and God extinguishes them. For annihilationists, the punishment for the lost is eternal extinction.

The second incorrect view is conditional immortality, which teaches that human souls are not inherently immortal and that at the judgment the wicked pass into oblivion while the righteous are given immortality.

While both of these views are certainly more appealing to the human mind, the Bible clearly teaches that punishment in hell will last forever. The Greek word *aionios*, which translated means "eternal" or "everlasting," appears sixty-six times in the New Testament. Fifty-one times it is used in connection with the happiness of the saved in heaven. It is used of both the quality and quantity of the life that believers will experience with God. The word is used another two times in connection with the duration of God in his glory. Six other times it is used in such a way that no one would question that it means forever. The other seven times it is used in connection with the fate of the wicked, and there should be no doubt to an objective mind that in these passages the word means "eternal," "forever," or "without end."

One of the clearest references in the New Testament to the eternalness of punishment in hell is Revelation 14:10-11: "They will be tormented with fire and burning sulfur in the presence of the holy angels and the Lamb. The smoke of their torment rises forever and ever, and they will have no relief day or night."

Matthew 25:46 describes both heaven and hell as eternal: "They will go away into eternal punishment, but the righteous will go into eternal life." To limit the meaning of eternity for the damned, one must also be willing to limit it for the saved.

I copied these words from a sermon by Charles Spurgeon many years ago. They powerfully express the terror and heart-wrenching despair of the eternalness of hell:

> *In hell there is no hope. They have not even the hope of dying; the hope of being annihilated. They are forever, forever, forever lost. On every chain in hell is written 'forever.' Up above their heads they read 'forever.' Their eyes are galled and their hearts are pained with the thought that it is 'forever.' Oh, if I could tell you tonight that hell would one day be burned out, and that those who were lost might be saved, there would be a jubilee in hell at the very thought of it. But it cannot be. It is forever. They are cast into outer darkness.*

Knowing the terrible judgment that awaits the lost should cause us to plead with them to be reconciled to God (2 Cor. 5:20-21).

Question 5: Will There Be Degrees of Punishment in Hell? When we considered the judgment seat of Christ, we saw that in heaven there will be varying degrees of reward for believers. Likewise, the Bible teaches that there will be degrees of punishment in hell for unbelievers based on the amount and nature of the sin committed and the light that was refused. Jesus himself taught that there will be degrees of punishment in hell:

> • *I assure you, the wicked cities of Sodom and Gomorrah will be better off on the judgment day than that place will be. (Matt. 10:15)*

> • *Jesus began to denounce the cities where he had done most of the miracles, because they hadn't turned from their sins and turned to God. "What horrors await you, Korazin and*

> *Bethsaida! For if the miracles I did in you had been done in*
> *wicked Tyre and Sidon, their people would have sat in deep*
> *repentance long ago, clothed in sackcloth and throwing ashes*
> *on their heads to show their remorse. I assure you, Tyre and*
> *Sidon will be better off on the judgment day than you! And you*
> *people of Capernaum, will you be exalted to heaven? No, you*
> *will be brought down to the place of the dead. For if the miracles*
> *I did for you had been done in Sodom, it would still be here*
> *today. I assure you, Sodom will be better off on the judgment*
> *day than you. (Matt. 11:20-24)*

- *The master will return unannounced and unexpected. He will*
  tear the servant apart and banish him with the unfaithful. The
  servant will be severely punished, for though he knew his duty,
  he refused to do it.

  But people who are not aware that they are doing wrong will
  be punished only lightly. Much is required from those to whom
  much is given, and much more is required from those to whom
  much more is given. (Luke 12:46-48)

At the Great White Throne Judgment, the Lord will open "the books," which contain all the deeds of the lost (Rev. 20:11-12). From these books the Lord will tailor the exact punishment to meet the crime.

Question 6: Is Heaven a Real Place? The word *heaven* occurs about 550 times in the Bible. It is a general word that describes three different "heavens" that exist. The first heaven is the atmospheric heaven, the second is the stellar or celestial heaven, and the third is the divine heaven (the abode of God). Contrary to popular belief, there is no "seventh heaven."

When we talk about heaven, we usually refer to the divine heaven or third heaven—the dwelling place of God. The Bible tells us that this third heaven is just as real as the first and second heavens that we can see. There are six reasons why I believe heaven is a literal place that exists right now:

1. Jesus called heaven his "Father's home" and said he was going there to prepare a "place" for his people (John 14:1-3).
2. Revelation 21:9–22:5 describes heaven in majestic, glorious, enthralling detail as a literal place with walls, gates, foundations, and a street.

3. Jesus taught that heaven is the present abode or dwelling place of God (Matt. 10:32-33).
4. Paul visited the "third heaven" where God dwells (2 Cor. 12:2).
5. Our citizenship is in heaven (Phil. 3:20-21).
6. Heaven is called our "heavenly homeland" (Heb. 11:16).

Biblical Terms for Heaven
• My Father's home (John 14:2)
• The city of the living God (Heb. 12:22)
• Mount Zion (Heb. 12:22)
• Paradise (Luke 23:43; 2 Cor. 12:4; Rev. 2:7)
• The third heaven (2 Cor. 12:2)
• A better place (Heb. 11:16)
• A heavenly homeland (Heb. 11:16)
• A heavenly city (Heb. 11:16)

Question 7: Will We Know Each Other in Heaven? Almost every person has probably asked this question at one time or another. We want to know if we will recognize our friends and loved ones in heaven and if they will know us. Well, I've got good news for you—we *will* know our friends and loved ones in heaven. In fact, we won't really know each other *until* we get to heaven. Only in heaven, when all the masks and facades are torn away, will we really know one another and enjoy intimate, unhindered fellowship.

The main passage that reveals that we will recognize each other in heaven is Luke 19:19-31. Remember in that parable the rich man recognizes Lazarus in heaven and remembers all the facts about their relationship on earth. The rich man even remembers his five brothers who are still on earth.

Moreover, Scripture indicates we will even recognize people we never met here on earth. At the transfiguration of Jesus, Peter knew that the two men with Jesus were Elijah and Moses (Matt. 17:1-4). Obviously, Peter had never met Moses and Elijah. How did he know who they were? It appears that he had an intuitive knowledge that enabled him to know immediately who they were. I believe that it will be the same way in heaven. All of the Lord's people will possess this intuitive knowledge that will enable us to recognize our friends and loved ones as well as the redeemed of all the ages. We will never meet a stranger in heaven!

Question 8: What Will We Do in Heaven? This frequently asked question takes various forms such as, Will there be football in heaven? Will I be able to golf in heaven? Will I get bored in heaven? Will I sit around all day on a cloud, strumming a harp?

While the Bible doesn't tell us as much as we would like to know about what we will do in heaven, it does focus on six main things we will do:[12]

1. We will worship without distraction (Rev. 4:8-11; 7:10; 11:16-18; 15:2-4; 19:1-8).
2. We will serve without exhaustion (Rev. 7:14-15; 22:3).
3. We will rule without failure (Luke 19:17, 19; 1 Cor. 6:3; Rev. 22:5).
4. We will fellowship without suspicion (Matt. 8:11).
5. We will learn without weariness (1 Cor. 13:12).
6. We will rest without boredom (Rev. 14:13).

Question 9: What Kind of Body Will We Have in Heaven? All of us look forward to getting a new body in heaven. This is especially true of those who suffer from one or more of "the five Bs of old age": baldness, bifocals, bridges, bulges, and bunions. All of us come to a point in life when we look in the mirror and say, "Mirror, mirror on the wall, you've got to be kidding!"

As our body begins to fall apart, we begin to groan for glory. We eagerly anticipate our new, remodeled, perfect body in heaven. As Paul says:

> *We know that when this earthly tent we live in is taken down—when we die and leave these bodies—we will have a home in heaven, an eternal body made for us by God himself and not by human hands. We grow weary in our present bodies, and we long for the day when we will put on our heavenly bodies like new clothing. (2 Cor. 5:1-2)*

But when we begin to think about our future, resurrection bodies, we often have more questions than answers. While the Bible doesn't satisfy our curiosity about every detail, it does give us a basic idea of what our new, glorified bodies will be like.

Generally, we know that our new bodies will be like the resurrected, glorified body of Jesus.

> • *We are citizens of heaven, where the Lord Jesus Christ lives. And we are eagerly waiting for him to return as our Savior. He will take these weak mortal bodies of ours and change them into*

glorious bodies like his own, using the same mighty power that
he will use to conquer everything, everywhere. (Phil. 3:20-21)

- *Yes, dear friends, we are already God's children, and we can't*
even imagine what we will be like when Christ returns. But we
do know that when he comes we will be like him, for we will see
him as he really is. (1 John 3:2)

225

What was Christ's resurrection body like? He ate food. His disciples
recognized him. He had scars. He was not limited by space. On two
separate occasions, Jesus walked right through the walls of the room
where his disciples were meeting (John 20:19, 26). Our future bodies
will be just like the resurrection body of Jesus, and we will be able to do
the same things he did in his body. Specifically, the Bible gives several
key facts about our future bodies in 1 Corinthians 15:35, 42-49:

Someone may ask, "How will the dead be raised? What kind of
bodies will they have?" . . . It is the same way for the resurrection
of the dead. Our earthly bodies, which die and decay, will be dif-
ferent when they are resurrected, for they will never die. Our bod-
ies now disappoint us, but when they are raised, they will be full
of glory. They are weak now, but when they are raised, they will
be full of power. They are natural human bodies now, but when
they are raised, they will be spiritual bodies. For just as there are
natural bodies, so also there are spiritual bodies.

The Scriptures tell us, "The first man, Adam, became a living
person." But the last Adam—that is, Christ—is a life-giving Spirit.
What came first was the natural body, then the spiritual body
comes later. Adam, the first man, was made from the dust of the
earth, while Christ, the second man, came from heaven. Every hu-
man being has an earthly body just like Adam's, but our heavenly
bodies will be just like Christ's. Just as we are now like Adam, the
man of the earth, so we will someday be like Christ, the man from
heaven.

Seven Fabulous Facts about Our Future Body
1. It will never decay or die. It will be imperishable.
2. It will be perfectly suited to our new environment. It will be
   a "heavenly" body.

3. It will be unique and diverse from everyone else's: "The stars differ from each other in their beauty and brightness. It is the same way for the resurrection of the dead" (1 Cor. 15:41-42).
4. It will be glorious—"full of glory." It will never disappoint us.
5. It will be powerful.
6. It will be spiritual.
7. It will be just like Christ's resurrection body.

The best thing about our new body is recorded in 1 Corinthians 15:43, where Scripture says that our new body will be full of glory and will never disappoint us. In this life there is some part of everyone's body (or maybe several parts) that he or she would like to change. Maybe it's your weight, your height, your hair, your facial features, or whatever. Our culture accentuates these imperfections by focusing so much attention on physical appearance. Ideal images of beautiful, well-built people bombard us daily. But in heaven, there will be no fad diets, no Weight Watchers, no aerobics, no exercise bikes, no personal trainers, no physical therapists, no StairMasters, no weight rooms, no saunas, no jogging tracks, no low-fat foods, no diet drinks, and no plastic surgeons. God will give every one of his children a glorious, unique, diverse, perfect, new body that will never disappoint. Think of how exciting that will be!

Question 10: How Can I Be Sure I'll Go to Heaven? I have saved this question for last because this is by far the most important question a person can ever ask. Knowing for sure where you will spend eternity is infinitely more important than any other issue you will ever consider. If you are still not sure you will go to heaven when you die, let me share a few very simple points with you.

God's Word declares that all people are sinners both by nature and by action (Rom. 3:23). The Bible also declares that God is infinitely holy, righteous, and just and cannot accept sinners into his holy presence. (Remember, it only took one sin for Adam and Eve to be expelled from the Garden of Eden.) As you can see, this is a major problem. How can a holy God accept sinful humans?

God in his infinite wisdom and grace formulated a plan to remedy this problem. God the Son agreed to step out of eternity into time, to take on human flesh, to live the sinless life we can never live, and to die as a substitute for sinful people. He took all our sins on himself and paid the eternal price for our sins, bearing the full wrath of the Father for us on the cross. Just before he died, Jesus cried out, "It is finished!" (John 19:30). The Father then raised the Son from the dead three days later to prove that he had accepted the full payment for our sins. Because of this finished work of Christ, it is now possible for sinners to have a relationship with a holy God. A full provision for sin has been made. "The Lord laid on him the guilt and sins of us all" (Isa. 53:6).

All that remains for you to have a relationship with a holy God forever is to recognize three key things: (1) *I am a sinner*—I recognize that I have sinned and have broken God's law; (2) *I need a Savior*—I admit that there is nothing I can do in myself to earn or merit salvation; my own good works can never take away my sins; and (3) *Jesus is my Savior*—I receive and accept Jesus Christ as my personal Savior from sin. It's as easy as that—just call upon Jesus, and ask him to be your Savior.

Carefully read these words from Scripture, and ask God to make them clear in your heart and mind:

- *To all who believed him and accepted him, he gave the right to become children of God (John 1:12).*

- *The wages of sin is death, but the free gift of God is eternal life through Christ Jesus our Lord (Rom. 6:23).*

- *God saved you by his special favor when you believed. And you can't take credit for this; it is a gift from God. Salvation is not a reward for the good things we have done, so none of us can boast about it (Eph. 2:8-9).*

You can receive Jesus Christ as your personal Savior right now, as you read these words, by following the three steps listed above. God offers you the free gift of eternal life. Don't wait. Receive the Savior now. Take the free gift God is offering you. It is the greatest decision you will ever make. When you trust Christ, you will immediately have a place reserved for you in heaven (1 Pet. 1:4). You can be sure from this time on that you will go to heaven either at the Rapture or when the Lord calls you home.

227

---

[1]John F. Walvoord, *Israel in Prophecy* (Grand Rapids: Zondervan Publishing House, 1962), 26.

[2]These statistics were cited at a leadership conference at Liberty University in October 1997.

[3]Thomas Ice and Randall Price, *Ready to Rebuild* (Eugene, Oreg.: Harvest House Publishers, 1992), 101–10.

[4]Mark Chalemin, *Deciphering the Bible Code* (Richardson, Tex.: Renewal Radio, 1998), 10.

[5]*Newsweek,* June 9, 1997, 67.

[6]Donald Grey Barnhouse, *Thessalonians: An Expositional Commentary* (Grand Rapids: Zondervan Publishing House, 1977), 99–100.

[7]These three points were adapted from Arnold G. Fruchtenbaum, *The Footsteps of the Messiah: A Study of the Sequence of Prophetic Events* (Tustin, Calif.: Ariel Ministries, 1983), 137-141.

[8]These five clues were taken from Fruchtenbaum, *The Footsteps,* 173.

[9]Ibid, 173.

[10]Jeane Dixon, *My Life and Prophecies,* (William Marrow & Co., 1969), 179–180.

[11]*Christianity Today,* October 7, 1998, 20.

[12]These six points were taken from Thomas Ice and Timothy Demy, *The Truth about Heaven and Eternity* (Eugene, Oreg.: Harvest House Publishers, 1997), 17–18.

A Proposed Chronology
of the End Times

I. EVENTS IN HEAVEN
  A. The Rapture of the Church (1 Cor. 15:51-58; 1 Thess. 4:13-18;
     Rev. 3:10)
  B. The Judgment Seat of Christ (Rom. 14:10; 1 Cor. 3:9-15; 4:1-5; 9:24-27;
     2 Cor. 5:10)
  C. The Marriage of the Lamb (2 Cor. 11:2; Rev. 19:6-8)
  D. The Singing of Two Special Songs (Rev. 4–5)
  E. The Lamb's Receiving of the Seven-Sealed Scroll (Rev. 5:1-14)

II. EVENTS ON EARTH
  A. Seven-Year Tribulation
    1. Beginning of the Tribulation
      a. Seven-year Tribulation begins when Antichrist signs a
         covenant with Israel, bringing peace to Israel and Jerusalem
         (Dan. 9:27; Ezek. 38:8, 11)
      b. The Jewish temple in Jerusalem is rebuilt (Dan. 9:27; Rev. 11:1)
      c. The reunited Roman Empire emerges in a ten-nation confedera-
         tion (Dan. 2:40-44; 7:7; Rev. 17:12)
    2. First Half (Three and a Half Years) of the Tribulation
      a. Jesus opens the seven seal judgments (Rev. 6:1-17; 18:1-5)
      b. The 144,000 Jewish believers begin their great evangelistic
         ministry (Rev. 7:1-8)
    3. The Midpoint of the Tribulation
      a. Gog and his allies invade Israel, and God decimates them
         (Daniel 11:40-45; Ezek. 38–39)
      b. Antichrist breaks his covenant with Israel and invades the land
         (Dan. 9:27; 11:40-41)
      c. Antichrist begins to consolidate his empire by plundering Egypt,
         Sudan, and Libya, whose armies God has just destroyed in Israel
         (Dan. 11:42-43; Ezek. 38–39)

    d. While in North Africa, Antichrist hears disturbing news of insurrection in Israel and immediately returns there to destroy and annihilate many (Dan. 11:44)

    e. Antichrist sets up the abomination of desolation in the rebuilt temple in Jerusalem (Dan. 9:27; Matt. 24:15; 2 Thess. 2:4; Rev. 13:5, 15-18)

    f. Sometime during these events, Antichrist is violently killed, possibly as a result of a war or assassination (Dan. 11:45; Rev. 13:3, 12, 14; 17:8)

    g. Satan is cast down from heaven and begins to make war with the woman, Israel (Rev. 12:7-13). The chief means he uses to persecute Israel is the two beasts of Revelation 13

    h. The faithful Jewish remnant flee to Petra, in modern Jordan, where they are divinely protected for the remainder of the Tribulation (Matt. 24:16-20; Rev. 12:15-17)

    i. Antichrist is miraculously raised from the dead to the awestruck amazement of the entire world (Rev. 13:3)

    j. After his resurrection from the dead, Antichrist gains political control over the ten kings of the reunited Roman Empire. Three of these kings are killed by Antichrist, and the other seven submit (Dan. 7:24; Rev. 17:12-13)

    k. The two witnesses begin their three-and-a-half-year ministry (Rev. 11:2-3)

4. Last Half (Three and a Half Years) of the Tribulation

    a. Antichrist blasphemes God, and the false prophet performs great signs and wonders and promotes false worship of Antichrist (Rev. 13:5, 11-15)

    b. The false prophet introduces and enforces the mark of the Beast (666) (Rev. 13:16-18)

    c. Totally energized by Satan, Antichrist dominates the world politically, religiously, and economically (Rev. 13:4-5, 15-18)

    d. The trumpet judgments are unleashed throughout the final half of the Tribulation (Rev. 8–9)

    e. Knowing he has only a short time left, Satan intensifies his relentless, merciless persecution of the Jewish people and Gentile believers on earth (Dan. 7:25; Rev. 12:12; 20:4)

5. The End of the Tribulation

    a. The bowl judgments are poured out in rapid succession (Rev. 16:1-21)

    b. Babylon is destroyed (Rev. 17–18)

    c. The campaign of Armageddon begins (Rev. 16:16)

    d. Antichrist kills the two witnesses, and God resurrects them three and a half days later (Rev. 11:7-12)

    e. Christ returns to the Mount of Olives and slays the armies gathered throughout the land, from Megiddo to Petra (Rev. 19:11-16; Isa. 34:1-6; 63:1-5)

    f. The birds gather to feed on the carnage (Rev. 19:17-18)

6. After the Tribulation (Interval or Transition Period of Seventy-Five Days—Dan. 12:12)

a. Antichrist and the false prophet are cast into the lake of fire (Rev. 19:20-21)
b. The abomination of desolation is removed from the temple (Dan. 12:11)
c. Israel is regathered (Matt. 24:31)
d. God judges Israel (Ezek. 20:30-39; Matt. 25:1-30)
e. God judges the Gentiles (Matt. 25:31-46)
f. Satan is bound in the abyss (Rev. 20:1-3)
g. God resurrects Old Testament and Tribulation saints (Dan. 12:1-3; Isa. 26:19; Rev. 20:4)

B. One-Thousand-Year Reign of Christ on Earth (Rev. 20:4-6)
C. Satan's Final Revolt and Defeat (Rev. 20:7-10)
D. The Great White Throne Judgment of the Lost (Rev. 20:11-15)
E. The Destruction of the Present Heavens and Earth (Matt. 24:35; 2 Pet. 3:3-12; Rev. 21:1)
F. The Creation of the New Heavens and New Earth (Isa. 65:17; 66:22; 2 Pet. 3:13; Rev. 21:1-8)
G. Eternity (Rev. 21:9–22:5)

Recommended Books for Further Study

GENERAL/OVERVIEW BOOKS

BENWARE, PAUL N. *Understanding End Times Prophecy: A Comprehensive Approach.* Chicago: Moody Press, 1995.

FRUCHTENBAUM, ARNOLD G. *The Footsteps of the Messiah: A Study of the Sequence of Prophetic Events.* Tustin, Calif.: Ariel Ministries, 1982.

HOYT, HERMAN A. *The End Times.* Chicago: Moody Press, 1969.

ICE, THOMAS AND TIMOTHY DEMY. *Fast Facts on Bible Prophecy.* Eugene, Oreg.: Harvest House Publishers, 1997.

LAHAYE, TIM. *Understanding the Last Days: The Keys to Unlocking Bible Prophecy.* Eugene, Oreg.: Harvest House Publishers, 1998.

LIGHTNER, ROBERT P. *The Last Days Handbook: A Comprehensive Guide to Understanding the Different Views of Prophecy.* Nashville: Thomas Nelson Publishers, 1990.

PENTECOST, J. DWIGHT. *Prophecy for Today: God's Purpose and Plan for Our Future.* Rev. ed. Grand Rapids: Discovery House Publishers, 1989.

———. *Things to Come: A Study in Biblical Eschatology.* Grand Rapids: Zondervan Publishing House, 1958.

RYRIE, CHARLES, ed. *Countdown to Armageddon.* Eugene Oreg.: Harvest House Publishers, 1999.

SWINDOLL, CHARLES R. et al. *The Road to Armageddon.* Nashville: Word Publishing, 1999.

WALVOORD, JOHN F. *End Times: Understanding Today's World Events in Biblical Prophecy.* Swindoll Leadership Library, gen. ed. Charles R. Swindoll. Nashville: Word Publishing, 1998.

————. *The Prophecy Knowledge Handbook.* Wheaton, Ill.: Victor Books, 1990.

————. *Prophecy: 14 Essential Keys to Understanding the Final Drama.* Nashville: Thomas Nelson Publishers, 1993.

WILLMINGTON, H. L. *The King Is Coming: A Compelling Study of the Last Days.* Wheaton, Ill.: Tyndale House Publishers, 1973.

WOOD LEON J. *The Bible and Future Events: An Introductory Summary of Last-Day Events.* Grand Rapids: Zondervan Publishing House, 1973.

DANIEL

CAMPBELL, DONALD K. *Daniel: God's Man in a Secular Society.* Grand Rapids: Discovery House Publishers, 1988.

JEREMIAH, DAVID. *The Handwriting on the Wall: Secrets from the Prophecies of Daniel.* Dallas: Word Publishing, 1992.

WALVOORD, JOHN F. *Daniel: The Key to Prophetic Revelation.* Chicago: Moody Press, 1971.

WHITCOMB, JOHN C. *Daniel.* Chicago: Moody Press, 1985.

WOOD, LEON. *A Commentary on Daniel.* Grand Rapids: Zondervan Publishing House, 1973.

EZEKIEL 38–39 (GOG AND MAGOG)

HITCHCOCK, MARK. *After the Empire: Bible Prophecy in Light of the Fall of the Soviet Union.* Wheaton, Ill.: Tyndale House Publishers, 1994.

REVELATION

HINDSON, ED. *Approaching Armageddon: The World Prepares for War with God.* Eugene, Oreg.: Harvest House Publishers, 1997.

JEREMIAH, DAVID. *Escape the Coming Night: An Electrifying Tour of the World As It Races toward Its Final Days.* Dallas: Word Publishing, 1990.

STEDMAN, RAY C. *God's Final Word: Understanding Revelation.* Grand Rapids: Discovery House Publishers, 1991.

THOMAS, ROBERT L. *Revelation 1-7: An Exegetical Commentary.* Chicago: Moody Press, 1992.

————. *Revelation 1-8: An Exegetical Commentary.* Chicago: Moody Press, 1995.

234

WALVOORD, JOHN F. *The Revelation of Jesus Christ.* Chicago: Moody Press, 1966.

THE RAPTURE

LAHAYE, TIMOTHY. *No Fear of the Storm: Why Christians Will Escape All the Tribulation.* Portland, Oreg.: Multnomah Press, 1992.

RYRIE, CHARLES C. *Come Quickly, Lord Jesus: What You Need to Need to Know about the Rapture.* Eugene, Oreg.: Harvest House Publishers, 1996.

SHOWERS, RENALD. *Maranatha: Our Lord, Come!* Bellmawr, N.J.: The Friends of Israel Gospel Ministry, 1995.

STANTON, GERALD B. *Kept from the Hour: Biblical Evidence for the Pre-Tribulational Return of Christ.* Miami Springs, Fla.: Schoettle Publishing Company, Inc., 1991.

WALVOORD, JOHN F. *The Blessed Hope and the Tribulation.* Grand Rapids: Zondervan Publishing House, 1976.

————. *The Rapture Question.* Rev. ed. Grand Rapids: Zondervan Publishing House, 1979.

THE BIBLICAL COVENANTS

PENTECOST, J. DWIGHT. *Thy Kingdom Come: Tracing God's Kingdom Program and Covenant Promises throughout History.* Grand Rapids: Kregel Publications, 1995.

BABYLON

DYER, CHARLES H. *The Rise of Babylon: Sign of the End Times.* Wheaton, Ill.: Tyndale House Publishers, 1991,

THE TEMPLE

ICE, THOMAS, AND RANDALL PRICE. *Ready to Rebuild: The Imminent Plan to Rebuild the Last Days Temple.* Eugene, Oreg.: Harvest House Publishers, 1992.

PRICE, RANDALL. *In Search of Temple Treasures: The Lost Ark and the Last Days.* Eugene, Oreg.: Harvest House Publishers, 1994.

SCHMITT, JOHN, AND J. CARL LANEY. *Messiah's Coming Temple: Ezekiel's Prophetic Vision of the Future Temple.* Grand Rapids: Kregel Publications, 1997.

SIGNS OF THE TIMES

DYER, CHARLES H. *World News and Bible Prophecy.* Wheaton, Ill.: Tyndale House Publishers, 1993.

HINDSON, ED. *Final Signs: Amazing Prophecies of the End Times.* Eugene, Oreg.: Harvest House Publishers, 1996.

HUNT, DAVE. *How Close Are We? Compelling Evidence for the Soon Return of Christ.* Eugene, Oreg.: Harvest House Publishers, 1993.

JERUSALEM

HUNT, DAVE. *A Cup of Trembling: Jerusalem and Bible Prophecy.* Eugene, Oreg: Harvest House Publishers, 1995.

PRICE, RANDALL. *Jerusalem in Prophecy: God's Stage for the Final Drama.* Eugene, Oreg: Harvest House Publishers, 1998.

THE JUDGMENT SEAT OF CHRIST

LUTZER, ERWIN W. *Your Eternal Reward: Triumph and Tears at the Judgment Seat of Christ.* Chicago: Moody Press, 1998.

WALL, JOE L. *Going for the Gold: Reward and Loss at the Judgment of Believers.* Chicago: Moody Press, 1991.

THE ANTICHRIST

HINDSON, ED. *Is the Antichrist Alive and Well? 10 Keys to His Identity.* Eugene, Oreg.: Harvest House Publishers, 1998.

PINK, ARTHUR W. *The Antichrist.* Swengel, Pa: Bible Truth Depot, 1923. Reprint, Grand Rapids: Kregel Publications, 1988.

THE MILLENNIUM

RYRIE, CHARLES C. *The Basis of the Premillennial Faith.* Neptune, N.J.: Loizeaux Brothers, 1953.

WALVOORD, JOHN F. *The Millennial Kingdom.* Grand Rapids: Zondervan Publishing House, 1959.

QUESTIONS AND ANSWERS

ICE, THOMAS, AND TIMOTHY DEMY. *Prophecy Watch: What to Expect in the Days to Come.* Eugene, Oreg.: Harvest House Publishers, 1998.

THE AFTERLIFE

BLANCHARD, JOHN. *Whatever Happened to Hell?* Wheaton, Ill.: Crossway Books, 1995.

LAWSON, STEVEN J. *Heaven Help Us! Truths about Eternity That Will Help You Live Today.* Colorado Springs: NavPress Publishing Group, 1995.

MACARTHUR, JOHN F. *The Glory of Heaven.* Wheaton, Ill.: Crossway Books, 1996.

MOREY, ROBERT A. *Death and the Afterlife.* Minneapolis: Bethany House Publishers, 1984.

PETERSON, ROBERT A. *Hell on Trial: The Case for Eternal Punishment.* Phillipsburg, N.J.: P & R Publishing, 1995

RHODES, RON. *The Undiscovered Country: Exploring the Wonder of Heaven and the Afterlife*. Eugene, Oreg.: Harvest House Publishers, 1996.

TADA, JONI EARECKSON. *Heaven, Your Real Home*. Grand Rapids: Zondervan Publishing House, 1995.

Index